The Emerging Self in Psychotherapy with Adults

By

Richard A. Mackey
Professor Emeritus
Boston College

FOR

Allie, Carter, Maddie and Joe

Contents

Acknowledgements

There are several individuals who helped me in the formulation, thinking through and the writing of this book. First, let me express my appreciation and love for the most supportive person in my life, my wife, Eileen, who offered, as she always has, astute feedback and encouragement at every step of the journey.

Colleagues who were of inestimable assistance included the late Dr Herb Goldberg, Dr Bruce Burnett and my long time friend and collaborator, Dr Bernie O'Brien, as well as Dr Esther Urdang and Dr Paul Kline.

The ideas in this book were germinating over the years and my primary place of employment, Boston College, provided the context in which they could develop. I especially want to acknowledge the Graduate School of Social Work and the Department of Counseling, Developmental and Educational Psychology.

I also want to acknowledge the following professional journals in which many of ideas in this book were originally published. These article provided a basis for some chapters, notably those on the biopsychosocial framework of the self, the importance of psychological intimacy in meaningful adult relationships, couples therapy and the significance of personal therapy to the professional self of a psychotherapist. The journals included Clinical Social Work, Sex Roles, The Psychotherapy Patient and Psychotherapy: Theory/Research/Practice/Training.

Individuals at Bentham who were most helpful were Sara Moqeet who guided me through the initial stages of the process of preparing a proposed book for publication and Bushra Siddiqui who offered valuable help in seeing the proposal become a book.

Prologue

No matter the specific theoretical orientation and technical approach to psychotherapy, this book present a perspective that the self of a practitioner tempered by professional values is the primary resource for helping troubled people, especially those who suffer from a damaged sense of self. The empathic use of self is the centerpiece of the role of a psychotherapist. In this introduction to the book, the context of psychotherapeutic practice both in the past and today are discussed, since context is so important in shaping ideas. The prologue also lays out the my values about theory and practice, which have an equally powerful effect on my orientation and approach to the practice of psychotherapy.

The adoption of theories for the practice of psychotherapy with adults is dependent on several factors, not the least of which is the professional context of particular historic eras. When I received my professional training in clinical social work in the late 1950's, the professional culture was shaped principally by psychoanalytic ideas, which in the 1960's and 70's were supplanted by family system theories. Beginning in the 1960's and extending to the present era, there has been an increased awareness and acceptance of cultural factors, especially those enlightening our sensitivities to social class, race, gender and age. Most recently, in response partly to changes in funding for mental health services and also to the availability of research findings about the effectiveness of cognitive/behavioral and time limited approaches, there has been a major shift toward short-term modes of intervention. Accompanying these changes in approaches to practice has been an explosion of theories about human behavior and psychotherapeutic models, some of which, such as cognitive/behaviorism, have a significant empirical basis.

No matter the orientation to practice, the point of view adopted in this book is that the self of the practitioner is the principal resource for integration of theoretical concepts with technique and for the development of therapeutic relationships with clients. The empathic use of one's self in professional relationships with troubled adults is the centerpiece of the role of a psychotherapist.

The self has been of concern to theologians, philosophers, social and behavioral scientists for centuries (Sass, 1988), and has received considerable attention from psychiatrists, psychologists and psychoanalysts (Lifton, 1993; Masterson, 1985; Kohut, 1971 & 1977) in recent decades. In the human services professions, the concept has served as a tool for describing how psychotherapists behave with clients as well as a theoretical tool for reminding us of the importance of being aware of our thoughts and feelings in professional relationships.

Today, there is a significant empirical evidence for the centrality of relational factors in successful psychotherapy that includes how clinicians integrate theories and skills into their professional selves. In summarizing the results of a task force of the American Psychological Association (APA), which spent 4 years examining empirical studies of factors that contribute to effective therapy, Norcross (2001 & 2002) observed " that the person of the psychotherapist is inextricably intertwined with the outcome of psychotherapy" (p. 346). Based on its analysis of the outcome literature on psychotherapy, the task force found " that specific techniques account for only 5% to 15% of the outcome variance " (p. 347) compared to relational factors that account for 40%. After reviewing the empirical evidence from more than 100 studies, Lambert and Barley (2001) concluded "that relationship factors correlate more highly with client outcome than do specialized treatment techniques" (p. 359).

The work of the APA task force underscores the importance of factors within psychotherapeutic relationships to treatment effectiveness. The research does not dismiss the importance of other factors, which include client expectations, technique and circumstances extraneous to therapy itself, but does suggest that factors in professional relationships common to a wide range of therapies occupy a central role in working with troubled human beings.

In addition, there is now a suggestion, based on early empirical evidence, of an important link between the quality of empathically informed therapeutic relationships and modifications in the underlying neural structures of clients who suffer from damaged selves. The research suggests that a new and potentially healing attachment between a client and a therapist is the vehicle for facilitating amelioration of damage from previous relationships (Attachment and related disorders, 2005). These data may extend the empirical evidence of a link between loving attachment relationships and the development of neurological structures in infants (Schore, 1994), despite the obvious differences in maturational levels of adults and children.

Because the relationship is always the medium for delivery of services, it is important, indeed critical, for students and practitioners to have a firm grounding in a concept of the self that encompasses bio-neurological, psychological and socio-cultural factors. While we focus on and deal primarily with psychosocial factors in psychotherapy, it is of critical importance to incorporate an understanding of biological factors in our work with clients. Not only may this grounding facilitate an empathic understanding of the people we serve, but may also become a resource for deepening and broadening awareness of ourselves in professional relationships.

This book is intended to complement existing theories by offering psychotherapists and students, who are preparing for careers in the human services, a perspective on the dynamic inner life of human beings as they live out their lives in the context of human relationships. Regardless of one's theoretical orientation and the professional suit one chooses to wear in practice, an understanding of the structure and development of the self are important elements in professional education and in successful therapy with clients.

In more than 40 years of practice as a clinical social worker, I have rarely known adult clients who did not suffer from significant damage to their selves as a result of abusive, neglectful, indifferent and oppressive relational experiences. These survivors, many of whom are some of the most vulnerable members of society, are increasingly the primary clients of social work and the other human service professions. They deserve practitioners who bring to therapeutic relationships an understanding of how the self emerges over the life span within the contexts of human relationships. There is no more effective route to such an understanding than theory based on relevant research complemented by an examination of one's own developmental and professional experiences.

I have listened to graduate students and experienced practitioners who have been open to exploring their professional development toward the goal of defining their sense of a professional self. They have been exceedingly generous in sharing what it has meant to them to become a competent psychotherapist (Mackey, R. and Mackey, E., 1994; Mackey, R. and Mackey, E., 1993 ; Mackey, R., Mackey, E. and O'Brien, B. (1993). At the heart of the learning process has been a genuine desire and openness to integrate ideas about the self into their professional roles. For the serious learner, that process involves a personal commitment to understanding how one's background, that has become part of the adult self, shapes professional roles and behaviors. The professional self builds upon the sense of self that has become a part of us from birth.

In my 1985 book, Ego psychology and clinical practice, a framework for practice was presented based on the structure and functions of the ego. The concept of self is more encompassing than that of ego, yet has continuity with the rich tradition of understanding human development from that perspective. While ego is defined by its psychological functions, a sense of self involves how one experiences - behaviorally, cognitively and emotionally - body and mind within the context of social roles and relationships, including professional ones. From birth, there is a quest for an integrated sense of self - biologically, psychologically and socially - that is only possible through involvement in meaningful relationships. Contemporary research points to the quality of child care, parental attunement to the needs of children, a positive emotional environment in the home and stimulation for cognitive development as the basis for that quest (Lewin, 2002).

What we are and who we become are shaped within relationships with others whose presence in our lives has significance for our well being. These experiences begin with primary figures in our families without whom we cannot survive and only with whom does a sense of self begin to emerge (Stern, 1985). That core of the self, shaped by interpersonal experiences with primary figures, serves as a resource for intellectual and emotional learning across the life span. That inner sense of who we are serves as a template, a "working model," for subsequent development (Bowlby, 1969, 1973 & 1980). Longitudinal studies (Karr-Morse & Wiley, 1997) suggest a connection between the quality of early attachments and subsequent behaviors, although the nature of that link is not well understood (Basham and Miehls, 2004).

As development unfolds, relationships with other human beings, who are experienced in the neonatal period as extensions of our rudimentary sense of self, change both in terms of quality and quantity. The enmeshed nature of these earliest attachments takes on a separate quality, both with original figures and with subsequent ones. If developmental experiences are optimal or "good enough" (Greenberg & Mitchell, 1983), we ingest psychologically the empathic gifts of those who love us. As this process of internalization unfolds, we emerge from earliest relationships with a sense of a consolidated self characterized by confidence, curiosity and initiative. After childhood and adolescence, the quest toward integration is facilitated through psychologically intimate adult relationships (Mackey, Diemer, and O'Brien, 2000).

So many of the adult clients whom we serve today have not had the kind of early experiences with primary figures to which all children are entitled. They may be the casualties of empathetically impoverished families, indifferent communities and societal hostility to their existence. As a consequence, so much of the development for these human beings may be a series of noxious experiences: instead of joy there is a persistent sadness, instead of optimizm there is nagging despair and instead of wholeness there is disjointed fragmentation.

In spite of differences in the clothing that we put on in our professional roles, we are similar to the people whom we serve in real yet invisible ways. Historically, several writers who have a humanistic orientation to understanding the self and relationships have recognized this: Towle (1955) referred to this connection in the concept of "common human needs," Berl (1988) in the idea of "human unity," and Buber in the "I-Thou" relationship (Smith, 1975). Constitutional factors, developmental experiences and contextual realities may differ but the emotional consequences of those experiences deep within ourselves may have a semblance to and may resonate with the inner world of others, especially those whom we call clients. That is, no matter how good the experiences with primary figures, they will never be "good enough" not to leave us with some residues of shame, guilt and doubt about ourselves. We all thirst for meaningful relationships throughout life with those who know and love us, who confirm our worth, who recognize our individuality and who respect us for what we are rather than what they and others may ask us to be. These meaningful connections with others are the basis for "human unity" and the "I thou relationship." The human capacity to attune to another individual while respecting that person's separateness from us is the essence of empathy, which, I believe, is central to understanding relational factors identified in the APA study (Norcross 2001).

How we think and feel about our bodies, our minds and our relationships is what shapes and gives substance to the sense of self. Themes of an emotional and cognitive nature that have become a part of us through processes of learning are significant components of the self. I have given much thought to the continuity of biological growth and psychosocial development and wonder about the connections between the self that emerges within the context of family, community and culture and the self which one begins to adopt during professional education and throughout one's career. My thoughts centered on the nature and importance of the continuity between the personal level of self and the professional level manifested in professional roles and relationships, the vehicles through which help is offered to another human being. There is a paradox between these levels. The use of ourselves in professional roles and relationships is an inherent part of our sense of self. Yet, there is a difference between the personal and professional just as there may be differences in the various roles that are adopted in life, including those of psychotherapist. To accept the similarities while respecting the differences is one of the most challenging tasks in developing a genuine professional self.

As empathic relationships are central to healthy development so too are empathic relationships central in the process of helping another human being, is not a new idea but one that may be secondary to technique in some models of practice. Constraints imposed by time and the pressure to produce results that are measurable empirically may also obscure the instrumental role that empathy and the therapeutic relationship play in the helping process. I believe that psychoeducational interventions based on cognitive/behavioral ideas need to be grounded in empathic relationships informed by respect, acceptance and understanding of clients. While technical skills change as a result of new knowledge based on sound research, relational skills informed by empathic understanding remain relatively constant over time. The empathic function within the professional self is the means for helping clients to integrate new learning about their selves and to modify undesirable behaviors. I have always believed that the process of integration is most effective when a client experiences a therapist not only as competent but also as empathic. That is the psychotherapeutic road for enabling a new sense of self to emerge. To this end, the book is organized as follows:

Chapter one presents a theoretical model for understanding the self as the sense of one's biological, psychological and social being in the context of time and space. Three theories that appear to be most germane to understanding how a sense of self develops, notably during childhood, are discussed in the second chapter. They are: attachment, self psychology and object relations theories. An essential aspect of understanding the self throughout life is meaningful relationships. One's sense of self is embedded in such relationships beginning with the nurturing parental relationship and extending into adult loving partnerships. Based on our research into understanding relationships, chapter three focuses on how meaningful adult relationships, characterized by psychological intimacy, are instrumental to the emerging self during adulthood (Mackey, Diemer & O'Brien, 2000).

The foci of subsequent chapters reflect the roles that I have played in my professional career: psychotherapist, teacher and researcher. In the fourth chapter, there is a discussion of the damaged self within adult clients who may confront us with considerable challenges in psychotherapeutic relationships. More often than not, these clients have been the focus of my practice. I have learned a lot from them, which is illustrated through a case study of one client. Chapter five focuses on the role of a therapist and on exploratory, supportive, confrontive, and educative skills that define the professional self. Again, psychotherapy with one of my former clients is used. Tape recordings from two sessions, one in the middle of therapy and the other a year later, are used to illustrate those psychotherapeutic skills as well as to show how the client viewed the helpfulness to non-helpfulness of our work. In chapter six, a model of therapy with couples based on our lasting relationships research is presented (Mackey, Diemer & O'Brien, 2000). This model of couples therapy is very timely in view of the confluence of recent studies that suggest the importance of working with the natural ways of how couples manage conflict rather than imposing a model of therapy on them (Jacobson et. al., 2000; Gottman, Coan, Carrere and Swanson, 1998). The final chapter focuses on the meaning of personal psychotherapy to the role of a psychotherapist, which is based on a study of graduate students and experienced practitioners in clinical social work (Mackey & Mackey, 1993). Although surveys indicate that most practitioners in the human services will be involved in personal therapy at some point in their careers (Norcross, J., et al, 1988), there is relatively little research on the topic. For many practitioners, regardless of their disciplines, personal therapy may be a valuable resource in the development of their professional selves.

References

Attachment and related disorders (2005). Conference: Harvard Medical School, Department of Continuing Education, May 6-7 Boston, MA.

Basham, K. and Miehls, D. (2004). Transforming the legacy: Couple therapy with the survivors of childhood. NY: Columbia University Press.

Berl, F. (1988). Social change and social work practice: Writings of Fred Berl. Hagerstown, MD.: Hagerstown Bookbinding and Printing Company.

Bowlby, J. (1980). Attachment and loss (Vol.3). NY: Basic Books.

Bowbly, J. (1973). Seperation: Anxiety and anger (vol.2). NY: Basic Books.

Bowbly, J. (1969). Attachment (vol.1). NY: Basic Books.

Erikson, E. (1950). Childhood and society. NY: W. W. Norton and Co., Inc.

Gottman, J.M., Coan, J., Carrere, S. and Swanson, C. (1998). Predicting marital happiness and stability from newlywed interactions. Journal of Marriage and the Family, 60, 5-22.

Greenberg, J. and Mitchell, S. (1983). Object relations in psychoanalytic theory. Cambridge, MA: Harvard University Press.

Hoffman, M. (1977). "Empathy, its development and prosocial Implications" In C.B. Keasey (ed.), Nebraska Symposium on Motivation,. University of Nebraska Press, 1977.

Joacobson, N. Christensen, A., Prince, S., Cordova, J. and Eldridge, K. (2000). Integrative behavioral couple therapy: An acceptance-based, promising new treatment for couple discord. Journal of Consulting and Clinical Psychology, 68 (2), 351-355.

Karr-Morse, R. and Wiley, M. (1997). Ghosts from the nursery: Tracing the roots of violence. NY: The Atlantic Press.

Kohut, H. (1977). The restoration of self. NY: International Universities Press.

Kohut, H. (1971). The analysis of self. NY: International Universities Press.

Lambert, M. and Barley, D. (2001). Research summary on the therapeutic relationship and psychotherapy outcome. Psychotherapy: Theory / Research / Practice / Teaching, 38 (4), 357-361.

Lewin, T. (2002). A child study is a peek, its not the whole picture. The New York Times, 07/21/2002.

Lifton, R.J. (1993). The protean self: Human resilience in an age of fragmentation. NY: Basic Books.

Mackey, R., Diemer, M. and O'Brien, B. (2000). Psychological intimacy in the lasting relationships of heterosexual and same sex relationships. Sex Roles. 43(3/4), 2000, 201-227

Mackey, R., Diemer, M. and O'Brien, B. (2000). Conflict management styles of spouses in lasting relationships. Psychotherapy:Theory/Research/Practice. 37(2) Summer, 134-148.

Mackey, R. and Mackey, E. (1994). Personal psychotherapy and the development of a professional self. Families in Society: The Journal of Contemporary Human Services 75(8), 490-498.

Mackey, R. & Mackey, E. (1993). : The value of personal psychotherapy to clinical practice (1993) with E. Mackey. The Clinical Social Work Journal. 21(1), 97-109.

Mackey, R., Mackey, E. and O'Brien, B. (1993). Personal psychotherapy and the social work student. Journal of Teaching in Social Work. 7(2), 129-146.

Mackey, R. (1985). Ego psychology and clinical practice. NY: Gardner Press, Inc. also published by Boston College Press, 1992.

Masterson, J. (l985). The real self: A developmental self and object relations approach. NY: Brunner/Mazel.

Norcross, J. (2001). Purposes and products of the task force on empirically supported therapy relationships. Psychotherapy: Theory / Research / Practice / Teaching, 38 (4), 345-356.

Norcross, J. (2002). Psychotherapy relationships that work: Therapists contributions and responsiveness to patient needs. NY: Oxford University Press.

Sass, L. (l988). The self and its vicissitudes: An archaeological study of the psychoanalytic avant-garde. Social Research, 55, 4 (Winter), 551-607.

Schore, A. (1994). Affect regulation and the origin of the self: The neurobiology of emotional development. Hillsdale, NJ: Lawrence Erlbaum Associates.

Smith, R. (1975). Martin Buber. Atlanta, GA: John Knox Press.

Stern, D. (1985). The interpersonal world of the infant. NY: Basic Books.

Towle, C. (1955).Common human needs. NY: American Association of Social Workers.

Chapter 01 - Toward an Understanding of Self

This chapter presents a theoretical perspective on the self that is not only essential for understanding the sufferings of clients but also for reflecting upon our roles in the therapeutic process. In addition to psychological and social factors, neurobiological factors are integrated into the discussion. My intent is to offer readers a conceptual framework for thinking biopsychosocially about clients. The framework underscores empathic understanding as the basis for the choice of specific interventive modes and techniques, and the centrality of a therapeutic relationship as the vehicle through which a new sense of self may emerge for clients. Biographies of three well known individuals are used to illustrate concepts.

The emergence of a sense of self is a life long process. Depending on endogenous factors, environmental resources, the personal will to engage life's challenges and to risk change, development may unfold from birth into old age. For many of us, one of the most important aspects of the emerging self in adulthood is the development of a professional self. The professional self that is at the center of the variety of roles, which may be adopted by a psychotherapist, is an extension of the personal self.

In this chapter, a concept of the self as the sense of one's biological, psychological and social being is discussed. The biological dimension is grounded on contemporary research in neurobiology, which includes empirical evidence for the connection between the quality of early attachments and the maturation of the brain. That evidence has critical implications for how an individual is able to regulate affect, to integrate new learning and to engage in the process of psychotherapy. Data from neurobiology underscore the importance of the psychotherapeutic relationship in working with adult clients (Shapiro & Applegate 2000) and offers a potential explanation for the substantial variance attributed to relational factors in effective psychotherapy (Nocross 2001). In addition to the neurobiological substrata, the inner world of the self is also home for innate human needs that include the need to be loved, to love, to be regarded by others with dignity and respect and to have one's individuality recognized and accepted. Discussion of the psychological dimension is based on my studies in ego psychology (Mackey 1985), specifically the functions of defense, cognition, empathy, relatedness and adaptation, which serve as intermediary resources as the individual strives to mediate the needs from the inner world with the expectations of the outer world. A sense of self is always shaped significantly by and is embedded in social context, which includes our behavior in social roles and relationships, the outer or visible dimensions of the self. As values become internalized from the external world, they have a powerful effect on how one views that world and how one regards her/himself in that world.

After presenting the biopsychsocial concept of the self, levels and principals that derive from that concept are discussed.

Defining self

For centuries, the search to understand and to find meaning in the concept, self, was the province of theologians and philosophers (Sass, 1988). In the twentieth century, the development of psychoanalytic theories resulted in new ways of understanding the self. Despite his dedication to understanding the mind, Sigmund Freud, the father of

Richard A. Mackey

psychoanalysis, paid little attention to the concept, seeming to equate it with the ego. In developing a theory of the structure and typography of the psyche, Freud had relatively little interest in developing theory that did not fit with his hypotheses about the pre-eminence of instinctual forces on consciousness.

In the 1930's, theory began to acknowledge relational factors in human development (Hartmann, 1939). Rather than focus almost exclusively on intrapsychic phenomena, theorists began to incorporate an interpersonal component into their models for understanding psychological development. There was a shift toward the inclusion of relationships with important "objects," notably the maternal object, into the writings of theorists. For example, Winnicott (1945) observed that children could not be understood without viewing their development within the context of the mother-child relationship, an idea that we may take for granted today but which, at the time, was a significant departure from extant ideas. Ideas about early or primary attachment relationships began to eclipse instinct in the writings of researchers and theorists (Bowlby, 1969, 1973 & 1980; Ainsworth, 1969). The hypothesis of self and object representations internalized from identifications with others also began to occupy a significant place in the evolution of theory. From the World War II era to the present, object relations theory has continued to have an important role in efforts to understanding the self (Jacobsen, 1964; Horner, 1984; Kernberg, 1980).

In the 1970's, a different perspective emerged for understanding the self. In his efforts to develop a theory to explain narcissistic personality disorders, Kohut, the father of self psychology (Kohut, 1971 & 1977), focused on the quality of early relationships between children and their primary caretakers. Empathic attunement of adult caretakers toward the child was considered essential for the development of a healthy sense of self. Kohut referred to the self that emerged from that empathic encounter as an "experience near phenomenon." The reference to "experience near" called attention to the centrality of primary relationships with empathic human beings as vital to the development of a positive sense of self. It also attended to the impact on the emerging self of verbal as well as non-verbal experiences in relationships with primary figures who are initially experienced as extensions of the self; that is, as selfobjects. Under optimal conditions, the emerging self gradually becomes the cohesive" center of initiative and creativity." Under less than empathic conditions, characterized by empathic hunger, an individual may remain at a narcissistic level of development. The more depriving and traumatic the deprivation, the more severe and chronic will be the narcissistic impairment. More than any other concept, empathy occupies a central place in the self psychological model of psychotherapy.

In recent decades, there have been other efforts among theoreticians, researchers and clinicians toward the development of theory to understand the self (Brown, 1998; Osborne, 1996; Lifton, 1993). Historically, research and theory focused mainly on male development. The sine qua non of maturity was to be found in the achievement of ego autonomy and a capacity for interpersonal separation. An important development since the 1970's, has been attention to how the self develops in females. Partly in response to the perceptions of a male bias in developmental research and the catalytic effect of the feminist perspective, there have been efforts to study female development and to identify potential differences between the sexes. One of the principal differences in the sense of self for females compared to males is the "centrality" of relationships in the development of the self over the life span (Surrey, 1985). Females are hypothesized to view their sense of self within relationships. Interpersonal attachments are valued over separations. Building and maintaining meaningful connections within mutually empathic relationships is viewed as the sine qua non of humanness for females. In our research on lasting relationships, we found a variation on that theme. While women in same sex relationships valued their attachments to their partners as central, rather than peripheral, in their lives, they valued as highly their autonomy within those relationships (Mackey & O'Brien, 1995; Mackey, O'Brien & Mackey, 1997).

More recently, there has been a renewed interest in attachment theory, as data become available about the potential links between the quality of early relationships and later disorders (Karr-Morse & Wiley, 1997) as well as the effect of early attachments on intimate adult relationships (Hazan & Shaver, 1994; Colin, 1996; Feeney & Noller, 1996; Feeney, 1999). In terms of the latter, our studies of lasting relationships (Mackey & O'Brien, 1995; Mackey, O'Brien & Mackey, 1997) found that a significant source of attraction of one partner toward the other was perceived differences in specific personal qualities. Individuals, whether straight or gay, reported an attraction to potential partners whom they perceived as having qualities different from themselves. The complementary relationships that resulted seemed to contribute to a sense of wholeness in each person, a fulfillment of their individual selves.

In this book, the self is defined as the encompassing sense of one's biopsychosocial being in time and space. Such a concept is highly useful for contending with the complexities of practice today. Even though our work with clients is focused primarily on psychosocial matters, one needs to frame understandings, on which interventions are grounded, in a wider context of bodily and culture realities. Understanding a client from a perspective that includes these three dimensions results in more informed practice.

The words that make-up this definition are important:

First, the idea of self is a concept, a useful tool to capture an understanding of human beings as they interact with their environments, especially the human environment. As a tool, this way of conceptualizing the self is a framework for organizing one's thinking about what may lie behind social behaviors. The model acknowledges that a wide range of factors may contribute to one's sense of self. Psychotherapy cannot change endogenous and historical factors that contribute to a damaged sense of self in the adult, but can be a valuable resource for helping people find strengths within themselves to lead more fulfilling lives (Smith, 2006).

Second, the idea of self refers to what is human about people in contrast to other living organisms. We refer everyday to people having a self yet we do not think of other animals, even primates, as having a self, at least in the same way that the concept is used in referring to human beings.

Third, the use of the term, sense, is meant to convey a central property of this idea, which is that our cognitive and emotional conception of who we are is a spiritual phenomena, invisible yet recognizable by us and by others. The word, spiritual, does not refer to a particular religious orientation but to a perspective on life that suggests a need within all human beings to find meaning in their lives that transcends observable realities. Religious teachings may fulfill that need for many individuals but, for others, they need to go beyond organized religion in the search for meaning in life. No matter what path one takes, the self emerges only through relationships that offer nurturance, stimulation and support for its emergence.

Encompassing means that we seek to experience ourselves with a sense of wholeness throughout life. This fourth component of the definition refers to a common human need to experience the bodily, psychological and social dimensions of the self as integrated rather than as fragmented. The congruent fitting together of mind and body within a social context that affirms the self characterizes consolidation of the self rather than fragmentation.

Fifth, time and space are the contextual aspects in this definition. The self in the present needs to be understood within the context of one's history, particularly the meaning of past experiences as those experiences have become part of the self through processes of internalization. Space refers to the physical environment and the culture of one's present existence. Although a focus on the self may propel one to look inward, the self is embedded in its surroundings. We cannot understand our own self or that of others outside of a heuristic context. For clinicians, that context includes the interactions in our relationships with clients (Nakkula & Ravitch, 1998).

Biological dimension

As potential contributors to one's sense of self, biological factors are grounded in genetic predispositions and neurobiological maturation. There is now impressive evidence for endogenous factors in many physical and psychological illnesses, such as schizophrenia and bipolar disorders. There is also a growing body of empirical evidence about the relationship of experiences in early attachments to the neurobiological maturation of the brain. That research has become an important component in shaping new models for working with children and adults who manifest attachment disorders (Hughes, 1997 & 1998; Shapiro & Applegate, 2001). No matter one's professional discipline, all clinicians need to have an appreciation and basic awareness of the advances in understanding how bodily factors, especially neurobiological ones, shape the emerging sense of self, especially during the first years of life.

Even though psychotherapeutic interventions may be focused principally on the psychosocial functioning of clients, many difficulties in psychosocial functioning may have their origins in the body. Although biological factors, including predispositions grounded in our genetic makeup and in neurological deficits because of less than optimal early developmental experiences, may not be "destiny," these factors have a powerful effect in shaping the sense of self as development unfolds. If our perceiving, evaluating and judging functions are constrained by theoretical myopia, we may fail to recognize the significance of these factors on the psychosocial functioning of an individual. As a consequence, we may formulate plans of intervention that are not as responsive to the needs of individuals as they should be.

A biopsychosocial perspective encourages us to view factors in any dimension of the self within the context of other dimensions. For example, biological predispositions on certain psychological states have been found to be contingent on the social environment. Although we have know for years about the etiological role of endogenous factors in schizophrenia and other severe conditions, we also know that acute psychotic episodes are associated with high volumes of family conflict. Teaching families about schizophrenia and helping them to understand the relational triggers that may result in repeated hospitalizations along with psychoeducational interventions designed to support families in reducing the intensity of conflict are important interventions in working with this population. Treatment of depression offers another example. When the debilitating effects of depression are controlled with medication, an individual may become more available for psychotherapy. The focus of intervention may then be to help individuals cope with a world that is perceived differently and to learn new and more adaptive ways of taking care of themselves in human relationships.

There is an inherent interdependence of biological, psychological social factors on the emerging self in human development. Even though the non-medically trained psychotherapist may not have as much competence as physicians and nurses in understanding the endogenous basis of many impairments in the psychosocial functioning of clients, we need to have enough knowledge to recognize their effect on psychological and social functioning, to assess their significance and to plan interventions that are grounded on the available research evidence.

Another aspect of the biological dimension is related to research on intelligence, notably the perspective that Gardner refers to as "frames of mind" (1985). This perspective broadens our understanding of strengths in individuals, their innate talents and skills. Historically, research in our culture has taken a narrow view of human intelligence. Although that perspective is changing, the belief system underlying the intelligence tests over other means of assessing personal competence persists (Murray & Hornstein, 1994). Such an approach to measurement of intelligence may not attend sufficiently to the influence of environmental factors and to other strengths within people that may be as important as intelligence quotients to overall functioning. Gardner hypotheses that there is not one type of intelligence but several "frames" that include linguistic, artistic, mathematical, spatial, bodily and interpersonal intelligences and skills. We do not know a lot about the origins of various frames. Even where there may be an endogenous predisposition to be "intelligent" in a specific frame, such as math, the unfolding of that gift and its development will be contingent on the social environment to stimulate and nurture its development. For example, is it not reasonable to assume that Mozart was born with a gift of musical intelligence? His genius as a composer can not be explained simply by the driving desire of his father, who saw in his son the potential for acclaim that had eluded the father throughout his own life. Any innate strength in one or more frames will be contingent on the resources of supportive environments for their development. Otherwise, the potential of an individual may never be realized. While it may be desirable that human environmental supports for the nurturance of various strengths be more empathic than those available to Mozart, optimal conditions may be the exception for many of our clients.

An important aspect of the biological dimension of the self has emerged from research on the interdependence of maturation of the brain and the quality of early relationships. Maturation of the brain occurs in sequential stages:

1. The brain stem matures first and regulates survival functions, such as the heart rate.
2. The midbrain becomes organized after the brain stem and controls functions such as sleep and appetite.
3. The limbic area, the center of emotional activity, matures next.
4. Finally, the cortex matures, the seat of rational and analytic functions (Goleman, 1995).

Prenatal damage to basic structures, such as the brain stem and midbrain, will compromise maturation of subsequent structures. Brain maturation in the neonate and young child occurs substantively at an emotional level based on relational experiences with caregivers (Goleman,1995). What is laid down as neurological structures during this critical time may have an important influence on psychosocial development over the life span (Karr-Morse and Wiley, 1997).

Data from neurobiological research offers evidence of the inter-relationship between early relationships and maturation of the brain (Schore, 1994). The quality of relational experiences with caregivers who are attuned to the needs of a child for emotional nurturance along with intellectual stimulation has a significant effect on the maturation of the brain. Schore extrapolates four "principals" related to these connections:

1. brain maturation "occurs in critical periods and is influenced by the social environment;"
2. brains of infants which mature "in stages" become "hierarchically organized;"
3. "genetic systems that program" maturation of the infant brain "are activated and influenced by the postnatal environment;"
4. the changing role of primary caregivers during the first two years of life "induces the reorganization of brain structures" (Schore, 1994: 9-20).

Development of an early sense of self, especially the feelings that become a fundamental part of anyone, is highly dependent on an empathetically attuned and responsive human environment. We have known for a long time how psychosocial functioning may be affected by the brain, as when neurological damage occurs. We now know that the maturation of the brain, including regions that control emotions and shape future behavior, is effected by the quality of early psychosocial experiences. The rudimentary thoughts and feeling that become the basis of a sense of self are incorporated into specific regions of the neonatal brain (Schore, 1994).

Based on a review of "recent advances in cognitive neuroscience neurobiology," Shapiro and Applegate (2000) identify the ways in which interpersonal experiences in early relationships affect neurological structures. While the aggregate of brain cells does not increase during the first three years of life, the connections among these cells through the development of synapses are contingent on the quality of early relationships. The connections or neural circuits are charged, positively to negatively, depending on early attachment experiences. That aspect of the relationship between maturation of the brain and caregiving responsiveness is particularly important in the neural links between the cortex, which houses cognitive resources, and the limbic region, which houses emotions. We "learn" emotionally through these early experiences before we become capable of understanding and being able to identify, verbalize and contain feelings through cognitive means. These relational realities set the stage for a child's capacity to manage affect in future relationships. Empathetically indifferent, neglectful or traumatic experiences during this critical period may have a damaging effect on the emerging sense of self as life unfolds from childhood through adulthood.

The development of a professional self and its use in therapy with adult clients need to be informed by an understanding of this research. The data point to the centrality of empathic relationships with these clients, which may serve as a vehicle for amelioration of damage to the self (Attachment, 2005; Shapiro & Applegate, 2000). New learning about old realities may result if these individuals feel accepted and understood. Therapeutic empathy may allow split off emotions, especially underlying rage and shame, to be confronted and reintegrated into a newly emerging sense of self.

Psychological dimension

The psychological dimension of the self refers to functions derived from the ego psychological paradigm. These functions include defense, cognition, empathy and relatedness, which are integral parts of the self and serve a vital role in mediating between the "push" of forces from the internal world and the "pull" of forces from the external world. The task of mediation is facilitated when functions of the ego are relatively intact and is impeded when one or more functions are impaired. They also serve as resources for synthesizing new learning with previously internalized learning. Ego functions are critical resources as a sense of self emerges over the life span.

<u>Defensive functions</u>

Defenses are the foundation upon which other functions are grounded. They serve as a check on the thoughts and feelings that might intrude into consciousness and compromise adaptation in social roles and relationships. The defenses contain or redirect the spontaneous expression of emotion into modes that are acceptable to significant figures such as parents, peers and others. In that sense, defenses are internalized through a learning process, which (unlike higher forms of learning) occur primarily at a level beyond awareness. Defenses look to the internal world and have the primary function of protecting one's sense of self from perceived threat or danger. Metaphorically, the role of defenses is to keep locked the emotional content stored in rooms in the inner world of the self. As a set of mechanisms acquired through a process of emotional learning over time, defenses tend to reflect identification with the characteristics of other people, who have an influential role in our psychosocial development.

Internalization of these mechanisms is reinforced through persistent patterns in relationships over time. Unlike many forms of learning at higher levels of development, non-verbal and "meta" messages are as important, or even more important, as overt verbal messages. Defenses become a part of us and are maintained only through a process, which exposes the individual to repetitious and persistent series of interpersonal encounters and cannot be attributed only to isolated events, although trauma may trigger their onset. They tend to be laid down early in the life cycle and remain more immune to modification than other functions. That is true because of their unconscious quality, the powerful emotional component in their adoption and because they serve as the foundation for other functions. Defenses are a crucial resource for the psychological well-being of individuals. In effective clinical work, we do not attempt to rob someone of their defenses without offering something better, which often is empathic acceptance and understanding.

The most generic of all defenses is repression, which Freud discussed extensively in his writings. Repression is employed unconsciously throughout life to contain the uncensored expression of affect. Freud thought that psychoanalysis was successful when unconscious material was raised to consciousness through the relaxation of repression. Based on theoretical and empirical developments since Freud, we know that this hypothesis cannot be generally applied to clinical work today and must be carefully evaluated in relation to understanding any individual's capacity for containing the threat to well being associated with uncovering work. In fact, we may rarely meet a client in typical outpatient settings today who may be appropriate for the level of therapeutic work to which Freud was referring. When we do encounter such people, the level of work may be determined by other factors such as motivation, availability of the client for long-term therapy, competing modes of intervention that may be appropriate and other conditions beyond the control of client or therapist.

Building on the work of her father, Anna Freud extended our understanding of other "modes of defense" while at the same time clarifying repression as "a special method of defense" (Freud, 1946). In addition to repression, she identified nine other mechanisms that protect the individual from the dangers associated with awareness of "forbidden" feelings that at one time, even for a moment, may have been conscious. She also contributed to our understanding of the origins and structure defenses by exploring their sources in various levels of anxiety:

> id anxiety (fear of engulfment or annihilation),
> object anxiety (fear of punishment),
> super-ego anxiety (guilt), and
> ego anxiety (fear of disintegration of synthesis in the adult) (Freud,1946, 58-70).

Anxiety is a catalyst that signals the self to mobilize defensive measures for its protection. It is a psychological phenomenon whose role is to mobilize defenses in order to avoid the pain of guilt, punishment, annihilation or disintegration. For the most part, becoming anxious contains a level of irrational anticipation out of proportion to the real consequences that might incur if the affect were allowed to reach consciousness.

The defensive system evolves in accordance with the state of biological maturation and with the level of psychosocial development. As a primary structure upon which other functions rest and upon which the emerging sense of self is grounded, different defenses become operational at particular points over the life span. The trigger or catalyst for early or primordial defenses is survival anxiety. Defenses that emerge as a consequence of that type of anxiety, referred to as primitive defenses, protect the person from anticipated engulfment of primordial instinctual forces. Examples include denial of reality, pervasive withdrawal from social relationships, dependency and helplessness inappropriate to one's maturational age. Generally, defenses at that level of development have an all-encompassing effect on the individual, and have a powerful narcissistic quality; they tend to distort reality in gross and persistent ways and may become ingrained as a syntonic part of the self.

The second level of defense is triggered by anxiety from early need gratifying relationships at a point when there is some recognition and rudimentary comprehension that other humans have the power and the means to punish us. At this level, the ego is defending against perceived pain at the hands of external objects such as parental figures. Defenses now take on a more interpersonal quality, which may be manifest in a fight, flight or splitting quality. Examples include splitting, projection, displacement and identification with the aggressor.

The third level of defenses evolves later in development after an individual has acquired the cognitive capacity for representational thinking and the skills to reflect upon the rightness or wrongness of behavior. The catalyst is shame and then guilt, rather than fear of external figures. Unlike earlier mechanisms, these third level defenses (often referred to as higher level defenses) have a more fluid quality and dystonic quality, and include a cognitive component. Examples are rationalization and intellectualization, reaction formation, and pervasive ambivalence. These third level defenses are more amenable to modification through psychotherapeutic interventions oriented to psycho-education, including self-awareness, insight and exploratory/reflective questions and comments.

The fourth level of defenses evolves after integration and consolidation have taken place in development of a sense of self. They may be triggered when an individual, who has previously achieved considerable success in coping with conflict, is confronted with an unusual and unexpected event that may stimulate feelings of loss, threat or challenge. Compared to other defenses, these mechanisms can be mobilized in specific, transitory situations that affect only a sector of one's life rather than overall functioning and a general sense of well-being. They also tend to have an adaptive quality by temporarily containing feelings from the internal world that might interfere with the capacity of an individual to cope with a period of upset or crisis. Although these fourth level defenses may include mechanisms from the other three levels, they are mobilized for limited periods of time and can be given up once an upsetting critical event(s) is negotiated.

Vaillant (1993) presented a somewhat different formulation for organizing defenses. He suggested four sources of defensive behavior, which were identified as the drives, guilt, relationships and reality. He then hypothesized that specific defensive "styles" are linked to different levels of impairment in the self. For example, psychotic impairment may result in denial, immature or characterological impairments such as projection, intermediate or neurotic levels of impairment in reaction formation and mature levels in the development of a sense of humor. The models of Anna Freud and Vaillant for understanding defensive behaviors and their connections to levels of psychosocial development and self impairments need to be treated with caution since individuals are highly variable in how they may respond to different stimuli, situations and developmental experiences.

Defensive behavior(s) inevitably involves other functions such as cognition and relatedness. The initial process of organizing the defensive system always occurs within a human context in which the individual is reinforced by significant figures for acceptable and unacceptable behaviors. Moreover, the development of this system is part of the socialization process that consists of identification with and introjections of characteristics of important figures, which may include their defenses; such learning takes place at levels of awareness below consciousness and beyond the influence of rational thinking processes (see next section).

Finally, what are most important about defenses is their raison d'être and modus operandi; that is, why they are used and how they are used. To distinguish various levels of defense and to understand their significance in the gestalt of the whole self is more critical to the process of understanding than is categorization.

In juxtaposition to defenses, which look inward to the internal world, the functions of cognition, empathy, and relatedness look outward to the external world. They rely on the defensive functions to maintain a sense of equilibrium between human needs and social expectations. Although each function can be identified by its unique contribution to their mediating role within the self, none can be understood outside of an inter-systemic perspective. Each function is interrelated with others so that impairment in one may have an effect on other functions and on one's sense of self.

<u>Cognition</u>

Cognition is a result of the interaction between genetic endowment and intellectual stimulation from the social environment. Although potential mastery in a cognitive sense may be limited by neurological structures already in place at birth, only social resources that stimulate and nourish intellectual understanding of the external world can activate that potential. Biological endowment may determine the minimal and maximal capacities of the individual's ability to think and to learn, but the environment controls the availability of opportunities for support of intellectual development. Historically, there has been no scientific consensus about the importance of "nature" and "nurture" in understanding intelligence. Over 20 years ago, Kagan observed: "the differences between species are fundamentally hereditary . . . but as for the differences within a species . . . in man . . . it is not clear how much can be attributed to heredity (Yahres, p.5)." He ascribed the same observation to other traits as well and concluded that "the evidence ... for a genetic cause is not any better than the evidence 30 years ago for an environmental cause" (Yahraes, 1978, p. 5). Today, the debate about the importance of nature and nurture continues, although there is now general recognition and acceptance of accounting for both aspects; thus, the critical importance of a biopsychosocial perspective for understanding not only emotional development but cognitive development, as well.

As individuals mature biologically and develop psychosocially, they acquire an increasingly sophisticated and complex apparatus for cognitive mastery of the world. That apparatus includes perception, memory, reasoning and judgment. While readiness for learning may be dependent upon the evolving neurological system within the individual, support for cognitive development is dependent upon the responsiveness of significant others to the child's physiological and psychological receptivity for intellectual mastery. The function of cognition is the result of the interaction among three spheres: biological readiness, psychological receptivity and social stimulation. Piaget suggests that this complex process may be organized into four principal stages (Piaget, 1952):

1. The first stage, which he referred to as the sensorimotor phase, lasts until age two (approximately) and is characterized by mostly narcissistic or, what he refers to as egocentric behavior. The early sense of self evolves during this period from a simple state of development characterized by reflexive behavior to a more complex state characterized by the beginnings of language (see Stern, 1985, for a different view on the evolution of the early emerging self). The cognitive operations of this stage lay the foundations for subsequent stages.

2. During the second phase—from two to six years—the child engages in continuing exploration of his world, including new experiences, relationships and an increasing capacity for intellectual recognition and understanding of different elements in the environment. Greater motor activity and mobility, development of language, play and identification with significant adult models facilitate the process. The cognitive function in this preconceptual phase is characterized by subjectivity of reasoning and judgment in which reality is limited to what is within their sphere of observation. For example, when talking on the phone to one of my grandchildren at this age, I've sometimes used the common expression "What's going on? " to which she replied "I'm talking to you, grandpa, on the phone." While I was thinking of how life was going beyond the immediate conversation and using the expression as a conversational opener, my four year old granddaughter was very literal and specific in her response, and appropriately so. Children, in general, cannot yet differentiate the more abstract meanings behind concrete events, which they observe and internalize as early representational images. During this second phase, the individual no longer considers all actions as originating from within him/herself and begins to attribute unusual power over events to others in his environment, a feature of human development that has profound significance for integrating values into one's sense of self. In this preconceptual period, the child is moving from a narcissistic orientation for being in the world to identification with human figures who are idealized (see Kohut, 1977, for another perspective on idealizing).

3. Around seven years of age the child enters a phase of concrete operations, which lasts until adolescence. During this period, the child develops a concrete and formal system of thinking in which she/he becomes able to understand conceptually the relationship between means and ends, a cognitive skill that contributes immeasurably to consolidating a sense of self prior to adolescence. The latency age child also develops systems for classifying objects and for seeing the relationships between parts and wholes. As a result, the individual is, for the first time, able to employ a deductive, rather than inductive, mode of thought, all of which facilitate a growing sense of

competence (Erikson, 1950, referred to this as industry, the flip side of which is inferiority). Positive reinforces are highly instrumental for individuals in negotiating this stage of cognitive operations in the journey toward a consolidate sense of self in adulthood. Adults who have not developed beyond this phase will function at a concrete level in their mode of thinking about the world and in their modes of solving problems.

4. The fourth stage, formal operations, extends from adolescence through adulthood. Cognition reaches its optimal potential for mastery during this period as the individual becomes ready (and receptive) to think abstractly, to reason creatively, and to engage in systematic modes of problem solving. Interpersonal differentiation and psychological integration become nodal issues in development, which are facilitated as the individual acquires the skills to formulate and test hypotheses and to derive knowledge through implication and inference. The cognitive function, which has developed on a horizontal plane up to this period, now takes on a vertical character in which the person is able to think about the significance of the present vis a vis the past and the future. This fourth level of cognitive development provides further intellectual resources for organization of adaptive functioning characteristic later of adult generativity. Rather than right or wrong, yes or no, black or white, the thinking process can now account for higher levels of complexity and variations as the individual thinks about herself/himself, social issues and the challenges of the external world.

Given the availability of certain resources or supplies such as adequate diet, socio-emotional nourishment in the form of empathy and intellectual stimulation at home and in school, the individual will negotiate through these periods in a progressive fashion. Each period will build upon preceding period(s) and lead to an adult with an integrated capacity for cognitive mastery, shaped by individual endowment interacting with environmental opportunities.

The development of this function is interrelated with all other functions. To be free to learn, an individual must have developed the capacity to defend against emotions that may interfere with a rational learning process. The adolescent and the adult need, as well, the sustenance of loving and caring relationships and humane systems that will recognize and support achievement in different frames of mind (Gardner, 1985).

An important aspect of cognition is reality testing, which is severely impacted when there is a disorder in cognitive processes within the emerging self. Reality testing is intact when a fit exists between the subjective and objective aspects of a personal encounter with the external world. Congruence between executive skills of perception, evaluation and judgment on the one hand and the real properties of external world on the other hand is the distinguishing characteristic of this aspect of cognitive functioning. That observation does not imply that an individual experiences a lack of fit as unreal. For example, the auditory hallucinations of the person who is impaired at a psychotic level, as in schizophrenia, is real for the person even though others may know that no voices exist outside of the individual's mind. Reality in that state is limited to interior processes which are damaged and reality testing within the self is impaired only because there is a lack of fit between subjective experience and objective fact.

The organization of the cognitive function is contingent on the processes of assimilation and accommodation identified by Piaget (1952). In the earliest stages of development the individual does not have the capacity to distinguish among environment inputs that tend to be absorbed in an undifferentiated way as long as they meet narcissistic needs. The infant's "outlook" on the world during this early period is based on the pleasure principle, which serves the process of assimilation. As development proceeds, the individual encounters increasing disparity between his self-centered needs and the responses of the human environment to those needs. He then must learn to accommodate to the world as it really is or to act on the reality principle. The process of accommodation, which evolves, from the process of assimilation, is the basis for reality testing. Although both processes continue to act together throughout life, accommodation becomes the master of assimilation as the individual learns to adapt to the realistic expectations of the external world.

As one travels through life, exposure to differing and expanding realities becomes a fact. The initial dyad becomes extended and soon enough involves the individual with widening groups of people outside of the nuclear and extended families. While the basic skills for appraising reality are laid down within the primary group of the family, the individual is soon exposed to and involved with other realities. How open or closed the individual will be to these new situations is determined by the quality of the accommodating process cultivated in the family. If the child has internalized the world as a dangerous place, that perception will influence his/her readiness to risk involvement in secondary groups. Consequently, individuals may be more closed to cognitive, emotional and social opportunities for expanding their realistic horizons and for accommodating to new situations. Appraisal of the objective world as a reasonably safe place of opportunity rather than threat will facilitate involvement in new social situations that may offer opportunities to learn about the unfamiliar world beyond the safe frontiers of the familiar primary group. Reality testing is inherently linked with cognition since the appraisal of reality involves a significant accommodating aspect. It is contingent, as well, upon the development of a repertoire of defenses which permit the individual to cope with new situations in dynamic, nonstereotypical and progressively open modes of reality testing rather than in rigid projections of one's inner reality onto others.

Empathy

Recent studies suggest that the empathic function may have a basis in neurobiology, namely the mirror neuron system in the brain. Research at the Neuropsychiatric Institute, UCLA, of brain activity of autistic and non-autistic children found a measurable difference in the abilities of each group to read basic human emotions, such as anger, fear, sadness and joy (Dapretto, 2005). Using MRI techniques, the mirror neuron system in the brains of autistic children, compared to non-autistic children, were less active as each group tried to recognize and then to imitate these emotions in the pictures of faces. While the research adds to our understanding of the neurobiological source of autism, the data may also point toward a neurobiological predisposition for empathic behavior.

Even if subsequent research supports the findings of a neurobiological substrata for empathy, which, of course would vary depending on the mirroring capacity of one's brain, early relational experiences cannot be underestimated in understanding the development of what Gardner (1985) refers to as interpersonal intelligence, a principal component of which is empathy. During the early period of primary narcissism infants are oriented and entitled to the self-centered satisfaction of their basic biological and psychological needs. These needs pull at the human environment for gratification and, depending on the quality of responsiveness of that environment, the individual will experience feelings of fulfillment to deprivation. For optimal development of interpersonal and cognitive functioning, there must be a combination of fulfilling and depriving responses from human caregivers appropriate to the developmental capacity of the child to tolerate increasing amounts of frustration. The process of helping the child develop a tolerance for frustration and to move from self-centered to object-centered modes needs to be accomplished gradually and within a consistent relationship with important human figures. As this process unfolds, the child begins to incorporate the capacity, once offered by others, to resonate with the feelings of others and, as a consequence, to become empathic with their emotional states, which may help in cultivating the mirror neuron system in the brain. Later, children develop the capacity to reflect sensitivity upon themselves and to become aware of intrapsychic, affective responses, which are the origins of the ability to self-sooth. In a real sense, the function of empathy is founded on a narcissistic base which is transformed through sublimation to the more altruistically informed behavior we call empathy. Empathy, then, is sublimated narcissism. No matter how altruistic an act may appear, it is never completely free of its narcissistic heritage.

Empathy is also the acceptance of our common humanity with others, the recognition that we are fundamentally no different from those we serve. At an inner level of the self, empathy is the freedom to feel within ourselves a semblance of what clients experience because their needs and ours are linked in a common human existence, a notion of empathy that represents an optimal level of sublimation.

As we grow and develop, not only may our capacity to engage in more altruistic behavior become real, but the nature of our needs change as well. For example, helplessness and the fulfillment of the accompanying need for basic trust insures well being and is essential to survival of the infant. The cry is a narcissistic signal for food. The unconditional response of the empathic caregiver to the primary narcissistic needs of the infant lays the foundation for the internalization of a sense of trust, which is a basis for future empathic attunement with others. The development of that function is contingent upon the experiences of the individual at each stage of psychosocial development, particularly in the quality of responsiveness of important caretakers to age appropriate needs. Too much gratification of primordial needs may lead to insensitivity and self-centeredness in the adult characterized by a sense of entitlement. Too much frustration, depending on the developmental level at which it occurs, may lead to feelings of apathy, shame, self-degradation and alienation, which may be manifested in helplessness, depression, sporadic violence, deviant behavior or psychosis. The core conflict in both situations is an underlying rage at having been cheated of essential empathic supplies by important caregivers, fear of one's impulses to act on that rage, shame for the intensity of one's emotional reactions and the persistent need to seek out and to replicate in new relationships the lost opportunities of earlier developmental ones. Early deprivation of the primary hunger for empathic love may result in deep and persistent shame, a more primitive affective state than guilt, which emerges at later developmental levels.

Hoffman suggests that the development of a capacity for empathy is related to cognitive mastery. He proposes a model of empathic development, which includes four stages:

1. Prior to differentiation of self from other(s), the infant responds to environmental stimuli by mirroring the distress of the other, such as an infant who cries in response to the crying of another infant.

2. When the capacity for differentiation has been reached, the child assumes that the inner emotional state of another individual is a mirror of his own inner state and responds to the other as if the latter's experience(s) were the same as his inner state.

3. Under optimal circumstances, children, between two and three years of age, can retain an image of loved figures, to acquire a sense of themselves as separate from other people, and to recognize that others have feelings and thoughts distinct from their own. With the development of representational intelligence during this period, the child can identify internally with another person and can imagine him/herself in the place of the other.

4. During the latter part of childhood, children gradually expand their awareness, affectively and cognitively, of the experiences of others. Empathic responsiveness then goes beyond specific interpersonal situations involving pleasure or pain to include the "context of a larger pattern of life experiences", (Hoffman, 1977, p. 182-184).

Endowment, interacting with human opportunities, plays a critical role in the development or inhibition of the empathic function. The family into which one is born and the social context within which one is raised channel our innate needs into different defensive and adaptive modes. Where emotional expressiveness is accepted within reasonable limits, the profound power of human needs may become sublimated into adaptive human relationships characterized by sensitivity to and empathy for the feelings of others. Sublimation is enhanced and true empathy results with the development of cognition. Where that potential is stifled through empathic indifference by caregivers, neglect and abuse or permitted unlimited expression, it may become a disabling defense and lead to debilitating behaviors.

Years ago I observed that:

"all people share the human condition which is undifferentiated in its primary core but which is manifested in various ways depending on the life experiences of each person as he first comes in contact with and is involved with the world of significant others, the family and the wider social milieu. Because there are no social statuses or pecking orders at this level of human existence, people are one: there are no teachers, no students, no (therapists), no clients, no healthy people, no deviants.... Differentiation occurs at one level and results in manifest differences ... among people while the interior world of all remains constant and is the repository of man's needs to be cared for, to grow and to become a somebody—a person of worth and dignity who needs the acceptance, respect and support of those around him" (Mackey, 1976, p. 623).

All of us are exceptions to this belief. No one escapes developmental experiences unscathed. Most of us are a complex mixture of narcissism and altruism, struggling to escape the narcissistic entitlement to our sense of self of powerful residual child-centered needs, while at the same time reaching to become more compassionate, sensitive and accepting adults. In fact, one of the great mysteries of the human condition is the capacity for empathic behaviors among some people despite overwhelming odds or absence of certain experiences. That reality may be a reflection of the resilience and adaptability of the human spirit, its capacity to deal with potential impairment in function through compensation by other intact functions, and to utilize developmental experiences, even very negative ones, to understand and connect with the suffering in others. The life histories of Maya Angelou, Eleanor Roosevelt and Frank McCourt, which are summarized in Appendix A, are testimony to that belief. Each of them, in their unique ways, transcended the realities of their oppressive, abusive and impoverished histories to become remarkably empathic adults.

It is challenging to empathize with a reality that one has not known. To have experienced what another has experienced may, with appropriate constraints, facilitate empathic contact with the feelings of the other, but empathic attunement can also be facilitated through other means. One does not have to be poor, for example, to appreciate the suffering that poverty inflicts upon an individual. Other examples related to race, ethnicity and sex may be found in contemporary life. In situations where basic difference s are obviously not subject to change, empathy may be cultivated and enhanced by cognitive and emotional understanding of others. One of the most empathic gifts that we may offer clients is to be open to learning from them about their backgrounds and cultures and to accept what they have to offer us. Perhaps there is no substitute for experience but a lack of experience may be ameliorated by genuine and responsible involvement in learning about other people who are "different." In the process, one may learn about one's self not only in relation to differentiation that promotes individuality but in relation to the collective needs of humans, which facilitates empathic attunement to the inner life of others.

The idea of compensation is critical for many people who have experienced deprivations that cannot be "made up" by therapy or therapists. The medium of the empathic relationship as a compensating experience may be a significant source of affective, cognitive and behavioral change for these people but can never become a substitute for the lost opportunity. Hughes (1997 & 1998) has developed a model for treatment of reactive attachment disorders that integrates empathy with confrontation. Its objective is to join therapeutic with parenting skills. This promising new approach to helping families will be referred to again in the chapter on therapeutic skills. Of course, our own psychic house must be in order so that we may "permit" that type of growth to become a possibility for it is most difficult for clients to grow beyond the developmental level of their therapists.

Relatedness

Relatedness is the capacity to become involved in human relationships without losing an internal sense of one's self. This function enables one to behave in a social role(s) appropriate to the realistic goals of different relationships. These relationships include parenthood, friendship, therapy and work. When intact, relatedness is a highly adaptive function. It is probably unrealistic, however, to think that any of us may become involved in relationships that maintain a rational focus on tasks appropriate to the goals of any relationships. Human relationships, no matter their agenda, are usually complex, often messy and rarely simple and straightforward. Our best efforts, as in the role of therapist for example, are to contain inappropriate behaviors that belong elsewhere and to struggle to focus on the appropriate agenda of a relationship.

The development of this function begins at birth when the infant is helpless and totally dependent on mother for survival. In response to that reality, mother and child become involved in a highly interdependent relationship that insures the child's survival and sense of psychological well being. During this period, the mother or another primary caregiver is the most significant human object in the child's world. In the day to day, moment to moment, interactions that make up primary attachments, we begin to internalize representations of those experiences. Those underlying images, which are the beginnings of object relations development, have a shaping effect on future relationships (Karr-Morse & Wiley, 1997; Hughes, 1997 & 1998).

Gradually, the child acquires a capacity to become more independent, not only as a result of physical and cognitive maturation, but also because the security and constancy of empathic caregiving offers one the psychological confidence for eventual independence. The natural thrust toward growth and psychological independence is facilitated by adult caretakers who are able to attune and respond empathetically to the bodily and psychological needs of the child, and later to a need for separateness within a different attachment relationship. That paradoxical process of integrating structure with empathy for differing developmental needs in human development is probably one of the most challenging tasks of parenthood.

Relationships with primary figures supply the individual with the "working models" (Bowlby, 1980) and "templates" (Ainsworth, 1969) that shape behavior in future relationships. The level and extent of "progressive internalizations" of empathic supplies from significant others and the capacity of significant others to let go at appropriate points is the vehicle through which the function of relatedness develops. Constancy of love, responsiveness to age appropriate needs, and sensitivity to individual differences by caregivers facilitate internalization. The journey toward "object constancy" (Mahler, 1975) is dependent on a consistent thread of positive regard, caring and love with room enough for progressive separateness. At the same time, a child needs to internalize the message that it is all right to return to familiar moorings.

One of the most critical aspects of moving developmentally toward maturity in relatedness is rapprochement. We must be able to return to home in order to continue the developmental journey. Integration of representations of supportive and reassuring figures into the emerging sense of self provides the confidence to move away. Early in development, rapprochement is characterized by a need for returning physically to the secure mooring for refueling (Mahler, 1975). Rapprochement may also meet needs for reassurance, reinforcement, reconciliation and life review over the life span. Transitional objects may also provide rapprochement-like resources as one reaches for an internal sense of developmental separateness (Winnicott, 1953).

As children enter the social arena of the world outside the primary family group, they are subjected to new relationships that contain their own agendas. At that development level, a child can not only recognize human figures in the environment, but can also differentiate among them. Differentiation within the self enables the individual to experience himself as well as other people as separate. Carrying with him internalizations from primary relationships informed by empathic attunement to his needs, which serve as a foundation for future attachments, the child is then ready to become involved in increasingly varied and complex social networks. Identifications with and internalizations from relationships at new levels may add to or modify earlier "working models" and "templates;" but these secondary experiences will never have the impact in shaping relatedness as primary attachment experiences. The latter point is particularly important for understanding the limits of any psychotherapeutic relationship with people who suffer from significant unfinished or negative business in early relationships. While the therapist may never make up for these deficits by "becoming" a substitute parent, although the power of the transference pushes the therapist to assume that role, she/he can provide a new experience with a real object who is available to accompany a client in the journey toward a sense of wholeness. In this frame of reference, the self of the therapist becomes a resource for supporting the integration of new understandings with behaviors appropriate to reality.

In transitioning to a discussion of the social dimensions of the self, a note needs to be made about secondary objects and the contemporary emphasis on role theory and concrete behavioral change in therapy. Role theory accounts for the pull of social expectations on the human being. Conformity to specific social roles which are in accord with normative expectations pulls on us and shapes behavior but does not account for the internal push toward wholeness in ones emerging sense of self. That push is as important in assessing the intactness to impairment in the function of relatedness as is an understanding of normative expectations about role behavior. Although a mature person will be capable of mediating most conflicts between the push of internalized needs and the pull of social expectations, no one ever reaches an optimal level of relatedness. The unfinished business in the process of reaching toward a sense of wholeness is manifested in various transferential reactions which, in fact, belong to previous relationships. When relatedness is intact, the individual is able to distinguish, cognitively and emotionally, between what is real and what belongs elsewhere. Internalized history of previous relational experiences is not dismissed but contained. In the unfinished aspects are the seeds for developing an empathic attunement to the sufferings of others.

Social dimension

The social dimension of the self is represented in one's "place" in the external world along with the need for relationships with other human beings. This dimension is manifested primarily in social roles and relationships, the most visible of the three dimensions of the self. One's sense of self is influenced significantly by environmental phenomena, human and non-human, which include one's community or neighborhood along with cultural expectations related to race, ethnicity, sex and social class that become internalized into the self. These factors always need to be understood within the social context of one's life, both now and in the past.

As a sense of self emerges over the life span, social realities become a part of one's psychic reality through processes of internalization. When biological predispositions and social supplies are "good enough" the individual will gradually begin to experience her/his emerging self as the center of initiative and creativity. Empathic gifts offered in "good enough" relationships empower the individual to experience a gradual shift in the locus of control from the external world to the internal world. No matter how complete the process, however, all individuals will retain a need for meaningful relationships with the human world. This notion of human development as a dynamic cyclical process embedded in a human context has eclipsed the traditional lineal model of development . The metaphor of "seasons" (Levinson, 1978 & 1996) replaces that of stages. No matter the heights of maturity, the consolidation of a sense of self remains a dream - a dream that fuels a quest for wholeness over the life span.

Compared to the biological and psychological dimensions, the social dimension of the self is more evident since we are able to observe behavior in social roles and relationships. Socially, individuals may become remarkably adaptive despite oppressive environments and less than optimal developmental experiences. It is a mystery how some people transcend developmental adversities and move beyond them, while others become their victims (see section on axioms for a discussion of adaptation in the lives of three well know individuals).

Adaptive role behaviors in social relationships mirros the intactness of psychological functions, which, when intact, constitute strengths. Adaptation looks outward to the external world in more conscious, rational, task-oriented and problem-solving modes that involves constructive attempts to accommodate to reality, and to confront what we might prefer to avoid.

As the defenses form the inner boundary of the self, adaptation in social roles and relationships forms the outer boundary at the intersection of the person and the environment. Adaptation relies on defenses to bind anxiety so as to contain troubling thoughts and feelings from intruding into social relationships. As a consequence, the person is freer to engage in purposive role behaviors appropriate to different relationships.

To understand adaptive functioning in an adult, one needs to examine their origins before development of higher level functions have progressed beyond a rudimentary level. To be adaptive, behavior does not necessarily have to be based on higher level functions such as those that emerge during the phase of formal cognitive operations. Thus, the cry of the infant may be considered adaptive although it is based initially on primary rather than secondary processes of "thinking." Individuals function in an adaptive way whenever they act to meet needs by way of age appropriate modes of behavior. Adaptive functions develop in accordance with the capabilities of an individual to accommodate to reality over the life span. In the adult, adaptive behavior is shaped by the process of sublimation, which permits us to contain our narcissistic needs in order to respond empathetically to the needs of others.

Adaptive role behaviors in human relationships is contingent upon the emergence of increasingly sophisticated function of cognition and on the readiness for engagement in more complex social networks. The change in function is facilitated by the availability of timely and meaningful positive reinforces from the human environment so that the individual experiences rewards from his successes and takes pleasure in their accomplishment. Although adaptation evolves throughout life depending upon the availability of human resources to meet biopsychosocial needs, adaptive functioning reaches an optimal level during adulthood when the potential for autonomy is at its peak.

Psychotherapeutic work is an example of adaptive functioning in a specific type of relationship. Because the professional self rests upon and is an extension of the personal self, it is critical for individuals who practice psychotherapy to be aware of their histories and how developmental experiences may affect their helping roles. We need to be free within ourselves of personal agendas that may compromise adaptation in the professional self. A generic element of our professional use of self, regardless of theoretical orientation to practice, is found in the principal that interventions are always supportive of the client's adaptive role functioning in relationships. Supportive treatment may result in cognitive, affective and behavior modifications.

In viewing adaptation as an important element in clinical work, a distinction must be made between the principles of therapy as always supportive and the differential use of support as a clinical skill. A supportive relationship is grounded on values of respect, acceptance and genuine regard for the well being of that other human being whom we refer to as a client. The therapist reinforces and promotes intact functions in order to enhance adaptive behavior and/or to enable intact functions to serve as a vehicle for restoring functions that are impaired. For example, cognitive awareness about alien feelings that were denied may lead to a greater sense of wholeness and integration within a client. The use of supportive, confrontive and psychoeducational skills to facilitate modifications in thinking, feeling and behavior are examples of adaptation role behaviors in professional relationships.

Levels

There are several ways of viewing the organization of the self. It is important to keep in mind that we are referring to hypotheses in this discussion, hypotheses that are shaped significantly by one's professional values, theoretical orientations, and experiences as a practitioner, which for me, included, not only psychotherapy but teaching and research, as well. Using a biopsychosocial frame for understanding the self, the simplest organization is to view the self from the inside and from the outside. We have been referring to inner and outer worlds as a way of addressing these two levels. Within this framework, there are additional layers of self that are defined by levels of awareness.

The traditional psychodynamic perspective suggests that psychic life has unconscious, preconscious and conscious levels, referred to as the topographical hypothesis. Structuralists argue that the organization of the self, once established, is, more or less, immutable. Orthodox psychoanalytic theory is based on the topographical and structural hypotheses. Freud thought that unconscious drives, eros and thanatos, act in tandem to control conscious life. They were immutable. Insight into their origins and manifestations, through free association and dream analysis, was the mode for enabling the conscious ego to exert rational control over their consequences.

A dynamic perspective argues against the idea that there is one self but suggests that many selves may emerge depending on the social context. Lifton (1993) adopted such a point of view, and argued that we put on different selves in modern society to adapt to the expectations of various situations. The idea of a core self having continuity over time is de-emphasized. At its extreme, this concept that Lifton refers to as the protean self is portrayed in Woody Allen's film, Zelig, in which the lead character assumes different identities because of a desperate need to be accepted by others. A sense of self is not just shaped but determined by one's perceptions of the expectations of others. The concept of a "pseudo self " contrasted to a "solid self" identified by Bowen in his theoretical model for family therapy appears to fit well with that perspective (Bowen, 1978). A solid sense of self is grounded on an acceptance and integration of one's talents and skills.

Several theorists suggest ways for understanding levels within the self. Winnicott (1965) hypothesized an individualized core nurtured by a "good enough" environment that he referred to as the "true self." (see: St. Clair, 2000; Greenberg & Mitchell, 1983) At another level, an individual may adopt various roles as a mode of coping with impingements on the true self. Winnicott labeled this level the "false self." As already noted, Bowen (1978) hypothesized that the self was organized onto two sectors: a "solid" sector made-up of one's convictions and values that are differentiated from those of others, and a "pseudo" sector that he referred to as an actor conforming to the expectations of others out of fear of loss of love, rejection and disapproval. Masterson (1985) also hypothesized two levels: a "real' self" that is the individuated center of creativity and initiative, and an "impaired" self that is a façade oriented to defending against the fear of abandonment

My way of thinking about the self attempts to integrate the work of others toward developing a model that is useful for clinical practice.

At its center, there is a core level of self that contains the potential for creativity and initiative as well as the fundamental need to experience the self as whole; that is, as integrated rather than fragmented. The core self, at the center of one's sense of being, has continuity over time and is not as mutable as the outer levels that include one's social behavior in roles and relationships. In addition to biological predispositions, the core self contains characterological themes that originate in experience near relationships, especially those in childhood and adolescence. Thoughts and feelings from experiences in these primary relationships become internalized via processes of identification and integration of messages from primary relationships and from the wider culture. These internal representations shape personal esteem, self-respect and feelings about risking involvement in new relationships. The latter constitute what Bowlby referred to as "working models," Ainsworth as "templates" and Horner as "schemas' (Horner, 1984). Substantial layers of the inner self are below awareness, particularly when a person has suffered developmental trauma, neglect or empathic indifference. It also may contain the narcissistic wounds, pockets or closed rooms of thoughts and feelings that are too painful to bear in consciousness for any period of time. They may emerge into awareness from time to time, especially when subsequent life experiences trigger a repetition of similar thoughts and feelings along with a breakdown in defenses that helped to contain them. The crisis may result in a post-traumatic disorder.

The outer world of the self refers to our behaviors in social roles and relationships. A level of the self most visible to others, these behaviors are shaped by internalized schemas from past relationships as well as by cultural expectations from current realities. The outer layer of the self may be adaptive or fragmented. When one is behaving adaptively, the self is responsive in a realistic way to social situations. That is, one's behaviors in social roles and relationships are shaped by conventions appropriate to differing contexts. For example, the professional role of being a psychotherapist requires us to behave with clients according to certain norms. The same person in another context, such as a good friendship, may behave very differently and appropriately so.

Fragmented selves emerge when the biopsychosocial dimensions do not fit together as they customarily do. Fragmentation results from several sources, such as physical and mental illness. Fragmentation may occur because of psychological wounds that have not healed, such as those inflicted by persistent empathic failures, neglect or abuse. Fragmentation may also occur from a current crisis that disrupts the balance in the biological, psychological and social dimensions of the self.

Fragmentation characterizes certain developmental periods, especially if those periods involve significant biological, psychological and social transitions. Adolescence tends to be characterized by fragmentation because of rapid sexual and other biological changes and because it is a critical transition from childhood to adulthood.

Axioms

The following ideas flow from this model for understanding the self and serve as a philosophical link to the discussion of therapy later in this book. These ideas are grounded on values that have become a part of my professional self over the years. They are beliefs that shape how one uses the self in a psychotherapeutic role. In addition to the life stories of clients with whom I have worked, an invaluable source in formulating these ideas came from the biographies of people who have overcome remarkable adversities to become generative adults. The life stories of three individuals are employed in the following discussion: Eleanor Roosevelt, Maya Angelou and Frank McCourt.

The life stories of these three individuals, summaries of which may be found in Appendix A, appear to have relatively little in common:

> an African-American woman, Maya Angelou, reared by her grandmother in a poor southern town when Blacks were overtly invalidated for being who they were;

a White woman, Eleanor Roosevelt, from an aristocratic upper class family who was offered minimal respect from her parents, both of whom along with a younger brother, died within 18 months of each other when she was nine years of age;

an Irishman, Frank McCourt, contending with overwhelming economic impoverishment and family pathology as he struggled to survive childhood.

Although the differences among Angelou, Roosevelt and McCourt are obvious in terms of their sex, race, ethnicity, socioeconomic backgrounds and life experiences, each of them shared a similarity in their resiliency to overcome adversities and to engage life in highly adaptive ways. While their stories are valuable in and of themselves, they also offer us an opportunity to identify several axioms on which this model of self is grounded:

1. The first axiom is that a sense of self emerges over the life span because of the interaction and interdependence of biological, psychological and social factors. At this point in time, we do not understand fully what all these factors are. We are even further from understanding how they may interact to result in different outcomes. For example, Angelou, Roosevelt and McCourt appear to have been endowed with certain talents and skills in their biological make-ups that were nurtured in relationships with key individuals. Each of them seemed to possess specific strengths, such as keen observational skills, a talent for writing about their experiences along with a creative way of examining life. Although we cannot be certain of their origins in any human being, these strengths or what is akin to Gardner's "frames" may have been grounded in genetic predispositions, temperaments, neurological substrata and other innate characteristics. Whatever their origins, these attributes served as valuable resources, coupled with key relational experiences, to the emergence of themselves in adulthood.

2. A heuristic orientation to understanding the self is a second axiom. That is, one needs to conceptualize the self as part of a larger context that includes the observer (Nakkula & Ravitch 1998). The sense that we have of our self today is imbedded in the present and shaped by relational experiences in the past that have been internalized as cognitive schemas and emotional images. This axiom is quite evident in the lives of Angelou, Roosevelt and McCourt, especially the impact of the social environment on their views of themselves at different ages. Consider, for example, how Eleanor Roosevelt may have felt about herself as a young child, when she was referred to as "wanting and unlovely" (p. 46) by her mother, with her feelings in middle age as Ambassador to the United Nations; or, the effects of being Black on Maya Angelou and being Irish on Frank McCourt. Although we now know that neurological maturation of the brain, including those areas which are the seat of talents and skills, is shaped by the quality of early emotional experiences with caregivers (Goleman 1995; Shore, 1994; Shapiro & Applegate, 2000), it is likely, although unconfirmed by empirical data, that other meaningful relationships may have an ameliorative effect on internalized experiences from earlier relationships. There certainly were such meaningful relationships in the lives of these three people.

3. The self is a multi-level phenomenon, some of which are modifiable while other levels are not as modifiable, a third axiom not shared by everyone who writes on the subject. For example, Lifton (1993) suggests that there is not a self but many different selves that one adopts depending on circumstances. The model in his book hypothesizes that aspects of the self are adaptable in the sense that we put on different psychological clothing and adopt different roles depending on social contexts. In other words, a substantial part of one's sense of self is defined by social role behaviors observable to others, especially those that persist over time. The model in this book hypothesizes deeper levels within the self that tend toward continuity over time and are not as changeable. That level includes the inner world of our human needs for love, acceptance, understanding and recognition of our thoughts, feelings and memories that are more similar than different for all individuals (Maslow 1962). We become differentiated at an outer level of the self in terms of observable behaviors in social roles and relationships.

4. A fourth axiom is that the sense of self is modifiable by current experiences. Current relationships have the potential to alter what past experiences mean to an individual, even though the most affirming of relationships can never change historical realities. Timely empathic gifts may be offered in any relationship, such as the one between Angelou and Mrs. Flowers, Roosevelt and Marie Souvestre , McCourt and the Franciscan priest. One gets a sense that Angelou, Roosevelt and McCourt all needed to be recognized, to be validated for who they were, to be offered support for expressing their inner strengths so as to find meaningful paths throughout their lives. Individuals who offered them these empathic gifts influenced each of them profoundly. For clinicians, the professional relationship is not just a technical vehicle of intervention to change behavior(s) but an empathic vehicle for acceptance, support, validation and understanding. Yalom's reference to existential factors in psychotherapy captures the meaning of this axiom (1989).

5. A fifth axiom, resiliency, may be derived from reflecting on the lives of Angelou, Roosevelt and McCourt. Individuals have a remarkable capacity to overcome enormous barriers and obstacles in their journey toward wholeness and fulfillment of their senses of self. One can outlive bad experiences but one can develop new modes for adapting to life as it is today and as life may be in the future. One of the great mysteries of human existence is to be found in the actualized potential of individuals who are able to move beyond unfortunate experiences, such as racism, abuse and impoverishment. It is likely that several factors and not a single one in our biopsychosocial makeup accounts for resiliency.

6. A sixth axiom is based on the idea of transformation. No matter how much an impediment to development of the self, adverse experiences may be transmuted into empathic resources for understanding the plight of others and helping them. Kohut (1971 & 1977) refers to the process of transmutations in the development of the self, or the capacity of individuals to modify social experiences so that they do not become incorporated directly into the self. We do not know how this happens or why one individual who has experienced oppression may develop compassion for oppressed groups, and of equal importance, the courage to act in behalf of those groups. That potential within the self was evident in the life of Eleanor Roosevelt who transformed her history of being oppressed into identifying

with the plight of African-Americans and Jews and then taking courageous actions on their behalves. It was also evident in the lives of Angelou and McCourt who helped us to see in their writings the human spirit beyond the scourges of racism, family pathology and severe economic poverty.

7. Related to resiliency and transformation is the idea of strengths, so evident in the generatively of Angelou, Roosevelt and McCourt in their adult years. It is fashionable today to speak of a strengths perspective in clinical practice. Sometimes, the idea of working with the strengths in a client is treated like a new idea. Respect for strengths has always been at the heart of interventions, no matter how impaired a client might be. Professional relationships are grounded in empathic connections with other human beings regardless of the mode of intervention: individual, family or group. An indispensable component of empathy is respect for strengths. While not denying the reality of impairments, respect for strengths within a relationship informed by empathic understanding is an inherent part of psychotherapy in general and is a centerpiece of the model of discussed in this book.

Summary

Self may be defined as the sense of one's bio-psycho-social being in time and space. The word 'sense' is used to convey what we think and feel about who we are, although that experience may not always be easy to communicate with words. We may experience ourselves in terms of our bodies, minds, social roles and relationships. We strive or reach for an integrated sense of ourselves biologically, psychologically and socially; that is, a sense of wholeness characterized by the integration among body, mind, social roles and behavior in relationships.

A sense of self needs to be understood within the contexts of time and space. Developmentally, the self of a child is obviously very different from that of an adult, that of an adolescent very different from that of an elderly person. Space, the physical as well as relational environment, also shapes the sense of self. Being poor may impoverish people economically but also psychologically. Individuals need different amounts of relational space. Consider, for example, the needs of the neonate who is dependent on the caregiving world for survival contrasted to those of the adolescent who struggles to negotiate the path to adult independence.

The three dimensions of the self are dynamically inter-related and interdependent. There is an innate thrust toward integration of biological, psychological and social dimensions into a holistic sense of self. When the dimensions fit together and are more, rather than less, at peace with each other, an individual may experience a state of consolidation. When an imbalance occurs in any dimension, such as a threat to bodily integrity by physical illness, the whole self will be affected. With one whose biopsychosocial functioning has been consolidated at an integrated level, impairment in one dimension may impact on other dimensions, thus threatening a sense of wholeness.

References

Ainsworth, M. (1969). Object relations, dependency and attachment: A theoretical review of the infant-mother relationship. Child development. 969-1025.

Attachment and related disorders (2005). Conference: Harvard Medical School, Department of Continuing Education, May 6-7 Boston, MA.

Bowen, M. (1978). Family therapy in clinical practice. NY: Jason Aronson.

Bowlby, J. (1980). Attachment and loss (Vol.3). NY: Basic Books.

Bowbly, J. (1973). Seperation: Anxiety and anger (vol.2). NY: Basic Books.

Bowbly, J. (1969). Attachment (vol. 1). NY: Basic Books.

Brown, J. (1998). The self. NY: McGraw-Hill.

Colin, V. (1996). Human attachment. Philadelphia, PA: Temple University Press.

Dapretto, M. *et al.* (2005). Understanding emotions in others: Mirror neuron dysfunction in children with autism spectrum disorders. Nature Neuroscience, 9, 28-30, (published online: 12/04/05).

Erikson, E. (1950). Childhood and society. NY: W. W. Norton and Co., Inc.

Feeney, J. (1999). Adult romantic attachment and couple relationships. In Handbook of attachment: Theory,research, and clinical applications. Edited by J. Cassidy and P. Shaver. NY: Guilford Press.

Feeney, J. and Noller, P. (1996). Adult attachment. Thiusand Oaks:Sage Publications

Freud, A. (1946). The ego and the mechanisms of defense. NY: International Universities Press.

Gardner, H. (1985). Frames of mind: The theory of multiple intelligences. NY: Basic books.

Gilligan, C. (1982). In a different voice: Psychologicial theory and women's development. Cambridge MA: Harvard University Press.

Goleman,D. (1995). Emotional intelligence. NY: Bantam Books.

Hazan, C. and Shaver, R. (1994). Attachment as an organizational framework for research on close relationships. Psychological Inquiry, 5 (1), 1-22.

Hoffman, M. (1977). "Empathy, its development and prosocial Implications" In C.B. Keasey (ed.), Nebraska Symposium on Motivation,. University of Nebraska Press, 1977.

Horner, A. (1984). Object relations and the developing ego in therapy. NY: Jason Aronson.

Jacobsen, E. (1964). The self and the objecy world. NY: International Universities Press.

Hornstein & Murray (1994). The bell curve. NY: the Free Press.

Hughes, D. (1998). Building the bonds of attachment: awakening love in deeply troubled children. Northvale NJ: Jason Aronson.

Hughes, D. (1997). Facilitating developmental attachment: The road to recovery and behavioral change in foster and adopted children. Northvale NJ: Jason Aronson.

Karr-Morse, R. and Wiley, M. (1997). Ghosts from the nursery: Tracing the roots of violence. NY: The Atlantic Press.

Kernberg, O. (1980). Internal world and external reality: Object relations theory applied. NY: Jason Aronson.

Kohut, H. (1977). The restoration of self. NY: International Universities Press.

Kohut, H. (1971). The analysis of self. NY: International Universities Press.

Levinson, D. *et al.* (1996). The seasons of a woman's life. NY: Alfred A. Knopf.

Levinson, D. (1978). The seasons of a man's life. NY: Alfred A. Knopf.

Lifton, R.J. (1993). The protean self: Human resilience in an age of fragmentation. NY: Basic Books.

Mackey, R., O"Brien, B. and Mackey, E. (1997). Gay and lesbian couples: Voices from lasting relationships . Westport, CT: Praeger Publishers.

Mackey, R. and O'Brien, B. (1995). Lasting marriages: Men and women growing together . Westport, CT: Praeger Publishers.

Mackey, R. (1985). Ego psychology and clinical practice. NY: Gardner Press.

Mackey, R. (1976). "Generic aspects of clinical social work, Social Casework, December, 619-624.

Mahler, M. *et al.* (1975). The psychological birth of the human infant: Symbiosis and individuation. NY: Basic Books, Inc.

Masterson, J. (1985). The real self: A developmental self and object relations approach. NY: Brunner/Mazel.

Nakkula, M. and Ravitch, S. (1998). Matters of interpretation: Reciprocal transformation in developmental relationships with youth. San Francisco: Jossey-Bass Publishers.

Norcross, J. (2002). Psychotherapy relationships that work: Therapists contributions and responsiveness to patient needs. NY: Oxford University Press.

Norcross, J. (2001). Purposes and products of the task force on empirically supported therapy relationships. Psychotherapy: Theory / Research / Practice / Teaching, 38 (4), 345-356.

Osborne, R. (1996). Self: An eclectic approach. Needham Heights, MA: Allyn & Bacon.

Piaget, J. (1952). The origins of intelligence in children. NY: International Universities Press.

St. Clair, M. (2000). Object relations and self psychology: An introduction (third edition). Belmont, CA: Brooks/Cole.

Sass, L. (l988). The self and its vicissitudes: An archaeological study of the psychoanalytic avant-garde. Social Research, 55, 4 (Winter), 551-607.

Schore, A. (1994). Affect regulation and the origin of the self: The neurobiology of emotional development. Hillsdale, NJ: Lawrence Erlbaum Associates.

Shapiro, J. and Applegate, J. (2000). Cognitive neuroscience, nerobiology and affect regulation: Implications for clinical social work. Clinical Social Work Journal, 28, 1 (Spring), 9-21.

Smith, E. (2006). The strength-based counseling model. The counseling Psychologists, 34, 1 (January), 13-79.

Stern, D. (1985). The interpersonal world of the infant. NY: Basic Books.

Surrey, J (1985). Self-in-relation: A theory of women's development. Wellsley, MA: Stone Center for developmental Services and Studies.

Vaillant, G. (1993). The wisdom of the ego. Cambridge MA: Harvard University Press.

Winnicott, D.W. (1953). Transitional objects and transitional phenomena: A study of the first not-me possession. International Journal of Psychoanalysis, 34, 1-25.

Winnicott, D.W. (1965). The maturational process and the facilitating environment. New York: International Universities Press.

Yahraes, H. (1978). Childhood environment and mental health: A conversation with Dr. Jerome Kagan. Rockville, MD: NIMH.

Chapter 02 - Development of the Self

Theory is a resource for informing one's practice. The concepts that are highly useful in understanding how a sense of self emerges over the lifespan are drawn from attachment, self psychological and object relations theories. These theories focus primarily on early development. The chapter also attends to the development in later childhood and adolescence and then introduces the emergence of the self in the adulthood. Beginning in this chapter, vignettes from psychotherapy with clients are used to tie concepts to practice.

Development of the self involves the internalization of attributes, values and functions of significant figures in the human environment that begins within the dyad with mother, and gradually extend to a widening array of relationships with other people. The emergence of a sense of self through the life-long processes of learning and internalization always includes a dynamic interplay of endowed potentials with environmental opportunities.

Developmental theories are useful in helping to understand how a sense of self emerges over the life span. This chapter reviews central concepts in attachment, self psychology and object relations theories that are germane to understanding the development of a sense of self over the life span. There is no pretense of comprehensiveness. Indeed, the discussion is parsimonious by focusing on those concepts, which appear to be meaningful to the theme of this book. Rather than discrete theories, attachment, self psychological and object relations concepts discussed here form a sequential model for understanding the process of the development of the self. The theories complement each other. Sometimes, a concept associated with one theory has a remarkable resemblance to another one. For example, the "dance" of connectedness, separateness and reunion that Kaplan (1995) discusses in relation to attachment is similar to Mahler's concept of rapprochement (1975) in separation/individuation when the child needs to return to mom for refueling and reassurance. Brief discussions of the emerging self in latency and adolescence and in adulthood follow the discussion of these three theories. The chapter concludes with a summary of developmental process extracted from those theories: attachment, identification, integration and consolidation.

Attachment

Throughout the life cycle, there is an innate quest toward a sense of wholeness within us. Under "good enough" conditions, the individual identifies with selective attributes of figures in the human environment and internalizes their affirming messages into the emerging sense of self. While the earliest and rudimentary origins of the self may begin prior to birth (Brazelton, 1980), we are more certain today of their origins in the moments after birth when mother and child are negotiating the first and most important relationship in life.

The paradigm for understanding early development of the self, which was initiated by Bowlby and elaborated upon by Ainsworth, had a significant boost in the 1980's. Drawing upon his studies and those of other researchers, Stern (1985) proposed that "infants begin to experience a sense of an emergent self from birth"(p. 10). His findings challenged prevailing hypotheses about the pre-differentiated state of the psychological infant in the first six months of neo-natal life (Mahler, 1975). Stern argued that there is no autistic or symbiotic stage of early development.

Richard A. Mackey

Table 1

Early object relations development

	Jacobsen	**Spitz**	**Mahler**	**Kernberg**
	(1954)	(1965)	(1975)	(1980)
2 months	undifferentiated	objectless	autistic	undifferentiated
	self		phase	self
		smile response		
	fusion of self and object representations	symbiotic phase	libidinal attachment	
6 months		rudimentary ego		
		stranger anxiety		
10 months	differentation	differentation	differentation	
			practicing	differentation of self and object representation
		semantic communication		
18 months			rapproachment	
36 months	integration of self and object representations		object constancy	integration

These individuals assumed that the infant entered the world in a state of fusion with mother and was not capable of differentiating from her or others until the latter part of the first year. We know that this assumption is not true and that children are able to differentiate in the early months of neonatal life when they are beginning the life-long process of developing a sense of self. As differentiation unfolds, the child begins to form mental images of human figures, referred to as object representations. The term, object, reflects the assumption in early theories that infants and young children were not able to recognize, even at a rudimentary level, the individuality of different figures in the human environment. Caregivers or what Kohut later referred to as selfobjects, were objects that met one's needs. The data, which are summarized in this table, have value today only if we incorporate recent research findings into the time lines. The capacity for differentiation is operational much earlier as are other processes. These data are helpful in understanding the process of object relations development, which evolves from differentiation to integration. At a differentiated level of development, the individual is able to form separate images or representations of self and the object world. At differentiation these representations are split and do not come together as integrated wholes unless the human environment provides the empathic resources for integration into whole images. The process of how one moves from a differentiated to integrated state is the focus of the following discussion.

Object relations may be thought of as the internal representations of our interpersonal histories (St.Clair, 2000). Internalization is the process of how experiences in social relationships become psychological schemas or representations (Horner, 1984) through the process of identification, introjection and integration. Identification has its origins in early attachments, in which considerable learning is already taking place. Optimally, identification confined to fondling homes, child evacuees from London during the blitz of World War II, and children separated temporarily from their parents because of hospitalization. Based on his observations, Bowlby hypothesized that attachment of the child to a loving caregiver was a central need and a critical component of healthy development. He hypothesized further that children form "working models" within their minds based on the quality of early attachment experiences. These models have a powerful effect in determining subsequent behavior. Bowlby identified three attributes of positive attachment relationships: proximity, safety and security. He argued that these attributes were optimally available in the relationships of biological mothers and their children. When a rupture occurred in a primary attachment relationship, Bowlby identified the following sequence of behaviors in the child:

protest,
despair, and
detachment.

Unless others who were empathetically attuned to the suffering of the child tempered reactions to the rupture, damage to the emerging self of the child was a potential consequence. Although Bowlby shifted attention away from the psychoanalytic focus on intrapsychic life to the relational aspects of early child development, his work reflected the prevailing cultural values of the period. That is, child rearing was the primary responsibility of mothers who were assumed to be better equipped, than were fathers, to nurture and care empathetically for children. Bowlby also assumed that the quality of early attachments between mothers and children had a significant effect on subsequent behaviors. The hypothesis of a link between early attachment experiences and subsequent behavior has received support in later research (Hughes, 1997 & 1998). Today, there is recognition of the significant effects of early experiences with primary caregivers on the emerging self of children and adults, although the link between early attachments and subsequent behavior is not as deterministic as Bowlby suggested.

The hypothesis about "working models" was the basis of research conducted by Ainsworth and her associates (Ainsworth, Blehar, Walters and Wall, 1978). She was interested in the effects on the developing self of early experiences with primary figures, especially when there was an alteration in the context of relationships. The response of an infant to separation was assumed to be contingent on the qualities of attachment relationships that had been identified by Bowlby.

Based on observational studies of hundreds of mother/child dyads using a research tool referred to as the "the strange situation," Ainsworth hypothesized three templates within the mind that result from different attachment experiences:

the secure template,
the anxious/ambivalent template, and
the anxious/avoidant template.

Subsequent research proposed a fourth, the disorganized/disoriented template. The mental representations that Bowlby referred to as working models and Ainsworth as templates are carried within the internal world of the self and may have a significant effect in shaping behavior in subsequent relationships. There are other factors, such as endowment, temperament and alternative attachment figures that also effect the emerging sense of self.

After reviewing research on early development, which included the studies of Stern, Schore and Greenspan, Hughes (1997) concluded that:

> attachment does not only consist of the magical moments of attunement during the first 10 months and the joy and vitality of the early practicing period. [The researchers] also stress the importance of the toddler's experience of separation and shame. Such experiences must lead to a reunion with the mother, one that is not a return to the earlier merging moments, but a more mature attachment that is able to integrate the autonomous self within the continuing bond. This attachment must integrate the "good" and "bad" in both the self and mother. Finally, it must move from the preverbal communion of the attachment experiences to the level of verbal communication, which greatly facilitates the child's ability to differentiate and integrate his affective experiences. The successful journey through this entire sequence is crucial for the child's development to continue in a healthy manner (Hughes, 1997, 18-19).

Hughes identified critical components of early attachment experiences that are the foundation of healthy development: connection, separation, shame, reunion and integration, all within the continuity of a loving relationship. Fraiberg may have been thinking of this sequence of attachment experiences when she talked of the birthrights of all children. Inevitable failures in this attachment dance (Kaplan, 1995) without the experience of reunion, may result in psychic ghosts (Fraiberg, 1975) rather than vitality in the emerging sense of self.

Empathy to the underlying needs of children is the most important aspect in early attachment relationships. That need persists throughout life, although its power is attenuated depending on how the hunger for it was satisfied in previous relationships. There is also an emerging body of evidence now available that point to the powerful role of early attachment experiences on subsequent behaviors (Karr-Morse, 1997; Cassidy & Shaver, 1999; Feeney & Noller, 1996; Sperling & Berman, 1994), although no "simple or direct link between early experiences and later development" has been found (Werner, 1989). Contemporary scholarship suggests that attachment theory is an important resource for understanding close relationships in adulthood and a relevant framework for research on those relationships (Hazan and Shaver, 1994).

Self Psychology

Self psychology, especially the concepts of mirroring and empathy, contributes to our understanding of what needs to occur in attachment relationships. All human beings have a natural hunger to be recognized, accepted and understood. These loving behaviors are the bedrock of empathy, which is the centerpiece of this theory. For infants and children, the need to be mirrored by caregivers who are attuned to that basic need is a narcissistic entitlement. Under conditions in which that entitlement is compromised - as in abusive, neglectful and/or empathetically indifferent attachment relationships - the grounds are set for future difficulties. Depending on the extent of empathic deficiencies, the child may remain stuck at a narcissistic level of development, be plagued by persistent rage and oppressed by enduring shame. Even when supplies of love are adequate, however, there needs to be failures of empathy, in gradual doses, for children to move ahead developmentally; that is, to learn to take care of themselves and not to rely on others to meet their needs.

Kohut (1971 & 1978), the father of this theoretical perspective, searched for a new way to understand and treat patients struggling with self acceptance and an underlying hatred toward themselves. Fragmentation and narcissism appeared to occupy the center of the psychological stage with these individuals who were diagnosed frequently with behavioral and personality disorders. Kohut hypothesized that the conflicts of these patients originated in a "pre-oedipal" level of development, a period when their needs for empathic attunement through mirroring by primary caregivers were not met. Despite their developmental deficits, these individuals were not so regressed and disorganized that they had no sense of a self. Rather, they possessed a very primitive sense of self that originated in the empathic impoverishment of their early experiences. These individuals were considered "non-treatable" with classic psychoanalytic intervention and frequently referred to clinical social workers for "relationship therapy."

In the process of formulating his ideas to explain the troubling symptoms of these patients, Kohut moved away theoretically from the dual drive hypothesis, which was central in the psychoanalytic model. Similar to the object relations school in ego psychology, the "new" psychology of the self hypothesized that infants were born with a fundamental need for attachment to and merger with a loving object. The object in the self psychological model was experienced internally by the infant as a "selfobject," a fused state between infant and caregiver(s). In this new model, aggression was not considered an innate drive, but an understandable reaction to selfobjects who were not empathetically responsive to the child's need for mirroring.

Early responsiveness of caregiver(s) informed by empathic understanding of needs for nurturance, soothing and attachment promote the formation of a core nuclear self within the child. While being empathetically attuned to the child and his/her needs, parental caregivers need to experience the infant and then the child as possessing a self if development is to proceed. The fused state of infancy gives way to differentiation of self and object and gradually to increasing comfort in being separate from one's caregivers.

Optimal "failures" in selfobject empathic responsiveness (i.e. S-O-E-R) are essential to building internal structures. Gradual failures that do not traumatize the emerging nuclear self result in "transmuting internalizations," through which external functions performed by caregivers become internal self functions. If one has experienced the selfobject relationship as soothing, one gradually internalizes the capacity to soothe the self without relying as much on the caregiver for meeting that need.

Needs may be understood as "poles" within the nuclear self. Kohut originally proposed a bipolar self but the self is now hypothesized to have at least three poles, the tri-polar self:

Pole one refers to the need for selfobjects to recognize one's grandiosity. That need is in ascendancy from 2 to 4 years. It may be represented in the transactional expression "I"M OK ... SEE ME!"

Pole two refers to the need for ideals that are met through identification with strong yet soothing self-objects. That need emerges from 4 to 6 years. It may be represented in the expression "YOU"RE OK and I WANT TO BE LIKE YOU."

Pole three, referred to as twinship, characterizes latency when the need for friends who are like one's self becomes central in development. It may be represented by "WE"RE OK."

It is important to keep in mind that these ideas are hypotheses and not empirical facts. The theory continues to develop. Self psychology suggests that needs - including the need to be recognized, to have values and to have friends - are life long pursuits, which may only be fulfilled through relationships that offer acceptance, empathy and understanding. Parents, other caregivers, siblings, peers, friends, teachers and individuals in the human service professions all have the potential to offer these gifts to an individual.

Interestingly, the theory of self psychology is based on clinical practice and not on systematic observations characteristic of research on attachment. Despite the differences in the sources of data, self psychology ideas appear to complement the findings of studies on early development. The centrality of the empathic relationship is underscored in research on healthy attachments and is the centerpiece of therapy informed by self psychology. Further along the developmental continuum, self psychological and attachment ideas are relevant to understanding intimacy in adult relationships that last, which is the focus of the next chapter.

Object relations

The early attachment relationship is the basis for development of a sense of self over the life-span. Self psychology provides the theory for understanding what needs to happen within attachment relationships so that development may proceed. Object relations theory offers a perspective for understanding the process of internalization of experiences in human relationships that facilitate an inner sense of separateness and individuation. While separate theoretically, the theories about attachment, the psychology of the self and object relations have a thematic continuity for understanding the beginnings of a sense of self and its emergence over the life-span.

Table 1 depicts early object relations development from the perspectives of four principal theorists: Jacobsen (1954), Spitz (1965), Mahler (1975) and Kernberg (1980).

Table 1				
	Early object relations development			
	Jacobsen	Spitz	Mahler	Kernberg
	(1954)	(1965)	(1975)	(1980)
2 months	undifferentiated	objectless	autistic	undifferentiated
	self		phase	self
		smile response		
	fusion of self and object representations	symbiotic phase	libidinal attachment	
6 months		rudimentary ego		
		stranger anxiety		
10 months	differentation	differentation	differentation	
			practicing	differentation of self and object representation
		semantic communication		
18 months			rapproachment	
36 months	integration of self and object representations		object constancy	integration

These individuals assumed that the infant entered the world in a state of fusion with mother and was not capable of differentiating from her or others until the latter part of the first year. We know that this assumption is not true and that children are able to differentiate in the early months of neonatal life when they are beginning the life-long process of developing a sense of self. As differentiation unfolds, the child begins to form mental images of human figures, referred to as object representations. The term, object, reflects the assumption in early theories that infants and young children were not able to recognize, even at a rudimentary level, the individuality of different figures in the human environment. Caregivers or what Kohut later referred to as selfobjects, were objects that met one's needs. The data, which are summarized in this table, have value today only if we incorporate recent research findings into the time lines. The capacity for differentiation is operational much earlier as are other processes. These data are helpful in understanding the process of object relations development, which evolves from differentiation to integration. At a differentiated level of development, the individual is able to form separate images or representations of self and the object world. At differentiation these representations are split and do not come together as integrated wholes unless the human environment provides the empathic resources for integration into whole images. The process of how one moves from a differentiated to integrated state is the focus of the following discussion.

Object relations may be thought of as the internal representations of our interpersonal histories (St.Clair, 2000). Internalization is the process of how experiences in social relationships become psychological schemas or representations (Horner, 1984) through the process of identification, introjection and integration. Identification has its origins in early attachments, in which considerable learning is already taking place. Optimally, identification builds upon the gains of early encounters with the human world. The gains of these early relational experiences stimulate a desire for continued contact with other familiar figures and confidence for expanded engagements with new figures. Unlike attachment, which was exclusively or primarily dyadic in nature, the process of identification involves the individual in multiple encounters with other members of the primary family group, with one's peer group and with secondary figures in the human environment. Internalized memories of attachment relationships remain central to the developmental process, especially when individuals can no longer return physically to their safe moorings.

With differentiation that begins within early attachment relationships the child is able to identify with loved ones and to ingest them psychologically as introjects. Imitation is a behavioral manifestation of that internal process, which in self-psychological terms may be thought of as mirroring. Over time and with appropriate support from primary figures, these representations of the object world are transmuted into a sense of self, the self-representation. Although imitation may remain as a critical factor throughout life, it eventually becomes less encompassing of the process of identification as a result of cognitive and emotional development. In fact, cognitive, emotional and behavioral alignments with figures to whom the individual is attached become more parsimonious at two years of age. Then, the child strives to become more self sufficient and independent through selective identifications. Thus begins the life-long process of alignment with others not only for narcissistic gratification of basic needs but, more importantly, for development toward a consolidated sense of self.

Throughout life, individuals tend to align with figures of identification to whom they cathect positively because of the attractiveness of qualities observed within those figures (Bandura, 1977). Depending on endogenous factors, earlier attachment experiences and the nature of subsequent relationships, the process of learning through identification may vary considerably from individual to individual. Bandura hypothesized that the desire to remain attached persists, however, only when there are rewards available within the encounter to sustain the relationship. These rewards are generally transmitted through the communication of respect, genuineness, empathy and support. For older children, adolescents and adults, learning through identification with models is not only contingent on the quality of earlier attachment relationships but also on the anticipation of future gain(s) from new relationships. Excessive deprivation or indulgence, internalized within the self as themes from earlier relationships, may tug at the individual to retain, to replicate, or to perpetuate the not-so-good-enough memories, which may interfere with developmentally appropriate identifications.

From an object relations perspective, a nuclear sense of self becomes organized if the constitutional endowments that push for expression, the developmental experiences already internalized within the self and the new encounters with the social world fit together in a complementary way. Under optimal conditions, the self representation will eclipse object representations. Individuals will then rely primarily on their inner convictions and values rather than on what they think others expect.

The importance of the quality of communications to the process of identification and object relations development has been implicit in this discussion. Continuity of supportive feedback patterns within primary and secondary groups facilitates the integration of positive esteem for the emerging sense of self. Conflicting messages of a degrading nature undermine integration, and are an affront to development of a positive sense of self. These compromising messages may target any dimensions of the emerging self, such as gender, race, religion and age.

Watzlawick and his associates have identified several "axioms" of communication that are useful in understanding the processes of identification and internalization in object relations development (Watzlawick, 1967). They suggest that in any human encounter that involves two or more people "one cannot not communicate." This axiom is not contingent on intention or mutual understanding of the participants. It means simply that people communicate, in the sense of transmitting messages to each other, whether they use words or non-verbal behavior and whether they are aware or unaware of their intentions. The second axiom suggests that "human communication is a multi-level phenomenon" which includes: a content dimension in which the sender (of a message) is defining the significance of the message, and a contextual dimension in which the parties are defining their relationship, one to another. This second axiom involves the concept of meta-communication, which attaches (usually at an implicit level) meaning to the importance of the overt message while at the same time defining the nature of the role relationship between ego and alter ego(s). Watzlawick observed that meta-messages define relationships as accepting of the receiver, rejecting of the receiver or as disconfirming the existence of the receiver. The latter two situations are the most undermining of an emerging sense of self since they discredit the very being of an individual or relegate the importance of his/her existence to insignificance. A third axiom hypothesizes that interactions within a social role relationship may be complementary or symmetrical; these are determined by the difference and similarities between ego and alter ego. Any constellation of factors - biological, psychological and/or social - may contribute to the symmetrical and complementary structure of relationships that are viewed as transactional encounters in which behaviors are evoked in a circular and interlocking way.

These ideas about communication are helpful in understanding the link between the social environment and internal object relations development. Identifications involve a dynamic interplay between the endowed potentials of the individual and the availability of social resources that are transmitted over time through human relationships. Messages from the figures in the external world that contribute to a sense of self are being exchanged continuously regardless of one's conscious wishes, a proposition which highlights the critical nature of preconscious and unconscious forces on development. In contrast to adults, children have less choice in escaping complementary relationships; as a consequence, they must develop defensive as well as adaptive mechanisms to cope with the impact of interpersonal and social forces on their developing selves and their internal images of others. The adolescent and adult may have more choice in contending with conflicting messages at different levels of communication.

Separation/individuation

The research of Margaret Mahler (1975) is often cited in attempting to understand how young children move psychologically from the secure moorings of early attachments to become progressively more independent. As valuable as Mahler's work was, it needs to be viewed within the context of the environment in which it was conducted. The research was designed to develop theory and not to test hypotheses. The ideas that emerged from her work are tools for understanding development of the self within various contexts. Social and cultural differences based on sex, ethnicity and economic status will have a significant impact on processes of separation/individuation. Other perspectives on early development of infants and children also need to be integrated into the hypothesis about separation/individuation. Figure 2 is an attempt to show that integration.

Mahler's beliefs about the first half year of neonatal life (autism and symbiosis) have been modified by more recent research (Stern, 1985). As has been said earlier, a rudimentary capacity for differentiation is available much earlier than she suggested. Mahler's most significant contribution was in identifying sub-phases of separation/individuation. Based on observations of the behaviors of children and their mothers, Mahler hypothesized that children are involved in differentiation from 6-12 months, practicing from 12-18 months, and rapprochement from 18-24 months. Around two years of age, children acquire the capacity for object constancy. Differentiation is facilitated by the acquisition of recognition memory, practicing by the maturation of mobility, object constancy by the maturation of representational memory through which the child can hold a reassuring image of the loved object(s) in her/his mind, especially when that person(s) is "out of sight."

Table 2

Stern's observations of the early self
with self psychological concepts and processes of separation/individuation

Emergent self

Early individuated self emerges within empathic bond

Core self

Validation of emerging self through mirroring self-object functions

Subjective self

Empathic bond supports individuation and gradual separateness

Rapprochement

Need to return to empathic self-object for
refueling, reassurance, reinforcement, reconciliation and review

Integration of a sense of self

Language facilitates the life-long journey toward wholeness;
Learning through identification and empathic bond with idealized self-object figures.

Rapprochement, Mahler's third sub-phase in separation/individuation, is fundamental to human development over the life-span. In order to move ahead developmentally, individuals need to return to the safe moorings of trusted attachments for re-fueling as Mahler suggested. Over the life-span, however, rapprochement has additional significancw related to other needs, which include reassurance, reinforcement, reconciliation and review. Reassurance and reinforcement encourage separateness; reconciliation attenuates guilt and review may facilitate moving on with life even as one negotiates old age and impending death. Development from birth to death cannot be represented by a straight line. It is uneven with many dips. Rapprochement represents the dips in the unevenness of the journey toward emergence, and eventually, of a consolidated sense of self.

Rapprochement needs may also be met through transitional resources, which are reassuring and soothing objects that temper anxiety associated with separateness (Winnicott, 1953). In children, these resources appear toward the end of the first year. Their appearance on the developmental scene may be associated with the availability of recognition memory when a child may need a reassuring object to remind him of the loved one who is no longer within visual reach. Transitional resources may begin to disappear as evocative memory and object constancy become consolidated. In various forms, rapprochement and transitional resources reflect life long needs to move back so as to move ahead developmentally

Latency

I will comment briefly on the most significant developments during these years to the emerging sense of self. Traditionally, the years from 6 to 12, more or less, have been thought of as a dormant or quiet period; thus, the use of the term, latency. The "quietness" of this period has usually been associated with physical maturation and sexual development that are quite different from the dynamism of earlier years and the impending changes of adolescence. These years may be relatively quiet sexually but this aspect of life for latency age children is undergoing dramatic changes because of earlier sexual maturation along with shifting cultural mores about sexual expression.

With the emergence of "concrete operations," there is an enhancement of adaptive functions characterized by significant gains in learning, problem solving, acquisition of task oriented work skills and the development of social relationships. The integration of values with cognitive development accelerates during latency, a development that facilitates at least a temporary consolidation of a sense of self. Socially, it is still ok to be a kid prior to pubescence unlike the ambivalent expectations of adults and the dominant culture toward the post-pubescent adolescent. Latency sets a floor for the adaptive regressions of adolescence (Blos, 1967).

Latency is also characterized by significant gains in adaptation, which are derived from the strengthening of cognitive functions, namely concrete operations. As a result of these gains, self-confidence is enhanced. Instinctual forces are attenuated and inner needs are now oriented to the enhancement of adaptive skills of rational problem solving, intellectual curiosity and pairing with others to achieve collective goals. While the defensive system continues to serve as a buffering resource, it tends to be relatively quiet except in those situations in which the child ascribes to new relationships those affects and defenses that originated in early childhood. These self-protective modes may be most apparent in peer groups and in relation to new authority figures such as teachers. Otherwise, latency is characterized by an ascending of adaptive functions over defenses.

The case of Paul

Paul, a nine-year-old White child, was referred to the clinic by his mother, who was concerned about his verbal and abusive behavior toward his two younger sisters, his association with older boys who were streetwise and tough, and his refusal to obey his mother. Her marriage of nine years to Paul's father was punctuated by numerous separations as a result of his physical and verbal abuse of her. Both parents are currently separated and in individual therapy.

Paul was an active yet manageable child and depicted by his mother in macho-like terms; his aggressive behavior toward her and his sisters has exacerbated over the past year, which coincided with the most recent marital separation. Although prenatal history was normal, Paul's first two years of life were plagued with severe bronchitis for which he was hospitalized three times during the first year. With medical treatment these symptoms abated by three years of age. Mother recalls that Paul was a happy and outgoing child despite these illnesses, but she also reports that he has always been afraid of hypodermic needles, of the dark, of being alone, and of sleeping by himself. No other developmental irregularities were noted in his history.

Despite abusive behavior toward his wife, the father was described as a loving person with the children and, in fact, seldom punished them. Much of the abuse took place while the children were present. At these times Paul would run to his mother in a panic, screaming and crying, and the father would chastise him for being a baby, and then walk away. Paul appeared to be caught between the need to protect his mother and retain her love while risking annihilation by his father whom he admired. To this day Paul has never been able to express anger directly and openly at his father. Despite these intrafamilial conflicts, Paul does well at school in his academic work and is not a behavioral problem in that setting.

His initial contact at the clinic was highly problematic. Notwithstanding a tough-guy demeanor characterized by crude language and a swagger to his gait, Paul refused to separate from his mother until the second session, when the therapist was able to get him into the playroom through a gentle but firm stance. Once alone with the therapist, he began to play spontaneously and related in an appropriate and warm manner which, according to the mother, corresponded to his behavior when he was alone with her. Although his play was characterized by an aggressive quality, Paul was not destructive and showed no signs of being overwhelmed by his anger. Themes in his verbalizations tended to revolve around associations of strength with masculinity, weakness with femininity, fears of bodily injury, fears of abandonment and covert guilt about his badness.

In her therapy, the mother expressed much anxiety about Paul's emulation of his father, particularly in his aggression toward her and his sisters, and fears that he would grow up to be a carbon copy of the father. Although she has some awareness of the significance of the most recent separation in increasing Paul's aggressive behavior, she does not appear to be empathetically in touch with the counterphobic elements of his macho-like behavior. In brief, mother seems to view Paul as a scaled-down replica of his father rather than as a differentiated individual, a little boy who needs firm and consistent limits. Father appears overwhelmed with shame for abusing his wife and worries that Paul is trying to emulate him. His preoccupation with feelings of guilt also seems to get in the way of recognizing the fearful little boy within the outer macho exterior of his son.

Discussion

This nine-year-old boy suffers from no physical or intellectual impairment at the present time and appears to be dealing with the task of learning in an adaptive manner. In spite of behavioral conflicts within the family, no complaints have been made by the school about Paul's behavior. He is an average student who is apparently getting along with peers and teachers.

Early physical illness, which required separations from the family, and a history of fears, which originated during that period are the precursors to current conflicts manifested in counterphobic symptoms and problems with separation. At the age of 22 months, for example, Paul experienced regressive enuresis when mother went to the hospital for the birth of the second child, but he regained bladder control when mother returned home with the new baby. In view of that regression occurring before, rather than after the baby and mother came home, his fear of abandonment may have prevented Paul from displaying any oppositional behavior that would have threatened, even more, the attachment relationship with mother.

We do not know how the father was available to him in these early years but we do know that Paul clung protectively to mother when the father was abusive toward her, also risking the verbal wrath of father if he retained the "safe haven" with mother. Rather than experiencing a gradual separation/individuation, Paul was confronted with a dilemma that resulted in identification with the aggressor to the exclusion of his attachment with mother. This interpersonal splitting along gender lines resulted in counterphobic behavior to keep his fears of abandonment from consciousness and in introjects of maleness inextricably associated with defeat of the weak female. His identification with the aggressive father was no doubt reinforced by the fact that he was the only male child and by the neighborhood, which was a tough place where boys are expected to learn to take care of themselves. His identification with older, streetwise boys, a pattern for the past year, serves to feed his tenuous sense of self as a tough kid who can take care of himself. Such a "false" outer self covered feelings of vulnerability and weakness, which were projected on to females. A hopeful prognosis that the splitting of self and object representations along gender lines can be modified is derived from the fact that Paul is able to relax this defense when he is alone with mother and with the therapist, who is also a woman. Under those conditions, he does not have to share the exclusive attachment to each woman. Another positive sign is that aggressive acting out associated with the splitting defense is confined to primary figures (mother and sisters) and has not contaminated his relationships with peers and other adults, such as teachers. Conflict-free ego functions, such as cognition and relatedness remain intact and facilitate adaptive involvement in the student role.

Paul's sense of self is tenuously grounded. Self and object representations are now compartmentalized by gender. For Paul, therapy may be an opportunity for relaxing his defensive need to preserve that split and of learning that the world is a safe enough place to be both strong and weak. These integrative gains will be contingent upon changes in mother's capacity to differentiate Paul from his father and as a consequence to relate to him as a separate little boy who needs love and firm control. Gain will be contingent, as well, on the capacity of father to make use of therapy to sustain recent changes in his relationship with mother and to support Paul in learning new ways of expressing his anger, especially towards females. The latter is contingent on father's ability to integrate similar learning into his own sense of self.

Adolescence

Adolescence is a transitional period between childhood and adulthood. Integrating the loss of being a child with the fears of becoming an adult is a major issue for adolescents and their parents. Propelling the transitional dilemmas of these years are the dramatic maturational changes compared to earlier periods. Bodily changes, especially genital maturation, may result in psychological fragmentation and disequilibrium in the adolescent search for a new sense of self. Another major change is the emergence of "formal cognitive operations" and the development of abstract reasoning, deductive thinking, analytic skills, vertical thought and a potential for empathic attunement. This new way of thinking supports a second round of separation/individuation on the road to an eventual consolidation of the self in adulthood.

Where the first round of separation/individuation resulted in a sense ... "that I am"... or capacity for separateness from attachment figures, the processes of separation/individuation in adolescence result in a social birth characterized by self constancy, which Erickson (1950) referred to as the attainment of a sense of identity. For the emerging self, adolescence is not so much "that I am" ... as ... "who I am?"

Attachments with peers facilitates separation from parents and the loosening of other object ties to the primary group of the family. Those social shifts in alignments contain potential conflicts as adolescents reach for social acceptance by conforming to the social expectations of the peer group and letting go of familial ties that may be devalued in the search for a separate identity. The significant challenge for the adolescent is in the struggle to integrate a sense of self while contending with messages from the outside world that may reinforce narcissism, inner conflict, upheaval and regression. Because they are trying to find an identity that fits with an inner world in transition, adolescents may engage in obsessive introspection. Anne Frank portrays the enhanced capacity for self observation, especially related to the struggle to integrate self and object representations, in the last passage of her diary:

> *I've already told you before that I have, as it were, a dual personality. One half embodies my exuberant cheerfulness, making fun of everything, my high spiritedness, and above all, the way I take everything lightly ... this side is usually lying in wait and pushes away the other which is much better, deeper and purer. You must realize that no one knows Anne's better side and that's why most people find me so insufferable...*
>
> *My lighter superficial side will always be too quick for the deeper side of me and that's why it will always win ...*
>
> *I'm awfully scared that everyone who knows me as I always am will discover that I have another side, a finer and better side. I'm afraid they'll laugh at me, think I'm ridiculous and sentimental, not take me seriously ...*
>
> *Therefore, the nice Anne is never present in company ... but almost always predominates when we're alone ...*
>
> *I try terribly hard to change myself, but ... I start by getting snappy, then unhappy, and finally I twist my heart round again, so that the bad is on the outside and the good is on the inside and keep on trying to find a way of becoming what I would so like to be, if ... there weren't any other people living in the world (Frank, 1952, pp. 240-241).*

This last passage in her diary, written the day before the family was captured, speaks to the process of negotiating the challenges of finding one's self during adolescence. It offers us a glimpse of the dialogue carried on in the inner world (Kaplan, 1995) during these years of transition from childhood to adulthood. The themes of fragmentation, lack of congruence between inner and outer worlds and the struggle to integrate the psychological and social dimensions of the emerging self are evident in her narrative.

During these years of transition from childhood to adulthood, there is a need for clear expectations from the adult world, which are reasonable and flexible enough for adolescents to experiment with new relationships and to try on different social roles. Rapprochement with love objects takes on a very different quality during adolescence; it is a critical resource in supporting the journey toward maturity, but the need may not be as apparent to the outside world as it is privately to adolescents, themselves.

Adulthood

The adult years offer opportunities to negotiate the unfinished developmental agendas of earlier periods as new developmental opportunities emerge; i.e.: to integrate: "young and old, masculine and feminine, destructiveness and creativeness, attachment and separateness" (Levinson, 1978 & 1996). The research of Levinson on the lives of men and women utilized the metaphor of "seasons" to convey the process of adult development. Their studies hypothesized a series of transitional and structural periods from early to late adulthood. During transitions, individuals are in the process of modifying dimensions of their lives and themselves. An example might be a decision to return to graduate school in order to pursue a career in human services. Structural periods are times of relative stability in which one may consolidate modifications underway during transitions. "Dreams," the distant realities beyond one's current reach, fuel development throughout adulthood. "Mentors" and models are the human resources that assist in the process of reaching for dream(s).

The work of the Levinsons and their colleagues provides a framework for considering how a sense of self emerges throughout the adult years. We have found their concepts useful in our research on lasting relationships (see Appendix B for a description of the methodology of our research). In particular, ideas about transitions and structures offer a framework for understanding how spouses adapt to marriage and same sex relationships. Structures are thought of as dynamic plateaus in which modifications in various dimensions of relationships are integrated and consolidated, albeit tenuously and temporally. Transitions involve change(s) as couples negotiate modifications in their relationships. The engagement period for married couples is conceptualized as a transition into the structure of early marriage. For same sex couples, at least in areas where marriage is not possible, a comparable transition is the time together before a mutual commitment was made to their relationships. Planning for children involves another transition into a new marital life structure, parenthood. In middle age, as children are leaving home, couples are on the road to another relational configuration, the post-parenting or "empty nest" structure. Differences based on gender, race and sexual orientation that were internalized as parts of one's self, shape the ways in which partners adapt to each other during transitional and structural periods.

Intimate relationships are indispensable for many people in the quest toward a consolidated sense of self during the adult years, a theme discussed in the next chapter. Meaningful relationships, as distinct from causal encounters and work oriented relationships, allow interpersonal space and support for the underlying levels of the self to emerge. In our culture, there are few opportunities where one may be one's self. Relationships, in which love predominates, may offer an opportunity for parts of one's self to emerge in a way that is not possible in day to day encounters with the rest of the world.

The meaning and value of adult relationships vary according to the developmental needs of each person that shape the quality of their relational attachment. The needs of each person and the level of the emerging self shape the symmetrical to complementary qualities of relationships. The more complete the internalization process and the higher the level of development, the more equipped are individuals to psychologically form and maintain a mutually empathic and symmetrical relationship in which differences are respected.

This point of view does not deny the capacity of people to transcend their histories. Although the past is always a part of the present, the past alone does not determine the quality of new relationships. The resiliency, creativity and strength of the human being to overcome adversity is one of the remarkable and reassuring derivatives of loving relationships that offer new opportunities for integration and consolidation of a sense of self. Development is continuous and close relationships to which individuals are committed support the quest in adult life for wholeness and fulfillment.

The case of the Timms

The Timms, a Black couple in their late twenties, applied for therapy because of mutual concern that they were growing apart rather than closer together in their relationship. Both were well established in their careers and recognized professionally for their competence. They met in graduate school and had been married for three years. Each described their relationship as mutually gratifying and supportive during the first two years of their marriage. Ms. Timms was employed full time in her profession for those two years, while Mr. Timms finished work on his degree. At that time, one year ago, they moved to this geographic area because of an exceptional professional opportunity for Mr. Timms. Since that time Ms. Timms has felt increasingly estranged from her husband and views him as a good person who is like a friend but not someone with whom she wishes to spend her life. She is not happy living in this area, misses friends and family, is troubled that her husband seems settled for life, and feels trapped. Ms. Timms had suggested a separation to have room to think through her situation, which precipitated his applying for therapy for both of them.

In individual interviews each appeared reasonably comfortable in talking about the situation. Mr. Timms was perplexed by his wife's behavior over the last several months. He expressed puzzlement about the change in her since the move. Neither felt at home in this area and both missed the camaraderie of the university neighborhood and closeness to her family. He came from a poor background and, like his older two brothers and a sister, had done well in school; as a consequence, he was able to obtain employment with a highly prestigious technological firm in this area. He describes his family as close and supportive; he is proud of their accomplishments. His father was a hardworking person who enjoyed his family. Mother was a loving and firm parent who had the primary role in disciplining and looking after the children. Ms. Timms describes herself as an expressive individual, in contrast to her husband whom she views as a very logical and conservative person. To her, he is more interested in his job than in her and, although concerned, he does not seem to understand how unhappy she is with the way the marriage has turned out. She came from a middle-class family that was composed of her and an older brother. Her mother was a housewife and father a successful lawyer who, she feels, spoiled her by giving her anything she wished. Like her husband, Ms. Timms remembered the family as close and cohesive; she thought that her father was the dominant figure and mother went along with what he wanted. She knew that they, particularly father, would be very upset if her marriage did not work out.

In conjoint interviews, this couple related initially in a reasonable and polite manner. There was a tightness and intellectual quality to their interaction that suggested a highly controlled and guarded relationship. Neither wished to hurt the other and, as a consequence, they avoided areas in their discussions that might provoke strong emotions, especially anger. Both reported that they had gotten along well before the move and attributed that happy period to the busyness of their lives as students as well as the supportiveness of friends and her family. Mr. Timms was attracted initially to his wife's carefree and independent life style and by her wit and intelligence She was attracted to his evenness in temperament and his goal directedness. Each recalled their relationship together as close and exciting, qualities, which had gradually disappeared over the past year along with a diminution in their sexual relations.

Discussion

This couple is experiencing the expected developmental conflicts of early marriage which have been exacerbated by the loss of familiar, collateral relationships which both valued, Ms. Timms more so than Mr. Timms. The conflict between them now (in contrast to the harmony which each says characterized their relationship prior to the move to an unfamiliar geographic area) is being defended against by a pulling-back from meaningful discussion of the issues that have created a change in their feelings for one another. Perhaps they fear that open discussion of their anger would destroy an already tenuous attachment. Historical data suggest that each developed a consolidated sense of self characterize by personal happiness and competence as well as success in preparation for their careers. Their attractiveness to each other, in fact, seemed based on a mutual perception of qualities that would contribute to a sense of wholeness: for her it was his autonomous and goal-oriented behavior in adapting to life; for him it was her empathy in relationships and her expressiveness. The stress associated with the transition of the move, along with the sense of isolation (particularly within Ms. Timms) created an imbalance in their relationship. One wonders if they would be experiencing this disequilibrium if there had not been such a dramatic change in the context of their attachment to each other.

As therapy progressed, it became increasingly clear that Ms. Timms resented the sacrifices that she thought she had made in helping her husband complete his professional education. She tended to dismiss these resentments as unimportant until they moved (in order for Mr. Timms to take advantage of an excellent employment opportunity in this area). During the past year, these resentments were increasingly on her mind, as the satisfactions of her work and the availability of supportive relationships with friends and family could not neutralize them. The loneliness associated with a strange environment fed avoidance of these feelings, which became manifested in sexual and interpersonal withdrawal from her husband. For his part, Mr. Timms was unaware of how his wife viewed the situation and he reacted with puzzlement and absorption in his work. The more she withdrew, the more he invested his energies into a highly interesting and rewarding career.

Ms. Timms was reluctant to confront Mr. Timms with her feelings, which were not compatible with her expectations of herself as a wife. She was modeling her role after that of her mother, who was devoted to the career of her husband. Mother never complained nor had she put her own needs before those of her husband. The difference for Ms. Timms was that she wished to pursue her own career, in which she had already experienced considerable success. In significant respects, Mr. Timms resembled her father, a competent, decent, logical and goal-oriented person. Mr. Timms saw in his wife much of the strength and warmth that he associated with his mother. Their symmetrical investment in the marriage was related to their race, cultural similarities and the levels of emotional and cognitive development that they shared. They appreciated these commonalties but tended to avoid dealing with differences. Her guilt for feeling resentful and her fear of loosing the relationship prevented Ms. Timms from sharing this part of her self with Mr. Timms. He resented the change in Ms. Timms, to whom he had been attracted by her warmth and support.

This couple was able to reestablish contact with one another by using therapy as a vehicle for opening doors that had begun to shut within their internal worlds, the result being an estranged attachment characterized by mutual avoidance and withdrawal. Each had brought into the marriage individual identities that reflected reasonably well consolidated senses of themselves. The precipitating event of geographic relocation had deprived Ms. Timms valued relationships upon which she depended and had triggered awareness of resentments toward Mr. Timms. Their individual levels of development and their commitment to the marriage were strong enough to absorb the threat to their relationship.

Summary

Themes from attachment, self psychological and object relations theories most germane to understanding the emerging sense of self over the life-span have been discussed in this chapter. These theories were the basis for the ideas presented in the first chapter. Parsimony guided the choice of concepts discussed. These ideas form a complementary matrix of the processes involved in the emergence of the self.

From birth to death, a sense of self emerges from empathic loving attachments that lead to subsequent identifications and internalizations. These object representations or schemes gradually become integrated into our sense of self as life unfolds. Under good enough conditions, the sense of self eclipses internal representations of objects so that we rely progressively on our own thinking and values in adapting to life rather than on the expectations of others. When bodily, psychological and social dimensions of the self along with inner and outer levels come together in a congruent fit, we may experience states of consolidation. Consolidation is the end point of a developmental journey when a significant pinnacle in life is reached. Such times may last or, as with many of us, they may be temporary. Life may consist of several consolidated moments in the journey of the emerging self. Maslow's concept of "peak experiences" (1962) comes as close as any other idea for capturing these pinnacles of development. Depending on individuals and their circumstances, consolidation may be realized in any number of ways.

While this approach subscribes to the notion that basic structures are activated and organized during the first few years of life, it also assumes that development is a life-long and dynamic process. At higher levels of development an individual is confronted with cognitive and affective themes which may spring from processes of earlier levels along with the human agenda of the developmental period of which he is then a part. As a consequence, except for the earliest levels of development, we are all confronted throughout the life cycle with the needs and demands of our current situation, as well as with the unfinished aspects of earlier levels. Development occurs within meaningful relationships that offer empathic attachment, timely differentiation, models for identification, internalization of qualities offered by models, and integration of these qualities into a consolidated sense of self.

References

Ainsworth, M., Blehar, M. and Walters, S. (1978). Patterns of attachment: A psychological study of the strange situation. Hillsdale, NJ: Lawrence Erlbaum Associates, inc.

Ainsworth, M. (1969). Object relations, dependency and attachment: A theoretical review of the infant-mother relationship. Child development. 969-1025.

Bandura, A. (1977). Social learning theory. Englewood Cliffs, NJ: Prentice Hall.

Berzoff, J., Flanagan, L. and Hertz, P. (1996). Inside out and outside in: Psychodynamic clinical theory and practice in contemporary multicultural contexts. Northvale, NJ: Jason Aronson, inc.

Blos, P. (1967). The second individuation process of adolesence. The Psychoanalytic Study of the Child, XXII, New York: International Universities Press, 162-186.

Bowlby, J. (1980). Attachment and loss (Vol.3). NY: Basic Books.

Bowbly, J. (1973). Seperation: Anxiety and anger (vol.2). NY: Basic Books.

Bowbly, J. (1969). Attachment (vol.1). NY: Basic Books.

Brazelton, G. 'The infant as focus for family reciprocity." In Harvard Seminar Series, The American Family (cassettes): Cambridge, 1980.

Cassidy, J. and Shaver, P. (1999). Handbook of attachment: Theorym research, and clinical applications. NY: Guilford Press.

Colin, V. (1996). Human attachment. Philadelphia, PA: Temple University Press.

Elson, M. (1986). Self psychology in clinical social work. NY: W.W. Norton & Company.

Erikson, E. (1950). Childhood and society. NY: Norton.

Feeney, J. and Noller, P. (1996). Adult attachment. Thousand Oaks: Sage Publications.

Fraiberg, S. (1977). Every child's birthright: In defense of mothering. NY: Basic Books.

Fraiberg, S. (1975). Ghosts in the nursery: A psychoanalytic approach to the problems of impaired infant-mother relationships. American Academy of Child Psychoanalysis, 14, 387-421.

Frank, A. (1952).The diary of a young girl. NY: Pocket Boohs.

Gardner, H. (1985). Frames of mind: The theory of multiple intelligences. NY: Basic Books.

Goleman,D. (1995). Emotional intelligence. NY: Bantam Books.

Greenberg, J. and Mitchell, S. (1983). Object relations in psychoanalytic theory. Cambridge, MA: Harvard University Press.

Hazan, C and Shaver, R. (1994). Attachment as an organizational framework for research on close relationships. Psychological Inquiry, 5 (1), 1-22.

Horner, A. (1984). Object relations and the developing ego in therapy. NY: Jason Aronson.

Hughes, D. (1998). Building the bonds of attachment: awakening love in deeply troubled children. Northvale NJ: Jason Aronson.

Hughes, D. (1997). Facilitating developmental attachment: The road to recovery and behavioral change in foster and adopted children. Northvale NJ: Jason Aronson.

Jacobsen, E. (1964). The self and the object world. NY: International Universities Press.

Jordan, J. *et al.* (1991). Women's growth in connection: Writings from the Stone Center. NY: The Guilforg Press

Kaplan, L.(1995). No voice is ever wholly lost. NY: Simon and Schuster.

Karr-Morse, R. and Wiley, M. (1997). Ghosts from the nursery: Tracing the roots of violence. NY: The Atlantic Press.

Kernberg, O. (1980). Internal world and external reality: Object relations theory applied. NY: Jason Aronson.

Kohut, H. (1977). The restoration of self. NY: International Universities Press.

Kohut, H. (1971). The analysis of self. NY: International Universities Press.

Levinson, D. et. al. (1996). The seasons of a woman's life. New York: Alfred A. Knopf.

Levinson, D. (1978). The Seasons of a man's life. New York: Alfred A. Knopf.

Mackey, R., O'Brien, B. & Mackey, E. (1997). Gay and lesbian couples: Voices from lasting relationships. Westport, CT: Praeger Publishers.

Mackey, R. & O'Brien, B. (1995). Lasting marriages: Men and women growing together. Westport, CT: Praeger Publishers.

Mahler, M. (1975). The psychological birth of the human infant: symbiosis and individuation. NY: Basic Books.

Maslow, A. (1962). Toward a psychology of being. Princeton, NJ: D. Van Nostrand.

St. Clair, M. (2000). Object relations and self psychology: An introduction (third edition). Belmont, CA: Brooks/Cole.

Schore, A. (1994). Affect regulation and the origin of the self: The neurobiology of emotional development. Hillsdale, NJ: Lawrence Erlbaum Associates.

Sperling, M. and Berman, W. (1994). Attachment in adults: Clinical and developmental perspectives. NY: Guilford Press.

Spitz, R. (1965). The first year of life: A psychoanalytic study of normal and deviant development of object relations. NY: International Universities Press.

Stern, D. (1985). The interpersonal world of the infant. NY: Basic Books.

Watzlawick, P., Beavin, J. and Jackson, D. Pragmatics of Human Communication: A Study of Interactional Patterns, Pathologies and Paradoxes. New York: W. W. Norton & Company, 1967.

Werner, E. (1989). Children of the garden island. Scientific American, 106-111.

Winnicott, D.W. (1953). Transitional objects and transitional phenomena: A study of the first not-me possession. International Journal of Psychoanalysis, 34, 1-25.

Chapter 03 - Intimate Relationships and the Emerging Self in Adulthood

The discussion of the centrality of psychological intimacy in meaningful adult relationships to the emergence of a sense of self in adulthood is based on our research into the meaning of psychological intimacy to 216 partners in 108 heterosexual and same sex relationships that had lasted for an average of 30 years. This study is also the basis of chapter 6 on therapy with couples. Factors that had a significant role in shaping the quality of psychological intimacy were the absence of major conflict, a confrontive conflict management style of one's partner, a sense of fairness about the relationship and the expression of physical affection between partners. These qualities are invaluable resources for development of the self during the adult years.

The hunger for a loving attachment to another human being is as important in adults as it is in children, although the actual dimensions of intimate relationships between adults is quite different (Hazan & Shaver, 1994). Prager (1995) summarized the research on the positive effects of being involved in psychologically intimate relationships. Citing several investigations from college students to Nazi Holocaust survivors, Prager suggested that well being is enhanced when individuals are able to share their thoughts and feelings about stressful events and receive support by someone who cares. Openness within a meaningful relationship has been found to reduce stress, enhance esteem and respect for one's self, and to reduce symptoms of physical and psychological impairments. Conversely, studies of isolated individuals who are unable to engage in relationships that promote openness and disclosure of inner thoughts and feelings are at risk for developing physical and psychological symptoms. Drawing from several studies, Prager concluded that "even people with sizable social networks are likely to develop symptoms of psychological disturbance in the face of stressful events if they lack confiding relationships" (pp. 2-3).

Other studies support a link between well being and relational satisfaction, on the one hand, and involvement in intimate adult relationships, on the other hand (Mroczek & Kolarz, 1998; Lane, 1998; (Horwitz et al, 1997; Coombs, 1991). Of equal importance, relationships that are troubled and stressful may have a negative effect on individuals (Kiecolt-Glaser et al, 1988). While there is a connection between involvement in intimate relationships and individual well being, the exact nature of that relationship is not settled: Are adults better off psychologically because of marriage, as Headly and Wearing suggest (1992), or are individuals with high levels of self esteem compared to others more likely to marry (Horwitz, White & Howell-White, 1996; Mastekaasa, 1995)? Perhaps, as Hendrix (1997) hypothesized, it may be that the benefits of intimacy accounts for the higher levels of well-being of married individuals compared to others. Although these studies focused on heterosexual relationships, we assume that intimate relationships to which individuals are committed, regardless of their sexual orientations, will have similar benefits.

In this chapter, I draw upon our research on adaptation in relationships that last (Mackey & O'Brien, 1995; Mackey, O'Brien & Mackey, 1997). These studies offer clues about the potential link between intimate relationships and the emerging self in adulthood. (Note: the methodology used in this research, which included in-depth interviews with 216 partners in 108 marital and same sex relationships that have lasted for an average of 30 years, is reported in

Richard A. Mackey

Appendix B). Based on our data, we suggest that relationships characterized by mutuality of trust, respect, openness and support - that is psychological intimacy - are instrumental to the developing self throughout the adult years (Mackey, Diemer & O'Brien, 2000).

Toward understanding psychological intimacy

Before discussing our findings and how they help to understand the emerging self during adulthood, previous studies on intimacy in adult relationships will be briefly discussed.

Summarizing a large body of research, Berscheid and Reis (1998) observed that:

> intimacy has been used variously to refer to feelings of closeness and affection between interacting partners; the state of having revealed one's innermost thoughts and feelings to another person; relatively intense forms of nonverbal engagement (notably, touch, eye contact, and close physical proximity); particular types of relationships (especially marriage); sexual activity; and stages of psychological maturation (p. 224).

Most frequently, intimacy has been used synonymously with personal disclosure (Jourard, 1971) that involves "putting aside the masks we wear in the rest of our lives" (Rubin, 1983, p.168). To be intimate is to be open and honest about levels of the self that usually remain hidden in daily life. The extent of personal disclosure is proportionate to how vulnerable one allows the self to be with a partner in revealing thoughts and feelings which usually are not apparent in social roles and relationships of everyday life.

Intimacy also has been thought of as companionship (Lauer, Lauer & Kerr, 1990) and has been associated with emotional bonding (Johnson, 1987). Others have defined intimacy as a process, which changes as relationships mature (White, Speisman, Jackson, Bartos & Costos, 1986). Schaefer and Olson (1981) considered intimacy to be a dynamic process, which included emotional, intellectual, social and cultural dimensions.

Several researchers have focused on the meaning of intimacy to individuals in varying types of relationships. Helgeson, Shaver and Dyer (1987) asked individuals to describe instances where they had experienced feelings of intimacy with members of the same and opposite gender. Self-disclosure, physical contact, sexual contact, sharing activities, mutual appreciation of the other, and warmth emerged as the major themes. Sexual and physical contact were mentioned frequently in descriptions of intimacy in heterosexual relationships but mentioned rarely in descriptions of relationships with members of one's own gender. Because of limitations in the study design, it is difficult to delineate the specific forms that intimacy takes in different types of relationship.

Monsour (1992) examined conceptions of intimacy in same and opposite gender relationships of 164 college students. Self-disclosure was the most salient characteristic of intimacy, followed by emotional expressiveness, unconditional support, shared activities, physical contact, and lastly, sexual contact. It is important to note that the low ranking of sexual contact in this study may have been due to participants describing platonic, rather than romantic, relationships. Also, this study focused (like others) on short term relationships of young adults.

Relatively little is known about non-verbal communication as an aspect of intimacy. Prager (1995) suggested that a glance or a touch may have great meaning between partners because of the mutual recognition of shared, albeit unspoken, experiences. However, "it is less well known how nonverbal factors influence the development of intimacy in ongoing relationships" (Berscheid & Reis, 1998). It appears reasonable to assume, however, that meta-communications in the form of non-verbal messages need to be congruent with the exchange of words, if a sense of psychological intimacy is to develop and be sustained between two individuals. At a minimum, meta-communications at a behavioral level cannot undermine or contradict words that may be used to enhance a sense of psychological intimacy between partners in a meaningful relationship.

Sexual involvement between partners in a relationship is another aspect of intimacy. The phrase "intimate relationship" has been equated with sexual activity in several studies (Swain 1989). For example, in a study of the meanings associated with close and intimate relationships among a sample of college students, 50 % of the participants referred to sexual involvement as the characteristic that distinguished intimate from close relationships (Parks & Floyd 1996). As mentioned above, Helgeson, Shaver & Dyer (1987) also found that participants in their research associated intimacy with sexual contact.

Although studies tend to support the observations of Berschid and Reis (1998) about the components of intimacy, a significant issue in studies of intimacy is the failure to control for relationship type, the effects of gender, and relationship duration. All of these factors impact how intimacy is perceived and experienced by individual partners.

Psychological intimacy and the self

Psychological intimacy emerged from our data as the sense that one could be open and honest in talking with a partner about personal thoughts and feelings not usually expressed in other relationships. During interviews partners talked of experiencing psychological intimacy when they were able to share their inner thoughts and feelings that were accepted, if not understood, by the partner. Such experiences were associated with feelings of mutual connection between partners. When interviewees talked of being psychologically intimate with their partners, a sense of peace and contentment within themselves permeated their remarks.

Clarifying the meaning of intimacy to these 216 partners involved an assessment of responses to questions that asked each of them to talk about their 106 relationships. These questions included a range of topics, such as what the partner meant to the participant, how their relationships may have been different from other relationships, how interviewees felt about being open with their partners, and what words best described the meaning of the partner to a participant. Of particular importance were question that elicited responses about the quality of communication, such as: How would you describe the communication between you? Positive communication was essential for the development of psychological intimacy. Although positive communication could be present without having a sense that the relationship was psychologically intimate, at least in a theoretical sense, the two factors were so closely linked that we combined them. Psychologically intimate communication captures what we are referring to as psychological intimacy that reflected themes of openness, reciprocity and interdependence between partners.

A lesbian participant discussed the meaning of psychological intimacy with her partner in a relationship that had lasted over 20 years:

I feel like I can be who I am. Now, she doesn't always like everything about that. But I can still be that way, and I don't have to pretend. That's never been something that we've had to do. I would be horrified if that had to be. I just can't imagine what that's like ... I don't see us as fused. It's important to me not to be. I don't like it. I don't think it's healthy ... I don't want to be in a relationship like that. It's important to me, for us, to be individuals as well ... She's my best friend ... There's peacefulness about that ... I can be whoever I am. I can say stuff to her that I would never say to anyone else. There are parts of myself that I don't particularly like, and I don't really share with other people, but it's OK to share with her. She'll take them in. She'll understand where it's coming from.

The partner spoke of how psychological intimacy had evolved throughout their relationship:

Although we like a lot of the same things, our interests are different ... I've appreciated the fact that she has been the one who will raise an issue or problem for the purpose of resolution, or improvement, and not just because she's angry. She seems to be willing to take that initiative. I didn't grow up in that kind of setting, so I think that's one reason this has worked. I think we both each really like the other one a lot ... There was a bond early on, in part because it was a different kind of relationship ... we were isolated for a long time, but that experience also bonded us ... I can be much more vulnerable now ... I look to her *for help with it which wasn't something I knew how to do before.*

As the couples in this study grew older together, the experience of psychological intimacy was marked by a deepening sense of relational communion between them, yet a respect for differences, as illustrated in the relationships of that couple.

A heterosexual couple reflected on the meaning of intimacy in their relationship that had lasted 30 years. The wife experienced her spouse as:

My best friend, best lover. The person I can come home to when something bad happens to me. Unfortunately, we have not had parents for many years. He is my parent as well as my friend. He is the person who most cares what is happening to me.

The meaning of intimacy to her husband was described by him:

I just like her to be next to me, near me. If you don't have that feeling, I think there is a piece that is missing. I think we are our own people, but we do it together. You just have to respect the other person...trust their decisions and beliefs and want to be with them.

The responses of these four partners reflected several themes that were central to understanding and defining psychological intimacy and its connection to the developing sense of self in these relationships. One theme, openness, reflected a sense of comfort in "being one's self;" to be able to reveal and say things to a partner that one felt could not be said to others; the use of the expression, "best friend," was often used by interviewees in describing this reciprocal dimension of their relationships. The second theme, interdependence, referred to maintaining separateness within the attachment to a partner. Maintaining interpersonal boundaries in these relationships apparently helped to sustain a sense of psychological intimacy; that is, individuals felt "safe" in revealing their inner thoughts and feelings because they could count on a partner to respect their separateness and to accept, if not understand, them. Third, psychological intimacy was not a constant in relationships but a sense or a representation in one's mind that one could confide in a partner if one needed to discuss personal matters. For both women and men, themes of connectedness, separateness and mutuality were apparent in their responses, although men tended to emphasize proximity and women mutuality in discussing how they experienced their senses of self in these relationships.

Gender and intimacy

Men and women may experience intimate communication differently. According to Prager (1995), "Few contextual variables have been studied more than gender, and few have been found more likely to affect intimate behavior" (p. 186). Whether there are endogenous factors that shape how males and females experience and value psychological intimacy is an open question. Research does suggest, however, that differences based on gender can be attributed to developmental experiences. The meaning of being psychologically intimate may be quite different to each gender, since males and females have been socialized to adopt different roles in relationships (Julien, Arellano & Turgeon 1997). Traditionally, males have been prepared for the "breadwinner" role, while females have been socialized "in ways that foster their abilities to maintain the emotional aspects of family life" (p. 114). Macoby (1990) catalogued some of the interpersonal behaviors that men may learn through socialization: competitiveness, assertiveness, autonomy, self-confidence, instrumentality, and the tendency not to express intimate feelings. Noller (1993) described some of the behaviors women may learn through socialization: nurturance, emotional expressivity, verbal exploration of emotions, and warmth. As a consequence, men may experience a sense of psychological intimacy through shared activities and women through verbal self-disclosure and shared affect (Markman & Kraft 1989). Changing cultural values toward androgyny in rearing children and in adult relationships are having significant impact on gender roles today and may be changing the meaning of intimacy to males and females in heterosexual and same gender relationships (Levant 1996).

In a self-report survey by Parks and Floyd (1996), 270 college students were asked what made their same and cross-gender friendships close and how this closeness was expressed. Across same and different gender friendships, the authors "found no support for hypotheses suggesting that women or those with a feminine gender role identification would label their friendship as 'intimate' more than men or people with a more masculine gender role identification" (p. 103). The findings of Parks and Floyd support their argument that "sharp sex differences in interpersonal behavior have always been scant" (p. 90). While helpful, this research, like many studies of intimacy, was conducted with a young adult and homogeneous sample that were reporting primarily on short-term relationships.

The extent to which men and women define and express intimacy differently remains ambiguous, not unlike the concept itself. Men may value shared activities as an instrumental means of experiencing relational connectedness that may lead to a sense of psychological intimacy, while women may place greater value on sharing thoughts and feelings about themselves. Even if these processes differentiate the meaning of intimacy to men and women in general, they cannot account for temperamental, contextual and intervening factors in relationships at different points over their life span.

Sexual orientation and intimacy

Compared to marriage, studies focused on the relationships of same sex partners are of fairly recent vintage. Peplau (1991) observed that "research on gay male and lesbian relationships dates mainly from the mid-1970's" (p.197).

Studies have found no significant differences between gay males and lesbians on measures of dyadic attachment and personal autonomy within relationships (Kurdek & Schmitt, 1986; Peplau, 1991). High dyadic attachment and low personal autonomy have been associated with the quality of relationships, a positive aspect of which was effective communication. Research is not conclusive about the quality of communication in same sex relationships, however. Some studies have found emotional distancing (Levine, 1979) and impaired communication (George & Behrendt, 1987) between gay male partners. Perhaps, those characteristics of gay male relationships suggest gender differences, rather than differences based on sexual orientation. That is, males may experience comfort in valuing separateness and autonomy in relationships, whether or not they are gay or straight, a hypothesis originally proposed by Gilligan (1982) in her studies of gender differences. In gay male relationships, distancing may become mutually reinforcing and lead to impaired communication between partners.

There has been much discussion about fusion in lesbian relationships based on hypotheses that have emerged from women's developmental research. Fusion, as an element in lesbian relationships (Burch, 1982), has been characterized by high levels of self disclosure between partners (Slater & Mencher, 1991). Elsie (1986) found that lesbian partners tended to merge emotionally compared to gay male partners who maintained emotional distance from each other. We (Mackey, O'Brien and Mackey, 1997) found that lesbian couples valued autonomy within attachment and rejected the idea of fusion in their relationships. Although these discrepancies may reflect gender differences within the context of these committed relationships, they may also be affected by how attachment and autonomy were defined operationally and how they were measured in these studies. Moreover, there is the issue of clarifying self-disclosure, fusion and differentiation as elements in psychological intimacy, especially in lesbian relationships.

The achievement of a sense of equity has been associated with mutuality in decision making among heterosexual and same gender couples (Howard, Blumstein & Schwartz, 1986), and equity has been identified as a central value in relationships that last, especially those of lesbians (Kurdek, 1988; Schneider, 1986). When partners in a relationship have felt relatively equal in their power to influence decisions, decision making has been characterized by negotiation and discussion (DeCecco & Shively, 1978). Fairness in decision-making about roles, household responsibilities and finances has been linked to relational satisfaction and potentially to perceptions of psychological intimacy.

Kurdek (1998) compared relational qualities among heterosexual, gay male and lesbian couples at one year intervals over a 5 year period. These qualities were intimacy, autonomy, equity, constructive problem solving and barriers to leaving the relationship. Of particular interest to our research were the scales that purported to measure "intimacy." Although there were many similarities between the three groups on other measures of relational quality, such as problem solving and conflict management styles, lesbians reported "higher levels of intimacy than partners in heterosexual relationships" (p. 564). That finding resonates with other studies on intimacy in relationships, including our own research, and has been attributed to the relational orientation of women. The valuing of mutuality, rather than autonomy within relationships (Surrey 1987), may nurture the development of psychological intimacy in women's relationships.

Factors that facilitate psychological intimacy

From our data, several factors were identified that help to understand the relational ambiance that nurtures psychological intimacy and the emerging self. The factors were:

conflict,
conflict management style of a partner,
decision-making,
equity,
sexual relations,
importance of sexual relations, and
physical affection.

There were questions that explored the nature of conflict. If disagreements and differences between partners had a negative effect on a participant and were viewed as disruptive to relationships, such as a cut-off in all verbal communication, conflict was coded as "major." Other conflictual matters between partners were coded "minimal."

Conflict management style was defined as the predominant way in which a participant and the partner dealt with differences and disagreements. Direct or face to face discussions of interpersonal differences between partners were coded "confrontive." If interviewees reported that they did not or could not discuss their thoughts and feelings in face to face encounters with their partners, such as denying their feelings or leaving the scene, the style was coded as "avoidant."

Interviewees were asked to discuss their " ways of making decisions." If decisions were usually made separately by one partner without the involvement of the other one, decision-making was coded "separate." If important decisions were made together, this variable was coded "mutual." The latter involved separate decision-making depending on circumstances. For example, mothers at home with children often made decisions about discipline without talking with their partners. The criteria were on predominant modes of making decisions about significant matters, such as major purchases.

Equity referred to the sense of fairness in relationships. The questions were framed as follows: Overall, have you felt a sense of fairness in the relationship? Despite differences, have things balanced out? Do you feel that your ways of solving problems, as a couple has been generally fair to each of you? If the responses to these inquiries were in the direction of an overall sense of fairness, this variable was coded "yes;" if not, it was coded "no."

Sexuality in relationships was explored through several inquiries. Interviewees were asked about physical affection that referred to bodily touching, such as hugging. If touching was regularly a part of relationships, physical affection was coded "yes" and if not a regular part of relationships, it was coded as "no/mixed." This factor was explored as part our explorations of sexual relations and included questions such as: How have you gotten along sexually? In terms of non-sexual intimacy like hugging and touching? Interviewees were also asked to assess the importance of genital sex in their relationships, which was coded as "important" or "not important." Genital sex that was very important early in relationships began to wane after several years. As the frequency and satisfaction with genital sex declined, psychological intimacy developed among most couples. For example, during the early years of these relationships, 76% of interviewees reported satisfaction with the quality of their sexual relations compared to 49% in recent years (the last 5-10 years). Comparable figures for psychological intimacy were 57% in the early years and 76% in recent years. Physical affection, such as hugging and touching, remained relatively constant throughout the years in contrast to the regression in sexual intimacy and the progression in psychological intimacy. Despite the change in sexual intimacy, genital sex continued to be seen as important from early through recent years.

<u>Relationship of factors to psychological intimacy</u>

Personal and demographic factors, such as gender, age, religion and socioeconomic status did not have a statistically significant relationship to psychological intimacy.

The following relational variables were related significantly to psychological intimacy. More than 9 out of 10 interviewees described their relationships as psychologically intimate in recent years if they also reported: positive sexual relations and physical affection between them and their partners. Among 8 out of 10 interviewees, psychological intimacy in recent years was associated with: minimal relational conflict, a confrontive conflict management style in one's partner, mutual decision-making, a sense of relational equity and the importance of sexual relations in their relationships.

Low to negligible correlations were found between psychological intimacy (i.e. more precisely psychologically intimate communication), and the independent variables of gender and sexual orientation.

Using these variables, two theoretical models were constructed and tested (See appendix B for a discussion of the research procedures). The first model contained the sexual orientation of couples along with the other significant relational variables; in the second model, the gender of interviewees was substituted for sexual orientation.

In the first model, which included sexual orientation, the following variables were predictive of psychological intimacy:

physical affection between partners,
seriousness of conflict between partners,
conflict management styles of partners as reported by interviewees, and
fairness or equity of relationships.

On the factor of the sexual orientation of couples, lesbians differed from both heterosexuals and gay males. Compared to the gay males and heterosexuals, lesbians were more likely to report that their relationships were psychologically intimate: 90% of lesbian, 75% of gay male and 72% of heterosexual interviewees reported that their relationships were psychologically intimate.

To clarify whether the differences between lesbians and the other two groups was a matter of sexual orientation or gender, a second model, in which gender was substituted for sexual orientation of couples, was constructed and tested. The factors that contributed to understanding psychological intimacy in the first model continued to have a similar effect in this modified model. The gender of interviewees had a moderate effect in contributing to reported psychological intimacy in recent years.

Sexual orientation, gender and psychological intimacy

To examine the interacting effects of gender and sexual orientation on psychological intimacy and its effect on the sense of self of individual partners, we returned to the original interview data. Four elements commonly mentioned in the literature (proximity, openness, reciprocity and interdependence) were useful in this task. Subtle differences were found in how these elements were weighed by interviewees as they talked about the meaning of psychological intimacy in their relationships.

Themes of proximity and interdependence were evident among males, as illustrated in the responses of a gay male:

emotionally, things are really good now ... it feels good knowing I'm growing old with [his partner] even though we're very different people, in that I'm very social, and I have a lot of friends, and he's not as social, and he doesn't have as many friends ... We both place a really great importance on togetherness. We make sure that we have dinner together every night and we have our weekend activities that we make sure we do together ... I think that both of us understand it's also important to be an individual and have your own life ... I think you become really uninteresting to each other if you don't have another life you can come back and share ... You need to bring things into the relationship ... that keep it growing and changing.

The importance of proximity in the connection to his partner was evident as this individual responded to our inquiry about psychological intimacy. At the same time, he noted the value that he placed on separateness from his partner. By implication, he was also talking about the element of interdependence as he expressed the joy of "growing old" with his partner in spite of the differences in their individual psychological makeups. He emphasized proximity along with interpersonal differentiation as he discussed the relationship and its meaning to his sense of self.

The responses of many women tended to reflect themes of openness and mutuality along with a respect for differences in the psychologically intimate connections with their partners. The significance of these themes to a woman's sense of self is conveyed in the words of this lesbian partner:

What has been good is the ongoing caring and respect and the sense that there is somebody there who really cares, who has your best interest, who loves you, who knows you better than anybody, and still likes you, and just that knowing, that familiarity, the depth of that knowing, the depth of that connection which is so incredibly meaningful. There is something spiritual after awhile. It has a life of its own. This is what is really so comfortable.

Variations by gender may have reflected how individuals perceived and valued different elements of psychological intimacy within themselves and in their partners. Because of the gender differences between partners in heterosexual relationships, these variations on the theme of psychological intimacy were manifested in a different way. The following observations of a heterosexual male illustrated those variations; he viewed his wife as:

very unselfish, and she would sacrifice so that I could go out and do my thing. One thing that we have always done, always, is talk constantly, to each other. I don't know what we talk about, and I don't know what we've had to talk about all these years, but we still communicate with each other ... We've had fights...when she gets mad at me, I stop talking to her. And then she feels very bad, and this may last a day or two, and then it passes and everything is fine again ... She's more open than I am. I keep a lot inside and I don't let it out, and that's probably not good. But, that's the way I am.

Many heterosexual males viewed observable qualities in their wives, such as support and their style of managing conflict, as important in developing and maintaining a sense of psychological intimacy in their marriages. Females, on the other hand, often commented on the observable and then went on to identify their understanding of the underlying dynamics, which shaped behavior. More than men, women talked about the interplay of relational dynamics. For example, the spouse in this marriage reported that:

I filled certain needs in him, and I know he filled certain needs in me ... he didn't have very high self-esteem. I may have boosted his confidence a lot ... He tells me I go ballistic over stupid things, and he outwardly is very calming ... I don't always agree with him, and he does not always agree with me ... but we're good friends through it all, and I think that if you have a good friend, you should be able to disagree, or agree, or get angry or be happy or any number of emotions, if that's your friend, that's your friend ... I don't even know how to describe it, you just have that closeness ... there has to be enough there so that when all these little outside things are finally gone, it's not: "Who are you? I don't know you, and we don't have anything." You have to really work at keeping that level of a relationship active ... not just a physical spark, but just the whole picture.

Themes of connectedness and separateness in these four interview passages were important dynamics in understanding the meaning of psychological intimacy to interviewees. The elements of proximity, closeness, mutuality and interdependence may have been shaped most significantly by the interaction of males and females in same and opposite gender relationships. That is, it may not be gender alone that may account for the differences between males and females. If women value attachment in relationships in a way different from men, then the data may suggest a mutually reinforcing process toward strengthening connectedness in lesbian relationships. In heterosexual and gay male relationships, the value that males place on separateness in relationships may temper the quality of attachment that develops over the years and result in different forms of psychological intimacy. What emerges from the data, regardless of the differences was the link between psychological intimacy and one's sense of self.

Psychological intimacy between lesbian partners had a different relational history from that of heterosexual and gay male partners. From the early years to recent years, our data suggest a progressive shift toward psychological intimacy between lesbian partners. Lesbians were as avoidant of face to face discussions of conflict as heterosexual and gay males during the early years of their relationships. For lesbians, the avoidance appeared to be the consequence of fearing abandonment by their partners if they openly confronted differences. Only as lesbian couples became increasingly disenchanted with their relationships did modification in conflict management styles occur. Usually, one partner took the risk of expressing her unhappiness. That encounter resulted in 85% of lesbians applying for therapy as a couple. Based on their reports, couples therapy appeared to facilitate the development of psychologically intimate communication between lesbian partners and the emergence of a positive sense of self within partners.

Discussion

The study of psychological intimacy in human relationships is a highly complex and dynamic process. Defining intimacy is a challenge, as is the importance of specifying the operational parameters. We defined psychological intimacy as the sense that partners had of their relationships as a place in which they could share personal thoughts and feelings about themselves and their relationships not expressed customarily with others. In this definition, positive communication was a quintessential component of psychological intimacy. We focused on cognitive themes about the meaning of relationships to individual partners rather than on specific interpersonal behaviors.

The results suggested that factors within relationships, themselves, had a more powerful effect in shaping the meaning of psychological intimacy than did social and demographic factors. The data suggested that a sense of psychological intimacy was nurtured: when interpersonal conflict was kept to minimal levels, when one's partner dealt with conflict in the relationship by initiating face to face discussion of differences, when one had a feeling that the relationship was fair and when there were expressions of affection between partners through touching and hugging. Perhaps, a reason that these relationships endured was that these factors nurtured a sense of psychological intimacy that contributed to relational stability.

In addition to the factors that had a shaping effect on psychological intimacy in recent years, subtle differences were found between lesbians and others. Differences based on gender and sexual orientation suggest a subtle interacting dynamic of these factors on psychological intimacy in relationships that last. Perhaps, a mutually reinforcing dynamic between two women who are committed to personal and relational development may explain the subtle yet important differences between lesbian couples and other couples in this study. Lesbians expressed a commitment to developing their relationships toward higher levels of psychological intimacy, which was qualitatively different from other couples.

The data support the hypothesis that psychological intimacy plays an important role in shaping the sense of self in adulthood and in supporting its emergence. How does this happen? One way is that a relationship in which one may feel safe may allow aspects of the self to emerge as they cannot or do not emerge in other relationships. Career oriented relationships usually demand that an individual contain personal thoughts and feelings that do not fit with the requirements of a job. Indeed, parts of the self that may emerge in intimate relationships may be inappropriate in other roles and contexts. Psychologically intimate communication characterized by acceptance and respect for individuality by one's partner may enhance esteem for the self. Such a relational ambiance may also be a refuge from the strains of everyday life, notably those associated with work roles.

The quality of psychological intimacy in these relationships changed as partners lived out their lives together. In other words, relational intimacy and its effect on the emerging self is a dynamic process between committed partners who remain together for many years. To capture that theme, passages from interviews with a Black couple who were married for 37 years are presented. As they spoke of the depth of their evolving love for one other, themes of adaptability, resiliency and commitment emerged. The husband remembered times of major conflict when:

the communication was broken down; it started breaking down real bad. She started going her own way and I started going mine and it went that way for quite a while...it almost tore us apart. We were just living and staying under the same roof ...today, every day ain't peaches and cream but it's a lot better than what it used to be. We laugh and talk about some of the things that almost broke our marriage up, all kinds of stuff. And I know she loves me and she knows that I love her. We just know that about each other...in my own way of thinking, I loved her all along but I didn't know how to say it... now I can say it but I still get a funny feeling. And I know it's true you know. It's just that I never knew what love was. When she hurts or has pain or something it bothers me. I don't think I even cared; I didn't know how to. So, I almost drove her completely away from me...I think about it even now, but I don't let it bother me because there's nothing I can do about it...we talk about some of that stuff now, and laugh about it. I think it really brought us closer together...Sometimes I'll be laying in bed at night and I'll just be running this through my mind. And I think that God must have wanted us to be together. With all the turmoil...we're still together today, and we love one another and care about one another more now than we did when we first started...the closeness has improved greatly over the last two or three years; we're more understanding and more respectful of one another. We've become like one. She means my whole life to me right now...when one of us has to go, pass away, I hope that it would be me. I want to go first... that's how much I love her...

Remembering her expectations of marriage as a young bride, his wife commented that:

most people who do go into marriage feel like the storybook romance is going to go on forever. But it doesn't. It's a thin line between love and hate. You can love in a marriage and you can hate in a marriage. But you got to be able to recognize it: "It's OK for me to hate. It's OK for me to love. It's OK if I tell you to go to hell. Fine, maybe tomorrow I won't." I had to learn that myself as I grew with him. I said these vows to this man, and half of them, I didn't mean because that was my ticket for out of the house. My love grew ...that's great in a marriage if two people can say: "it's OK, we can grow with one another"... We've had good times and we've had bad times. But that's life, you know...I think the best thing in life about two people is when they're able to come back and say, "I'm sorry," or "I did see it wrong." He has been a real human being for me...as we grew, we grew stronger. I knew that he was good...you can feel when people love you. I just loved my husband and he loved me. There's been times in our lives when I could say: "I don't think this is what I want out of life. " But we always sit down and we talk about it and we give it another go... as you grow, and you're with someone for so long, you learn to get all that nurturing from them. He's my world. That's what he means to me. You know, the world out there is the world, but he's my world.

Conclusion

The human propensity to think stereotypically may preclude the development of psychological intimacy in many relationships. George Harrison spoke to this when, at the age of 52 in a rare interview, he observed that he was "not really 'Beatle George.' 'Beatle George' is like a suit or shirt that I once wore on occasion and until the end of my life people may see that shirt and mistake it for me"(Newsweek, 12/10/01, p. 82). How we define ourselves is a complex process and is shaped by the perceptions of others, which may persist even as time goes by and life changes. The clothing, which we wear in the form of social roles and behaviors, including professional ones, is as much a part of our self as is our inner and often private world. However, only in specific types of relationships, such as the close and committed relationships in our research, may there be support to look beyond what we are wearing. Psychologically intimate relationships are an invaluable resource in consolidating a whole sense of self during the adult years.

References

Berscheid, E. and Reis, H.T. (1998). Attraction and close relationships. In D.T. Gilbert, S.T. Fiske & G. Lindzey (Eds.), The handbook of social psychology (4th ed., Vol 1, pp. 391-445). New York: McGraw-Hill.

Blasband, D., and Peplau, L.A. (1985). Sexual exclusivity versus sexual openness in gay male male couples. Archives of Sexual Behavior, 14 (5), 395-412.

Burch, B. (1982). Psychological merger in lesbian couples: A joint ego psychological and systems approach. Family Therapy, 9, 201-208.

Coombs, R.H. (1991). Marital status and personal well-being: A literature review. Family Relations. 40, 97-102.

DeCecco, J.P. and Shively, M.G. (1978). A study of perceptions of rights and needs in interpersonal conflicts in homosexual relationships. Journal of Homosexuality, 3 (3), 205-216.

Duck, S.W. and Wright, P.H. (1993). Re-examining gender differences in same-gender friendships: A close look at two kinds of data. Sex Roles, 28: 1-19.

Elise, D. (1986). Lesbian couples: The implications of sex differences in separation-individuation. Psychotherapy, 23 (2), 305-310.

George, K.D. and Behrendt, A.E. (1987). Therapy for male couples experiencing relationship problems and sexual problems. Journal of Homosexuality, 14 (1-2), 77-88.

Gilligan, C (1982). In a different voice: Psychological theory and women's development. Cambridge, MA: Harvard University Press.

Gottman, J., Coan, J., Carriere, S. and Swanson, C. (1998). Predicting marital unhappiness and stability from newlywed interactions. Journal of Marriage and the Family, 60, 5-22.

Hazan, C. and Shaver, R. (1994). Attachment as an organizational framework for research on close relationships. Psychological Inquiry, 5 (1), 1-22.

Headly, B. and Wearing, A. (1992). Understanding happiness: A theory of subjective well-being. Melbourne Australia: Longman cheshire.

Hegelson, V.S., Shaver, P.R. and Dyer, M. (1987). Prototypes of intimacy and distance in same-sex and opposite-sex relationhips. Journal of Social and Personal Relationships, 4, 195-233.

Hendrix, L. (1997). Quality and equality in marriage: A cross-cultural view. Cross-Cultural Research: The Journal of Comparative Social Science, 31, 201-225.

Hesse-Biber, S., Dupuis, P. and Kinder, T. S. (1992). HyperRESEARCH: A tool for the analysis of qualitative data. (Computer Program). Randolph (MA): Researchware.

Hill, C.E., Thompson, B.J. and Williams, E.N. (1997). A guide to conducting consensual qualitative research. The Counseling Psychologist, 25(4), 517-572.

Horwitz, A. V., White, H.R. and Howell-White, S. (1996). Becoming married and mental health: A longitudinal study of a cohort of young adults. Journal of Marriage and the Family, 58, 895-907.

Howard, J.A., Blumstein, P. and Schwartz, P. (1986). Sex, power, and influence tactics in intimate relationships. Journal of Personality and Social Psychology, 51 (1), 102-109.

Jourard, S.M. (1971). Self-disclosure: An experimental analysis of the transparent self. New York: Wiley.

Julien, D., Arellano, C. and Turgeon, L. (1997). Gender issues in heterosexual, gay male and lesbian couples. In Halford, W. K. amd Markman, H.J. (Eds.), Clinical handbook of marriage and couples interventions, (pp. 107-127). Chichester, England: John Wiley & Sons, Inc.

Kiecolt-Glaser, J.K., Fisher, L.D., Ogrocki, P., Stout, J.C., Speicher, C.E. and Glasser, R. (1988). Marital discord and immunity in males. Psychomatic Medicine, 50, 213-229.

Kurdek, L. (1998). Relationship outcomes and their predictors: Longitudinal evidence from heterosexual married, gay male cohabiting, and lesbian cohabiting couples. Journal of Marriage and the Family, 60, 553-568.

Kurdek, L.A. (1988). Relationship quality of gay male and lesbian cohabiting couples. Journal of Homosexuality, 15(3/4), 93-118.

Kurdek, L. A. (1991). Correlates of relationship satisfaction in cohabiting gay male and lesbian couples: Integration of contextual, investment, and problem-solving models. Journal of Personality and Social Psychology, 61(6), 910-922.

Kurdek, L.A., and Schmitt, J.P. (1986). Relationship quality of partners in heterosexual married, heterosexual cohabiting, and gay male and lesbian relationships. Journal of Personality and Social Psychology, 51 (4), 711-720.

Lane, R.E. (1998). Searching for lost companions in the groves of the market. In D. Kahneman, E. Diener and N. Schwartz (Eds.), Understanding well-being: Scientific perspectives on enjoyment and suffering. NY: Russell Sage foundation.

Lauer, R.H., Lauer, J.C. and Kerr, S.T. (1990). The long-term marriage: Perceptions of stability and satisfaction. International Journal of Aging and Human Development, *31,* 189-195.

Levant, R. (1996). The new psychology of men. Professional Psychology: Research and Practice. 27, 259-269.

Levine, M. (1979). Gay male men: The sociology of male homosexuality. New York: Harper & Row.

Mackey, R., Diemer, M. and O'Brien, B. (2000). Psychological intimacy in the lasting relationships of heterosexual and same sex relationships. Sex Roles. 43(3/4), 201-227.

Mackey, R.A.,O'Brien, B.A. and Mackey (1997). Gay male and lesbian couples: Voices from lasting relationships. Westport, CT: Praeger.

Mackey, R.A. and O'Brien, B.A. (1995). Lasting marriages: Men and women growing together. Westport, CT: Praeger.

Mackey R. and O'Brien, B.A. (1998). Marital conflict management: gender and ethnic differences. Social Work: Journal of the National Association of Social Workers. 43(2) March, 128-141.

Mackey R. and O'Brien, B.A. (1999). Adaptation in lasting marriages: A multi-dimensional prospective. Families in Society: The Journal of Contemporary Human Services, 80 (6), 587-596.

Macoby, E.E. (1990). Gender and relationships. American Psychologist, 45, 513-520.

Markman, H.J. and Kraft, S.A. (1989). Men and women in marriage: Dealing with gender differences in marital therapy. Behavior Therapist, 12, 51-56.

Mastekaasa, A. (1995). Age variations in suicide rates and and self-repoted subjective well-being of married and never married persons. Journal of Community and Applied Social Psychology, 5, 21-39.

Monsour, M. (1992). Meanings of intimacy in cross- and same-sex friendships. Journal of Social and Personal Relationships, 9: 277-295.

Mroczek, D. K. and Kolarz, C.M. (1998). The effect of age on positive and negative affect: A developmental perspective on happiness. Journal of Personality and Social Psychology, 75, 1333-1349.

Newsweek, 12/10/01.

Noller, P. (1993). Gender and emotional communication in marriage. Journal of Language and Social Psychology, 12, 132-154.

Parks, M.R. and Floyd, K. (1996). Meanings for closeness and intimacy in friendship. Journal of Social and Personal Relationships, 13(1), 85-107.

Peplau, L.A. (1991). Lesbian and Gay male Relationships. In J.C. Gonsiorek & J.D. Weinrich (Eds.). Homosexuality: Research implications for public policy, (pp. 177-196). Newbury Park, CA: Sage.

Prager, K.J. (1995). The psychology of intimacy. New York: Guilford Press.

Reilly, M. E. and Lynch, J. M. (1990). Power-sharing in lesbian partnerships. Journal of Homosexuality, 19(3), 1-30.

Rosenbluth, S.C. and Steil, J.M. (1995). Predictors of intimacy for women in heterosexual and homosexual couples. Journal of Social and Personal Relationships, 2(2), 163-175.

Rubin, L.B. (1983). Intimate strangers. New York: Harper & Row

Schaefer, M. and Olson, D. (1981). Assessing intimacy: The PAIR Inventory, Journal of Marital and Family Therapy, 47-59.

Schneider, M. S. (1986). The relationships of cohabiting lesbian and heterosexual couples: A comparison. Psychology of Women Quarterly, 10, 234-239.

Slater, S., and Mencher, J. (1991). The lesbian family life cycle: A contextual approach. American Journal of Orthopsychiatry, 61, 372-382.

Strauss, A., and Corbin, J. (1990). Basics of Qualitative Research. Newbury Park (CA): Sage.

Surrey, J. L. (1987). Relationship and empowerment. Work in Progress, No. 30. Wellesley (MA): Stone Center Working Paper Series.

Swain, S. (1989). Covert intimacy: Closeness in men's friendships. In B. Risman & P. Schwartz (Eds.), Gender in intimate relationships: A microstructural approach. Belmont, CA: Wadsworth.

White, K., Speisman, J., Jackson, D., Bartis, S. and Costos, D. (1986). Intimacy, maturity and its correlation in young married couples. Journal of Personality and Social Psychology, *50,* 152-162.

Chapter 04 - The Damaged Self and the Process of Psychotherapy

Often, I have treated individuals who have had previous therapy, sometimes years of it with therapists of different orientations. As a result, there may have been rather specific behavioral changes yet the individual continues to experience feelings about themselves that are troublesome. This chapter focuses on such individuals and uses a case to show the beginning to ongoing process of psychotherapy.

In the past three decades, impairments in the self and their treatment have received increasing attention in the professional literature (Basham & Miehls,2004; Berzoff, Flanagan & Hertz, 1996; Jackson, 1991; Elson, 1986). These disordered states, which cover a spectrum of damage in one's sense of self, may be conceptualized along a diagnostic continuum bounded at one pole by the psychoses and at the other by the neuroses (Mackey, 1985). Rather than a diagnostic group, the concept of damage or impairment refers to persistent thoughts and feelings that compromise the emergence of a whole sense of self in adulthood. These inner messages may demean esteem for the self that may be obscured by ingrained defenses, although many of these individuals function very adaptively in specific roles and relationships.

This chapter focuses on people who suffer from impairments in their sense of self as a result of historical damage that has become a part of them. It is concerned with a method of psychotherapy with individuals who feel highly vulnerable in personal relationships yet have the capacity to contain their affect with a fair degree of cognitive control. They may "know" what their central conflicts are; yet their feelings do not match their thinking. It is not uncommon for these people to function well, even exceptionally, in certain social roles and relationships such as work, yet to experience disabling anxiety in other roles and relationships, such as loving and close friendships. Skills and inner resources that are highly adaptive in one context are impediments in another context.

Two characteristics need to be understood in working with these clients. Each is critical in deciding upon the method of intervention and the way in which the therapist uses her or his professional self in the therapeutic relationship. The client's sense of narcissistic vulnerability is one characteristic. Psychosocial histories reveal considerable deprivation of appropriate empathic attunement by critical figures during childhood and adolescence. A sense of loneliness and depletion often characterized inner affective life during those crucial developmental periods. The resulting rage, bred out of prolonged and intense disappointment, is often expressed in aggressive behaviors that inevitably have a severe self-defeating consequence. Excessive drug use, teenage pregnancy, and suicide attempts are not unusual. A second characteristic about these clients is their cognitive and other personal resources, which may be utilized in certain contexts where there is clear structure and cues for success. It is not surprising to find that these people have achieved unusual success at school and work, although the psychopathology associated with impaired development of the self may undermine adaptive successes from time to time. Indeed, the sense of emptiness associated with emotional deprivation often fuels the need to be successful. Those achievements serve a compensatory function but also insure an illusionary sense of protection against the dangers inherent in their perceptions of interpersonal relationships.

Richard A. Mackey

Less available to the early exploratory phase of therapy is the intense shame or primitive guilt that these people carry within themselves into adulthood. Rage at empathetically unattuned figures of childhood and adolescence is shamed by these same figures, which results in an inner harshness, which may lead to perfectionist strivings to appease their shame, to compensate for inner turmoil and to avoid replication of disappointing and painful relationships. It is not unusual to hear projective complaints of others being distant. Another manifestation is cognitive rigidity in which theses individuals literally cannot understand why others cannot be more like them. The latter also suggests difficulties in differentiation of self and object representations.

Although borderline features may characterize the psychic structure of these clients, the nuclear conflicts, which become the focal points in therapy, revolve around issues of integration rather than of differentiation. That is, the predominant concerns tend toward containment of fragmentation of self and a longing for personal wholeness. Their interpersonal world is grounded on a narcissistic need to feel more fulfilled internally yet shame for being so needy. Because of their excessive expectations, these clients may become disillusioned with relationships that inevitably cannot be responsive enough to their inner depleted states. As with the borderline client, there is an internal fear of losing a sense of one's self in relationships. Because of the intactness of cognition including the ability, although distorted, to assess reality, these individuals become highly anxious about relationships. Closeness and ambiguities threaten differentiation and may lead to flight-or-fight reactions. In highly structured relationships where parameters are explicit and in which they have control, these individuals may function quite adequately and productively.

Feeling vulnerable in relationships produces a specific quality to the self-containing structure of the self. The structural effect in adult clients will vary depending on how well parenting figures were able to respond to their bodily, affective, and cognitive needs during childhood. Within these midrange disorders, especially with people who experience the world as threatening, fragmentation will be avoided only by maintaining control or distance in human relationships. A sense of self is achieved only at the expense of developing false, illusionary selves, which contain frightening and painful affect.

Theoretical framework

Despite a common motivation to understand the psychological mysteries of the human condition, development of theory has tended to proceed along separate and independent lines in which theorists develop their ideas within a specific framework. For the practitioner of psychotherapy, these independent lines of theoretical development pose a challenge. One may adopt a narrow perspective by adhering to a specific framework and developing techniques based only on that framework. The choice here is to use concepts discussed earlier in this book (see chapters 1-3) to formulate an empathic approach to these people, who are being seen increasingly in clinical practice.

In chapter 1, we explored the notion of the dualism within the self (Winnicott, 1965; Bowen, 1978; and Masterson, 1985. We also talked of a fourth model in which the outer level of the self was conceptualized along a continuum from defensive and false to adaptive and generative. Taking these notions of self, we may think of the biopsychosocial dimensions of self as becoming organized into a bimodal structure. That structure, fueled by aspects of one's biological endowment will be shaped by the responsiveness of those people who play crucial parenting roles in the socialization process. Although the self is an open system with the potential to change throughout life, the substantive structures are laid down early and are less amenable to change after adolescence. Throughout life we experience a sense of cohesiveness when the biological, psychological and social dimensions and their constituents are more rather than less at peace with each other. Thus, cohesiveness implies an integration of the dimensions, which is carried out through the mediating functions of the self. An integrated sense of self may be lost if the dimensions do not fit as they need, as in a crisis; fragmentation may result. The fragmented self has an impaired, false, and pseudo quality which serves both a defensive/protective as well as adaptive/survival function. Both modes of self exist in all of us, to some degree, no matter how well endowed our potential or how optimal the developmental resources available in the environment; thus, the importance of attending to both strengths and liabilities in the therapy.

If there is an inherent thrust to preserve a cohesive sense of self, as is proposed in this model for understanding the self, there is also an equally important struggle to contain fragmentation. For the child nurtured in an optimally attuned environment that is empathetically responsive to developmental needs, the external world will be experienced internally as a safe place - a place where one can be free and secure enough to learn both in a cognitive and emotional sense. In other words, the external world will contain the supplies in the form of emotional nurturance, cognitive stimulation, and reasonable boundaries based on an empathic understanding of the child's needs. In this context, the child gradually internalizes the containing features of the environment so that he is eventually able to take care of her/himself rather than rely on external figures. Conversely, the more unattuned, intrusive or indifferent the internal experience of the external world, the more one will feel propelled to rely only on the emerging self as the only source of safety. When this pathological process begins early in childhood, the emerging self of a child may not contain the resources for coping with threats to cohesiveness. Safety is to be found only within the self and not in human relationships that create a culture for the emergence of false and impaired selves.

The child with good enough potential for intellectual functioning may respond to culturally unattuned environments by relying too pervasively on cognitive skills for coping with empathic deprivation. These skills, which may be highly adaptive in certain contexts, will be employed defensively to protect the fragile self in other contexts. This process will be reinforced if the child's only sense of adequacy comes about from the rewards associated with intellectual competence. Intellectualization and rationalization may compensate for inner emptiness and protect the emerging self from the hunger, rage, and shame at being cheated out of crucial narcissistic supplies to which each child is entitled.

Adler (1985) and Masterson (1985) help us understand the internal processes and external factors that compromise the emerging self of these individuals. Their ideas, coupled with those of Gardner (1983) about human intelligence, provide a theoretical framework for understanding the specific constellation of dynamics at play in the lives of clients who suffer from narcissistic depletion yet possess intact cognitive skills. Adler proposes that a primary source of pathology (in borderline character disorders) is a "primary inner emptiness" which is attributable to a "relative absence of positive introjects." This insufficiency of internal self-soothing resources may be traced to a "real loss, relative neglect, or overindulgence alternating with neglect" in the early histories of these people. Thus, the individual does not achieve solid evocative memory of critical libidinal objects and remains vulnerable to stresses, which may lead to fragmentation of the self. If these childhood fragments persist into adulthood, the individual will remain caught between a need to depend on external objects to maintain psychological stability, on the one hand, and an inner panic that these same relationships may lead to annihilation of self, on the other hand. In this limbo-like state the core of one's identity is experienced as an "intensely painful aloneness."

In trying to understand what is at stake for these people, Masterson proposes that a real self exists which he defines as the "sum of self and object representations with their related affects" (Mastcrson, 1985, p. 221). The realness of self would appear to be more than this and to include, as well, the individual potentialities of each child present at birth as part of her/his constitutional endowment. Under optimal circumstances one's sense of realness emerges as a self-contained structure. That is, when empathic supplies are available in loving relationships, the child will have the opportunity to integrate individualized characteristics with the reasonable and appropriate expectations of loved ones about social role behaviors. In families where parenting is not attuned to and respectful of an individual's potentials, impaired selves may emerge to "defend against painful affect" whose source, according to Masterson, is panic associated with the fear of abandonment. To preserve tenuous attachments and to avoid abandonment, the child must conform to the intrusive demands of others. Thus, the potential for the individuated self to emerge as a whole and separate entity is submerged in the interest of conforming to expectations. The psychic price, Adler suggests, is a profound aloneness.

People who enter adulthood with an insufficiency of childhood empathic supplies will experience pervasive inner loneliness and live their life in anticipation of being abandoned or rejected in any relationship that is of importance to them. When people with this configuration of unfinished emotional business are also endowed with “good enough” intelligence in one or more frames of mind (Gardner, 1983), they may cope with the inner threat of rejection or abandonment by a particular combination of primitive and seemingly high-level defenses. That is, in the interest of binding the anxiety and denying the threat, these people may employ fairly high-level defenses, which may include rationalization and intellectualization. This defensive structure seems to occur when there are available in the environment persistent patterns of reinforcement for intellectual achievement. In many of these clients, that form of achievement may be the only source of esteem for the emerging self. Positive reinforcement for success in specific contexts may temporarily neutralize inner loneliness. These defense mechanisms may serve the individual in a highly adaptive way in certain contexts such as school and later in work. The clinical observations leading to this hypothesis do not imply that these clients do not employ lower defenses, such as splitting, projection, and denial. It does suggest, however, that cognitive resources and skills, which are highly adaptive in learning and work, will become defenses in containing the painful affect associated with intense inner aloneness and panic about abandonment. While the substratum of the defensive structure is built upon more primitive defensive needs organized at earlier levels of development, the primary defenses that are most available to modification in therapy are of a nature which have traditionally been connected with higher level neurotic structures. These defenses serve a vital self-containing function and protect the individual from the constant anxieties about fragmentation. It is, therefore, critical to be empathetically attuned to the powerful forces beyond what is observable in social role behaviors. In that substratum these individuals suffer from a very fragile sense of self.

The Therapeutic Process

When these people apply for therapy, they usually present with a specific configuration of defensive and adaptive structures. At an adaptive level, they may appear as reasonably well contained. At a defensive level they may need to distance themselves and to resist our efforts to explore affective components of life, especially interpersonal relationships, which are of an intimate rather than work or task oriented nature. Exploration may reveal significant accomplishments in relationships that are more structured and less personally demanding than those that involve psychological intimacy. Their sense of confidence in being able to take care of themselves and to contain fragmentation is grounded on a capacity to deal with threats, challenges, and losses in a cognitively oriented problem-solving mode of adaptation. "The idea" of feeling, except for experiencing satisfaction at accomplishing tasks, may be quite foreign to them. Although the reason for seeking therapy may involve concerns that are quite specific, there is an accompanying message of something missing within the self and in relationships.

Inevitably, something has changed in life to challenge the mode of coping which may have "worked" in the past to contain any affective threat to self-esteem. As one listens to their concerns, the missing pieces become evident. Empathic and relatedness functions have not developed sufficiently to enable the individual to experience an inner sense of competence in situations that cannot be controlled. As a consequence, the individual is unable to contain powerful feelings intruding into their sense of a competent self.

While initially cooperative and compliant, the client may soon become difficult to manage. Questions about the therapist's competence, demands for expert advice, intense anger and disappointment with anticipated results along with acting out are not uncommon. The need to control others in the interest of protecting the fragility of the self undermines exploration and clarification about the meaning of their behavior. Techniques oriented to interpretation and education are not timely at this point in the therapeutic process. When employed, they may heighten resistance rather than facilitate involvement in therapy. These so-called resistive behaviors of these clients need to be redefined as the only way in which they can allow an important yet threatening person to know of the intensity and frightening quality of their struggle to contain fragmentation.

Empathic attunement is a critical resource in the efforts of therapists to be helpful to these psychologically damaged clients. One of the challenges in making empathic contact is that the client's defensive and adaptive functions may be fused. As a consequence, a therapist may encounter considerable rigidity in exploring how the client feels. The fusion may create a self-containing structure that will only begin to soften after a considerable period of testing the trustworthiness of the therapist. Behind the outer adaptive resiliency, which has enabled these individuals to survive, may lie an inner world of emptiness, narcissistic rage, and intense shame.

Empathy is to psychodynamic work with this population what free association is to psychoanalytic work with neurotically impaired clients. To be empathic is to resonate vicariously with the inner affective world of these clients while respecting their need to deal with our attunement to that world as their developmental state permits. Empathy, a natural human sensitivity informed by theory and tempered by professional ethics, is primarily a tool of exploration and a means of observation as the therapist is getting to know a client. Building upon that supportive foundation, educative modes of intervention may be integrated into the clinical work as the client experiences and internalizes trust in the relationship.

With these individuals, one needs to be empathetically available in other ways as well. While attunement to the inner world of an impaired self is critical, it is equally important to be empathetically respectful of the client's need to take care of her/himself through false or pseudo selves. Understanding the need for particular defensive styles neutralizes the temptation to move too rapidly toward confrontive and educative modes of intervention. To challenge an existing self-containing structure may overwhelm the person with an inner aloneness and leave her/him with a sense of abandonment. Early in therapy the goal is to engage the client in a mutual effort of exploration for the sake of understanding and not to change her/him. Firm parameters, empathetically informed, are valuable resources for accomplishing that challenging task. Consistency, tolerance, and patience informed empathetically by their absence in the client are indispensable to the therapy during this period.

Because of their intense neediness, rigidity, as well as agility at controlling the world, these clients are a challenge to engage in treatment. As with disorders of the self, in general, the transference reflects the developmental deficits, which have been internalized by the client. They may be demanding yet rejecting of our help; they may idealize us only to later question our competence; they may persistently seek rational explanations to neutralize frustrated narcissistic needs. It may be difficult to maintain empathic neutrality because of the intensity of transference needs in the relationship. The temptation may be to strike back by using premature confrontations/interpretations, to collude in the client's resistance by keeping the dialogue at an intellectual level, or to dismiss the client as unready or not a suitable candidate for therapy. No other clients probably challenge our capacity to contain negative reactions. In part, success is achieved through the client's experiencing the capacity of the therapist to contain countertransference and to put her/his feelings to work in the interest of understanding how the narcissistic needs of the client are manifested in human relationships. Through this mutual experience the therapeutic relationship may become ameliorative of an impaired sense of self.

As the therapeutic process unfolds and the client feels empathetically heard, understood, and respected, opportunities evolve to engage the client in modes of exploration that are increasingly oriented to confrontation and education. The development of awareness of self through educative modes needs to be grounded on and inextricably part of the exploratory/supportive process. Integration of new learning about the self will be compromised unless the client feels accepted and understood. The skill of doing this type of therapy with this population involves the empathic dexterity in slipping behind the defenses of clients, which are part of the false self, and to invite them to use their cognitive resources to become more attuned to their narcissistic injuries. Rather than confront false selves as resistance, the approach is to use this part of the self to push back the boundaries of awareness; in other words, to enable the client to use what had served him defensively for an adaptive purpose.

The case of Ms. G

The client, a thirty five year-old White, single professional woman, with a successful career in business, was referred by her former therapist who was leaving the geographic area. In exploring the referral, the previous therapist reported that the client had presented many obstacles to engagement in therapy. She had applied for help 6 months before the referral. Her use of therapy was intermittent and characterized by a help-rejecting attitude. She demanded late-evening treatment hours and was generally critical of this therapist's and previous therapists' capacity to help her. Past treatment included psychodynamic as well as cognitive/behavioral therapies, all of which the client said were "failures."

<u>The exploratory phase</u>

In the initial interview Ms. G presented as a competent and articulate individual who readily identified her major concerns. She said that she would like to be more herself but was not sure what that meant. To the inquiries of the therapist, Ms. G reported that she did not feel good about who she was but was quite frightened to find out what lay behind this. She was particularly concerned about her relationships with men, with whom she could not get involved beyond superficial friendships. She also said her relationships with women were very distant; she did not have any close friends but several acquaintances. In addition to her most recent therapy, she had consulted several other psychodynamic and cognitive/behavioral therapists over the previous ten years, none of whom, she reported, had been able to help her. Although the referring therapist had indicated that a major concern of the client was in weight reduction, Ms. G did not identify weight as a major concern in this initial interview.

As the client discussed her concerns about herself and her relationships, the exploration led to a discussion of her family. She described her mother as a domineering and tyrannical individual who was very controlling and critical of Ms. G during her childhood. She was constantly put down by mother, as were her siblings. She has a younger sister by 2 years and an older sister by 2 years; mother treated all three in a very similar way. The client described how her mother was equally withholding and demeaning of the three children throughout childhood and adolescence. In contrast, father was described as a quiet and passive individual whom the children looked to for care and nurturance. He took care of them and was available as a sympathetic listener when he was at home, which was rare, since his job required significant travel. The description of the father was in stark contrast to the mother, who was described as the polar opposite of him.

Ms. G was quite open in the initial interview about events in childhood and adolescence, which were characterized by several serious incidents. She recalled being a high achiever in school, yet the mother was never pleased with her accomplishments no matter how well she "performed." She recalled an attempted suicide at 13 after coming home with all A's on her report card only to have mother warn her that the client could not afford to settle for all perfect grades only one time. She ran away several times during adolescence but always with a specific destination in mind, usually a friend's home where she knew she would be accepted, comforted, and protected. There was also a pregnancy that ended in abortion when the client was around 16 years of age. In general, the life of this client from latency through adolescence was depicted as very lonely, volatile and unhappy.

The client said that her father died after a lengthy illness 2-1/2 years before this interview; since his death the relationship with mother has become even more conflicted. Father had served as a buffer and mediator in the family who stood between the children and mother; he would intercede for them and protect them from her wrath. Ms. G said that her personality and role in the family was somewhat different from that of the other siblings. She saw herself as a highly sensitive child who also had a keen mind and was very perceptive of hurts and slights. To this day, she feels more affected by mother than do her siblings. The older sister has been able to escape the orbit of hostility and recriminations by living in another state; she is raising a family of her own and has only occasional contact with the nuclear family. The younger sister has remained single and lives close to the mother yet has been able to maintain a sympathy for mother that is uncharacteristic of the client. The younger sister is seen as fused with mother while the older sister is disengaged; the client sees herself in the middle experiencing tremendous guilt about wishing that she could be emancipated from the bind of this hostile dependent type of relationship.

The client described herself in this initial interview as a "doer." She said that she was confused because she understood what her problems were, attributing some of that understanding to her previous therapy, yet seemed bogged down by feelings of unhappiness. Her goals for accepting the referral and for pursuing therapy now were to feel and experience herself in a different type of way. In depicting her childhood as unhappy, Ms. G saw herself as someone who never developed much confidence in self. She also thought that feelings were never acknowledged or tolerated within the family so she has difficulty even getting "in touch" with feelings. To feel was strange and foreign to her. One of the things she had learned in her previous therapy was that she takes action to avoid feelings so that she would like to focus more on her reasons for that behavior in the current therapy. A noticeable characteristic about her was the intellectual and detached manner in which she described her life along with a propensity to tell me of her "insights" about herself.

In summary, this woman applied for therapy in order to understand herself, particularly to become more aware of her feelings and how they affected her current relationships. She has been able to use her cognitive skills to function in a highly adaptive way previously in school and recently in the business field. Yet, she is troubled by the reality of having few close friends and being unable to maintain a loving relationship with a man. While she presents as a competent, self-assured, and engaging person, there is an underlying sense of fear, depression, and apprehension that appear contained only when she is in control of relationships. This may help to explain why she has become so competent in her career and why she functions so successfully in task oriented relationships. She is a highly goal oriented individual who is quite productive when the parameters of relationships are explicitly clear, time limited, and goal oriented. Although splitting is a prominent feature of her family relationships and seems evident in her internal world of self and object relations, the client conveyed a higher level of psychic organization in other aspects of herself. She views the world through a highly narcissistic lens. When she is in command of situations, the client functions optimally, but experiences a sense of fragmentation when she is not in control of relationships. The initial data suggested that treatment, if it were to be successful, would have to focus on the client's sense of vulnerability in relationships, including the therapeutic relationship. Her mode for taking care of and protecting herself was reinforced by intact cognitive functioning. Containment of disabling anxieties was achieved by remaining in relationships in which she felt in control.

Beginning Phase of Therapy

The first 3 months of therapy were devoted to further exploration of the client's concerns, which included the problem of weight. The major work was done on clarifying the therapeutic contract and building an alliance. These 12 sessions focused on: the reciprocal roles of client and therapist as they were played out in sessions, the client's fears about therapy as a threat to cohesiveness, her increasing frustration and intolerance of the therapist's nondirective behavior, and persistent demands for answers. As the therapist attempted to slip behind the client's cognitive defenses in order to explore the fears and vulnerabilities of becoming involved in therapy, the client was able to talk about her difficulties in relationships; she expressed the belief that no one could live up to her values. She entrapped them with her generosity. She felt shame in receiving and security in giving. Although Ms. G was able to discuss the significance of these observations to the experience of therapy with this particular therapist, the connections were difficult to hear and to integrate. Therapy confronted her with overwhelming threats to self-esteem and a fragile sense of cohesiveness. Considerable support in the form of acknowledging the risks for her of becoming involved in exploratory/dynamic therapy was a prominent theme. The client was also offered assurance that the therapist respected her need to control the content of their discussion and would not push her to talk about anything before she was ready to discuss it.

The therapeutic role was repeatedly clarified as one of understanding her as to assist Ms. G in accomplishing her goals. The therapist suggested often that their task was to look at what got in the way of her feeling better about herself—a perplexing task for Ms. G since she already had her problems figured out yet continued to experience unhappiness, which she complained was getting worse instead of better. The frustration with the slowness of therapy led to a questioning of the therapist's competence and devaluing of his methods. She persistently questioned why her "knowing" what was good for her (i.e., losing 30 pounds) did not translate directly into behavior change. She could not understand the incongruence between thinking and feeling. She talked, for example, about her false conforming self that inevitably went "along to get along," her awareness of that behavior, her inability to change, and her anger that the therapist would not or could not help her.

Ms. G began to talk about her dating patterns and expressed a disdain for usually 'giving into guys" for sex on the first date or shortly afterwards. As the therapy unfolded, she talked not only about her fear of men leaving her if she did not do as they wished but her feelings that she had nothing else of value to offer them in a relationship except her body. Exploration of her inner emptiness and low self-regard became prominent themes in the therapy.

Concurrent with the referral for her individual therapy, Ms. G had independently consulted a family therapist whom she saw conjointly with mother. The client feared that the mother would die and leave her with a lifetime of painful guilt. Having been with father throughout his suffering prior to death, Ms. G felt at peace with him but carried an "awful fear" that her life would be ruined if she did not reconcile with her mother before the mother died. The concurrent family therapy offered another opportunity to explore the conflicts with her mother and those with the individual therapist. Because the family therapist talked and told her more than I did, the client felt cheated and enraged. As this was explored, it became clear that anger, as well as weight (mother was significantly overweight) were the only ways that the client could feel connected to her mother. They rarely talked of anything but the frustrations of loosing weight. At one level, the frustration and anger at the individual therapist were a reflection of Ms.G's efficient and active problem-solving skills, which were invaluable resources in her career. At a deeper level, her response was the only means available within herself to cope with the dangers inherent in the relationship. She was frightened of the ambiguities of individual therapy and her perception of the therapist's power; the mode for self-protection was to fill the dangerous space between them with anger, which prevented him from getting too close to her. The fear of fragmentation and shame for neediness and the resulting sense of vulnerability fostered her resistance. A break in the treatment relationship because of the therapist's vacation 3 months into therapy fed abandonment anxiety, which also contributed to resistance. With the exception of father who had always been there for her, men were portrayed as either helplessly incompetent, exploitive, or betrayers of her trust.

Another important aspect of this beginning phase was her references to her previous therapy and therapists. Ms G had been involved in cognitive, behavioral and weight reduction therapies, none of which had helped. It appeared increasingly evident that the potential gains of these previous interventions were compromised by the underlying thoughts and feeling about herself that were a significant focus of her current therapy. She both needed yet feared attention to that inner world. Exploration of that world informed by mutuality and acceptance were critical ingredients for keeping this client in therapy.

Ongoing Phase

The process of building a relationship and its inherent difficulties characterized the early months of therapy. These dynamics also characterized subsequent work with this client. However, the nature of the interaction gradually took on a different quality. The treatment process reached new plateaus, as issues were resolved in the therapeutic relationship. While the initial stage was characterized by more intense conflict related to issues discussed in the preceding section, the ongoing phase was less volatile. Two changes may account for that observation: As elements in the alliance—such as boundaries, reciprocal roles, trust, and safety—were negotiated, the client felt potential value in a new structure that earlier had been a threat. In addition to empathic support, the client was able to take in a new perspective of an affective nature on old cognitive defenses. Her confidence in taking care of herself by confronting and understanding feelings rather than explaining them away was a second shift in the ongoing phase.

A modest shift occurred early in this phase when the client recognized a persistent defensive pattern and asked the therapist for help with it. This happened after they had explored the significance of her anger at the therapist. Ms. G identified how she jumped around verbally whenever the therapist asked how she felt or commented on her feelings about a subject. She was then able to express how difficult it was to experience affect and to find words to express her feelings. Her mother was intolerant of her feelings and devalued her whenever she tried to put feelings into words. This made her feel incompetent and vulnerable—similar to her feelings in the therapeutic relationship with its lack of familiar structures. She reacted by demanding action from the therapist to reduce the threat and by questioning his competence. She gradually began to understand this behavior as a defense that had led to premature terminations in her previous therapies.

Exploration with the goal of understanding her feelings about how she used sex to hold on to relationships with men, her need to control relationships and the use of flight when sex or fight did not work were prominent themes in this phase of ongoing phase.

Other themes in the therapy in the ongoing phase were the client's need to hold on to her anger at her mother. She felt connected through anger but, more important, she harbored a revenge fantasy since childhood that one day she would get even. As she felt more trusting of the therapist, Ms. G was able to reveal, for the first time, her bitterness at father's death, feeling that mother should have died before him. She never forgave mother and experienced intense shame for what she perceived as a primitive wish. What had been understood as a problem in separation now was understood as a need to hold on to a very destructive attachment in order to gain revenge. As the meanings associated with these events were explored through a supportive- mode of intervention, the client was able to extract herself partially from this enmeshed relationship and to begin to integrate new learnings into her emerging sense of self. With each small gain, the therapy paused at a new plateau.

Discussion

In the context of this framework for understanding the self, therapy is considered a resource for supporting human development. When human environments provide essential biological, cognitive, and social supplies within empathetically attuned relationships, the individual gradually internalizes their own inner resources, which facilitate adaptation. Under conditions in which early experiences with primary figures are significantly less than optimal, the sense of self as an integrated biopsychosocial structure will become fragmented. Integration that results in a sense of cohesiveness will be compromised as the individual struggles to protect the self from the perception of dangers in the external world. Clients who have suffered less than adequate experiences with emphatically attuned caregivers will be vulnerable to fragmentation. Cognitive structures, which become organized adaptively in the interests of learning, will also become a means for controlling relationships that have the potential for undermining a fragile sense of self. False selves will emerge as dominant parts of the character structure in which the functions of adaptation and defense become fused to protect the individual.

With Ms. G, early experiences were significantly less than optimal in facilitating the development of cohesiveness. The client's way of coping with the non-attuned mother was to turn to father who provided nurturance and protection. This psychic split in object relations mirrored a perception of social reality differentiated between the all-good father and the all-bad mother. Her cognitive resources enhanced the struggle of the client in persistently reaching for a higher, more integrated sense of self. The former facilitated the development of what appeared to be higher level defenses. These defenses functioned to maintain distance and control of relationships that were experienced as threats to self-cohesion and esteem. The seemingly high level defenses became a syntonic means for containing fragmentation in the client's fragile internal world.

In the process of accommodating to the role of client, these individuals tend to replicate early developmental and other life experiences. As a consequence, the nature of the therapeutic process needs to be communicated to these clients within the context of an empathically attuned relationship. The adaptive resources of the client need to be acknowledged and respected by the therapist who concurrently maintains a therapeutic stance of helping the client look beyond current modes of coping to discover the emotional lesions in development that contribute to a lack of wholeness. The treatment process gradually moves from an exploratory/supportive/understanding mode to an exploratory/confrontive/educative one. Because of the dynamics involved, the therapist needs to be particularly attentive to the importance of respecting the need of the client to control the pace of their work together. While one moves optimally at the proverbial pace of the client, the distinctions between that adaptive ideal and the reality of colluding in defensive avoidance are often murky.

The use of self by attunement to countertransference is one of the most effective tools available for engaging these clients in this type of therapy. They try to do to us what they have done and continue to do to others in the interests of their psychosocial survival. They maintain distance and control of relationships. When people get too close the client may resort to fight and then to flight. The most antitherapeutic behavior is to engage the aggressive defense with a counterattack; in other words, to fight with the client who possess an unusual talent for provoking such behavior. Interestingly, this client reported that several of her previous therapists had become angry with her so she "fired them." To attune to anger as an expression of scariness in being with a therapist is to let the client know, in an accepting way, that we are trying to understand. This paradox of accepting aggression and understanding its underlying dimensions also lets clients experience that it is not only safe to show that part of themselves but to talk about that part. They will not be "treated" as they expect but will be asked to look beyond the fight to understand the feelings that fuel their reactions. This approach, carried out with a reasonable degree of consistency, will help to define the reciprocal roles of client and therapist and to set the tone of their subsequent therapeutic work together.

There is a unique challenge in trying to engage these individuals in psychotherapy. The task is to meet them developmentally where they are, to respect their accomplishments often against overwhelming odds, and to invite them to use their adaptive strengths to understand their vulnerabilities. The road is inevitably conflicted. Out of this conflict, clients may begin to relax self-defeating modes of defense and to discover new ways of caring for themselves.

References

Adler, G. (1985). Borderline psychopathology and its treatment. New York: Jason Aronson.

Basham, K. and Miehls, D. (2004). Transforming the legacy: Couple therapy with the survivors of childhood. NY: Columbia University Press.

Berzoff, J., Flanagan, L. and Hertz, P. (1996). Inside out and outside in: Psychodynamic clinical theory and practice in contemporary multicultural contexts. Northvale, N.J.: Jason Aronson, inc.

Bowen, M. (1978). Family therapy in clinical practice. New York: Jason Aronson.

Elson, M. (1986). Self psychology in clinical social work. NY: W.W. Norton & Co.

Gardner, H. (1983). Frames of mind: The theory of multiple intelligences. New York: Basic Books.

Jackson, H. (Ed.) (1991). Using self psychology in psychotherapy. NJ: Jason Aronson inc.

Mackey, R. (1989). Containment of self in the narcissistically vulnerable yet cognitively agile client. The Psychotherapy Client, 4, 3/4, 1988, 119-138.

Mackey, R. (1985). Ego psychology and clinical practice. New York: Gardner

Masterson, J. (1985). The real self: A developmental self and objects relations approach. New York: Brunner/Mazel.

Winnicott, D.W. (1965). The maturational process and the facilitating environment. New York: International Universities Press

Chapter 05 - The Professional Self

The role of a psychotherapist is operationally defined by the techniques and skills that are employed in working with troubled individuals. Using a single subject design, this chapter focuses on my work with one client by presenting two transcripts of interviews one year apart. This individual suffered from a chronic sense of depletion in herself that resulted in feelings of depression and inadequacy. The empathically informed relationship along with psychotherapeutic skills of support, confrontation and psychoeducation are explored.

The professional self refers to the role of a psychotherapist, which is:

to offer the client a respectful hearing of her/his story,

to listen empathetically to the themes that give meaning to the story,

to accept the client as a fellow human being, and

to base treatment planning and therapeutic interventions on professional understanding of what the client needs.

That role is defined by a set of therapeutic skills that include exploration, support, confrontation and psychoeducation. We are introduced to these skills in professional education, and they become a part of our professional selves as we move through our careers. Compared to techniques, therapeutic skills are more generic and are the foundation on which specific interventions may be grafted. For example, the skill of psychooeducation may include interpretation informed by psychoanalytic theory, explanation by self-psychological theory and cognitive restructuring by cognitive/behavioral theories. The attitudinal dimension of skills is as important, perhaps even more important, than what is manifest in our words and actions.

Skills may be understood as:

exploratory

exploratory > supportive

exploratory > supportive > confrontive

exploratory >supportive > confrontive > educative

There is a sequence to the use of these skills. The thoughts and feelings of a client about the difficulties that brought her/him to therapy need to be explored in a supportive manner before other types of interventions are employed. Exploration and support are the basis for understanding a client and developing an empathic alliance with him. Confrontive or educative modes of intervention are most effective when they are grounded on an exploratory/supportive relationship through which clients are involved in setting the goals of treatment.

In this chapter, the human context of professional practice and the goals of psychotherapeutic intervention are reviewed. The skills of exploration, support, confrontation and psychoeducation are discussed and illustrated by using excerpts from 2 interviews with a client who is referred to as Catherine.

Richard A. Mackey

The human context of psychotherapeutic work

At a core level of the self, the level of basic human needs, people are more similar then different. At this level, all people share a common heritage. Because a substantial part of this basic level of the self is relatively unaffected by the social environment, people are one: there are no teachers, no students; there are no clinicians, no clients; there are no therapists, no patients. This innermost world of all remains relatively constant and is the repository of our needs to be loved and to love, to be cared for by others and to care for others, to grow and to become a person of worth and dignity who needs the acceptance, respect and support of those around her/him. Attunement to and acceptance of this common level of the self within people is the basis of empathy.

At the level of the core self, therapist and client may be quite different from each other in temperament and innate talents and skills. Endowment coupled with opportunity play an important role in the development of our personal assets and liabilities. The family into which one is born and the social environment in which one is reared play the most fundamental roles in nurturing an individuated sense of self.

Differentiation of thoughts, feelings and social role behaviors may also result from life experiences in the family and the wider social milieu that have not been responsive to the needs and endowed strengths of an individual. In situations that oppress and victimize people, as in neglectful and abusive parenting relationships, individuals internalize defensive modes of dealing with the human world in order to protect themselves from further damage. It is often a challenge for the clinician, who may wear different defensive clothing, to hear the fear and shame that lies behind the exterior facade of a client. One's exterior behaviors may be quite different from and even the opposite of how one thinks and feels in the privacy of the inner self.

In clinical work, empathy is conducive to making emotional and cognitive contact with the inner life of the client and for facilitating an attachment to a therapist and involvement in a therapeutic relationship. Empathy is the acceptance of our common humanity with the people we serve, the recognition that we are fundamentally no different from them at one level of existence, and the choice to feel within ourselves a semblance of what they experience because their needs and ours are linked in a common human existence. Empathy is, secondly, the humility to accept our differences as an accident of endowment and as a consequence of opportunities over which we had little choice or control. Finally, empathy is the realization that the most effective clinical resource we possess is our human commonality tempered and disciplined by the acquisition of knowledge and professional skill. Empathic attunement and connectedness characterize the therapeutic alliance with a client along with separateness and respect for that person's autonomy, no matter how tenuous. That paradox is the basis of the skillful use of the professional self.

Goals

The responsibility of a therapist throughout the helping process, but more particularly during the beginning phase, is to listen to the applicant and to evaluate the meaning of her/his conflict within a vertical and horizontal context. That is, to understand the person in terms of her/his current life situation and how the conflict developed for the purpose of working toward mutual goals. The attention to goals is a critical aspect of the process for the following reasons:

goals provide *structure* for clients who may experience fragmentation in their lives;
goals provide clients with a sense of *control* over a process that may be concerned with discovery of the unknown which is, by definition, not controllable and, therefore, provocative of anxiety;
goals involve the exercise of executive and adaptive functions that reinforce ego *strengths*;
goals convey *respect* for the autonomy of the client and hope that she/he can be in charge of her/his life;
goals establish *boundaries* between therapist and client that help to define the client's responsibility for taking an active role in his own behalf;
goals establish the *reality* that the means for resolving conflict, suffering and pain lay within the client and not in the therapist;
goals are an essential part of the therapeutic *alliance* and offer the therapist an opportunity to decide whether she/he can work with a particular individual.

While the goal of therapy may be renegotiated independently of other contractual aspects, the setting of at least tentative goals is an important part of the beginning of the therapeutic process. It is easy to drift into the ongoing phase of intervention without attending to this important aspect only to find powerful resistance as therapy unfolds. Resistance is a natural part of therapy but will be manageable if the client has been encouraged to set her/his own goals toward which she/he and the therapist are working. Today, with the reality of time limits on therapy, goals need to be parsimonious and oriented to what may be realizable, especially in brief psychotherapy. Only when the applicant and therapist come together in a mutual understanding of goals does a therapeutic alliance exist between them.

Skills

Exploration is a parsimonious inquiry on the part of the therapist into the thoughts, feelings and experiences of clients that are germane to understanding them and their situations. Such inquiry is tempered by an empathic appreciation of the readiness of another person to share various aspects of her/his life with us. Readiness will vary according to the state of that person's emerging self and her/his trust in the therapist. The nature of data that become available through the exploratory process is contingent upon our respect for meeting the client where she/he is and in working with her/him toward realistic and mutual goals.

In this model exploration is, by its nature, a supportive skill which is intended:

to illicit data upon which understanding will be grounded;
to involve the client in a therapeutic relationship which is the vehicle through which change may be realized;
to serve as a vehicle for setting mutual goals;

to establish and then to reinforce the expectation that the primary source of change is within the client and only secondarily in the client-therapist relationship;

to convey respect for the right of the client to engage in the process of therapy at a level that is congruent with her/his motivation and capacity for change; and

to neutralize the natural human wish that change may come about without significant personal investment of the client in the process

Exploration in the beginning of a therapeutic relationship may be quite different from its use later in the helping process. In the beginning, the therapist tries to connect empathetically with the client and to develop an understanding of how that person is troubled. That professional attachment usually begins with some definition of the conflict that triggered the request for help. As the client and therapist arrive at a mutual albeit beginning awareness of the conflict and its different aspects, the process naturally moves in the direction of considering how the conflict began and how it may affect the individual at the present time. As exploration focuses on horizontal and vertical dimensions of the person's life, the therapist needs to hear the cognitive and affective themes associated with the client's experiences in the present and their links in the past. The timing and depth of beginning explorations must be tempered by an empathic understanding of the developmental level of different clients and their readiness to privilege us with their stories.

Support is oriented primarily to conscious thoughts and feelings, which the client has communicated to the therapist, verbally and behaviorally. It is defined as those therapeutic behaviors that build upon and reinforce those personal assets which the client brings to the relationship in order to help her/him sustain a present level of functioning or to assist her/him in moving to a more adaptive level. Support is grounded on listening to the narrative of a person's life experiences and hearing the emotional themes associated with those experiences. We serve as an empathic yet dispassionate witness as clients tell their stories. In that sense of using the self professionally, acceptance, respect, listening and empathy are essential components of support and are powerful reinforces of the emerging self throughout adulthood. Although a therapist may respect and accept defensive behavior in the interest of developing a working alliance with clients, we do not overtly support defenses that compromise the journey toward development of the self. Rather, the supportive therapist resonates with adaptive attempts to cope with life as it may be today. This notion of the supportive use of self is the foundation of the helping process and is an inexorable component of any other skills including confrontation and psychoeducation. . A client's sense of being empathetically understood is an essential therapeutic prelude to other forms of intervention (Kohut, 1977).

The supportive use of the professional self is a matter of attitude as much as it is a matter of overt behavior. Support is of value when we hear and connect empathetically with cognitive and affective themes within clients through an accepting, respectful and understanding psychological posture. When clients experience a therapeutic attitude informed by these values, conveyed verbally and behaviorally, it may be highly supportive to their emerging sense of self. Optimally, support will be most effective when there is a congruence of verbal and non-verbal messages at different levels of the professional self.

Confrontation is a process of assisting the client to face currently unacceptable thoughts and feelings about her/himself and toward internalized representations of significant figures now or in the past that compromise the emerging self. Support is part of the confrontive process in the sense that the therapist must be attuned to and accepting of those thoughts and feelings before moving to engage the client in talking about them. Support also provides the trustful matrix through which these affects and thoughts may become part of the therapeutic conversation. Supportive interventions, in themselves, may lead to a type of confrontation. In that sense, confrontation by a therapist may be considered a secondary option when interventions to engage the client in confronting himself through supportive exploration has failed.

Confrontation of thoughts and feeling that have been avoided by way of any defense(s) always involves a loss. In facing the unfaceable, the client is sacrificing or separating himself from accustomed pattern(s) of thinking and feeling. A piece of the self that has served a useful purpose in the past is being discarded. Although that piece may have served more of a defensive rather than adaptive purpose, it likely contributed to personal and/or interpersonal equilibrium. Robbing a person of defensive functions that contribute to equilibrium requires an understanding of the person as a whole human being and empathic attunement to the significance of defense(s) to their sense of self. Otherwise, confrontation may be an expression of our goals for the client rather than a respect for her/his goals. We need to be careful that it is not a means of punishment but a resource for liberating the client from those forces that encumber the development of the self. The importance of self-awareness of the therapist and empathic understanding in utilizing confrontive techniques cannot be overemphasized.

Traditionally, confrontive skills were considered appropriate for clients with moderate levels of impairment whose integrative capacities were intact. In the 1970's, a shift in thinking took place. Kernberg (1980) argued that confrontation was useful in working with the borderline client who falls within a moderate to severe level of impairment. Impairment in the client at a borderline level of development involves failure of integration of self and object representations although they are differentiated sufficiently to offer the individual a sense of separateness from others. Generally, representations of self and others tend to be split and imbued with an all-encompassing sense of aggression or idealization. For Kernberg, splitting is differentiation without integration. To reach a developmental level of integration, the client needs to be helped to explore and to eventually confront the split-off representation(s) as they are manifested in the relationship with the therapist and in other relationships. A strictly supportive orientation to therapy may reinforce the splitting defense and perpetuate the developmental arrest.

With the client who is impaired severely (at a psychotic level), confrontation may be therapeutic when it is focused on the reality testing function. The expression of "lending the ego" to these severely impaired people may be another way of expressing this intervention. In lending the ego, the therapist serves as a real object to the client and, in the process, supportively confronts them with the discrepancies between their inner representations of reality and the external world as a therapist understands those discrepancies. First, however, severely impaired persons need to experience the acceptance and respect of the therapist for the psychic realness of delusions and hallucinations. Such realness was portrayed elegantly in the film, A beautiful mind, based on the biography of the Nobel laureate, John Nash, by Sylvia Nasar (1998).

Responding to the challenge of time limits on the practice of psychoanalysis, Davanloo (1980) introduced the use of confrontation in psychoanalytically oriented short-term psychotherapy. He suggested the use of "gentle but relentless questioning and confrontation of the defenses against true feelings (p. 46)." His approach was a significant departure from orthodox psychoanalytic technique. Instead of maintaining a dynamically passive mode of intervention, the analyst assumed a very active role from the first contact with a patient. This departure from classic technique was helpful to many patients according to Davanloo.

In the 1990's, Hughes (1997) developed a model of psychotherapy focused on children who suffered significant psychological impairments as a result of traumatic attachment experiences. The approach integrates empathy with confrontation to help children with attachment disorders and their parents find new ways of adaptation. The therapy focuses primarily on the here and now, similar to the work of Kernberg and Davanloo, and reaches beyond conventional techniques with children to confront underlying feelings that are being avoided. Because of the nature of impairments originating in disordered attachment experiences, Hughes hypothesizes that conventional techniques of a verbal nature are not effective with these children. Therapists are active, creative and confrontive as they work with children and their parents who are essential participants in the intervention.

Given the realities that practitioners face today, Kernberg, Davanloo and Hughes offer new modes of confrontive interventions that may be used early in a therapeutic relationship. These developments in technique may suggest that we have been too conservative in the past in our thinking about the constructive use of confrontation early in a therapeutic relationship. Several clients may have the inner resources to engage in confrontive work and as a result to integrate new learnings into their emerging sense of self. We may also underestimate how quickly an empathic relationship may be established that will be good enough to absorb the dynamics of confrontive work.

Psychoeducational skills, like confrontive ones, may never be isolated from their empathic, exploratory and supportive base. One critical aspect of support as it relates to psychoeducation is the safe therapeutic environment, which may permit the client to explore parts of self that were previously off limits to consciousness. These thoughts and feelings may have been so potentially disruptive to self esteem and psychic equilibrium that they were relegated to a level of non-awareness. The use of empathic listening, purposive questioning and a confrontive intent within the therapist may accelerate the process of integrating new learnings into one's sense of self.

Psychoeducation ranges from interpertative/explaining to cognitive/behavioral interventions. In psychoanalysis, interpretation is defined as a process of assisting the ego of the client to become aware of the linkage of one level of conscious experience to another level beyond awareness with the intent of expanding the perimeters of self-understanding. In self psychological treatment, the empathic relationship of therapy may loosen themes contained within the inner levels of the self, which may become more accessible to awareness and thus available for validation and explanation by the therapist. Until that accessibility evolves, the client is not ready to have her/his hidden world exposed. Prior to that time, interpretation of the unconscious is a narcissistic exercise for the therapist, which is not in the interest of enhancing development of a new sense of self within clients.

While confrontation is primarily an emotional process, which involves loss, psychoeducation involves a significant cognitive gain. This is especially true in cognitive/behavioral work with its variety of techniques for learning new ways of thinking, problem-solving and modification of patterns of behavior (Scott, Williams & Beck, 1992). My practice has generally focused on working with individuals who have significant difficulties with integration of new learnings until the shame and guilt associated with their thoughts and feelings have been shared and understood. Unless these troubled feelings of a client are received by a therapist with acceptance, empathy and respect, they will compromise the emergence of a more adaptive sense of self. That principal was illustrated in the therapy of Ms G that was discussed in the previous chapter.

Another option involves collaborative work. Some of colleagues and I have found that the model of therapy discussed here works well in collaboration with other approaches. For example, a referral to another therapist is made for treatment of a specific behavioral dysfunction. Concurrent cognitive/behavioral therapy for sexual dysfunctions, eating disorders and other specific behavioral disorders, such as phobias, has been successful. As part of the treatment contract, I have also required individuals with addictions to be involved in other forms of intervention, such as Alcoholics Anonymous.

The case of Catherine

The following case from transcribed tape recordings of two interviews with the client illustrates many of the concepts that have been discussed in this chapter as well as those in previous chapters. The client gave permission for random tape recordings of her individual therapy with the understanding that they could be used for professional education and publication(s). The actual clinical data have been carefully disguised to protect her privacy. The passages are presented as they happened except for minor editing to protect confidentiality.

Introduction

Catherine, a 35-year-old mother of 6 children, suffered from chronic depression since her mid adolescence. As a young adult, she was treated as an inpatient with electroshock therapy and has been seen for the last 15 years by psychiatrists for medication and intermittent psychotherapy. None of these treatment modes had a significant impact on her sense of depletion, the persistent pattern of devaluing self, and her resignation to this pathology as inevitable.

In the current setting, Catherine had initially been seen by a female social worker who treated her briefly as an individual and then invited her to join a woman's group. She withdrew from the group a few months into the therapy for the birth of her sixth child. Shortly after that time, the original therapist left the agency and asked a colleague, a male clinical social worker, to assume leadership of the group. At that time, Catherine was invited to return to the group, which she did. The group remained together for approximately another two years, at which time all of the members, except Catherine, felt ready to terminate. Their concern for Catherine was that she seemed different and had made no progress in "getting in touch" with her anger and asserting her rights as a woman, especially in relationships in which the group members had felt exploited. She persisted in idealizing males, including the therapist, and was perplexed about the anger of other women, especially toward the male therapist, whom she experienced as a kindly and supportive individual.

Catherine was interested in continuing therapy. The group leader offered to refer her to another therapist or to continue with her as an individual client. She opted to continue with him. The interview excerpts take place several months into her individual therapy when she is beginning to talk for the first time in her life about the deep sense of loneliness and unhappiness in her family of origin. She is also beginning to talk of the rage within her that has been carefully controlled throughout her adult life. As the therapy unfolded, there was consultation with a psychiatrist about the advisability of using medication since her depression was deepening as she talked about these troubling feelings. Because of a history of medication not being effective as well as the positive quality of the therapeutic relationship, medication was not recommended and she continued in individual therapy. A little over one year later after considerable gains in her individual therapy, Catherine struggled with the issue of whether to terminate treatment or reach out to her husband by inviting him to join her in conjoint marital therapy. For the proceeding several weeks, the issue of the husband's involvement was a prominent theme in her therapy and one that she appeared to have considerable ambivalence about. The husband did accept the invitation to become involved in conjoint treatment and they continued in therapy as a couple.

Family History

Catherine was born into an extremely impoverished family, both emotionally and financially. She was the second oldest of two daughters in an Irish Catholic family of five children. Standards related to emotional expressiveness, sexuality and independence were harshly suppressed, especially for female children. Although the family remained intact throughout her childhood and adolescence, a pervasive pattern of disengagement, isolation and unhappiness characterized the family atmosphere. Aspects of the family history, which emerged throughout Catherine's therapy, were confirmed later when another family member was referred for therapy to the same clinical social worker that had treated Catherine.

Although she reported never experiencing physical punishment or overt abuse and was considered a perfect child, Catherine felt smothered by her mother's overprotectiveness and ignored by her father's indifference. Although he appeared to be a detached and aloof figure in the family, Catherine felt that he took some interest in the achievements of her brothers but showed no interest in her. No matter how good she was as a person or as a student, he ignored her. As she talked about him more fully in therapy, he began to emerge as a rather disturbed individual who probably functioned at or near a psychotic level for much of his life. His personal hygiene was poor which made him repulsive to others. Her memories were of a man who worked in a menial and dirty job in a factory. He would come home in dirty clothing and smelling of body odor, and sit in the same chair near their coal stove without talking to anyone in the family. The only communication between the parents took place through the children who would serve as conduits for any kind of menial request that either parent wished to make of the other. She remembers no physical affection nor does she remember any between mother and father.

In contrast to a father who was experienced as an isolated and mysterious figure, mother was remembered as an overly involved and smothering figure. The picture that emerged as therapy unfolded was of a person who suffered from a deep and persistent insecurity and needed to live out much of her unfilled life through her two daughters. The enmeshed relationship with them promoted unusual dependency until late adolescence and adulthood. Yet, she was also experienced as an unusually good and charitable individual with whom no one could get angry. At the same time, Catherine talked of her as someone who was never satisfied with her second daughter's accomplishments nor did she ever convey much respect for her struggle to separate and individuate during late adolescence. To Catherine, mother had subtle but powerful ways of reminding her of incompetence no matter how successful the accomplishments. Within this atmosphere, Catherine developed a very harsh conscience, which permitted no imperfections and an ideal of motherhood and womanhood that was geared to pleasing others and sacrificing her own needs to serve them.

Given the rather severe nature of impairments in both parents, one of the remarkable aspects is that Catherine, as an adult, despite her impairments, was quite adaptive in specific aspects of her life, notably in parenting her children. Perhaps, because of her own suffering as a child, she had a remarkable capacity for nurturing her children with empathy. Certain functions were quite impaired such as her capacity to think for herself, to stand up for her rights by taking reasonable stands against the infringements of others on her time, and her persistent pattern of presenting herself to the world as a pleasant, loving and ever generous individual. She could tolerate no awareness of aggression within herself, particularly anger at disappointment toward her husband whom she tended to idealize. She seemed very frightened of relationships, a theme that was explored throughout her individual treatment. Self esteem was very fragile and she tended to put herself down continually by always taking the blame and seeing herself as one who was very inadequate and inferior to others. Throughout much of her therapy, Catherine complained of a feeling of "deadness" and not being able to experience any kind of feeling whether of an aggressive or loving nature. One way of dealing with this inner painful world was to assume and hold on to a nurturing and caregiving, role, not only with her children but also with the extended family. She was always available to serve others and felt a sharp remorse whenever she began to experience feelings of anger about the tendency of others to exploit her generosity.

The treatment process

As noted in the introduction, the clinical social worker who treated Catherine first became acquainted with her when she was a member of a woman's therapy group, which he led. As the group moved toward termination, a primary issue for many of the members was their concern for leaving Catherine behind; they felt that they had profited from the group experience and were conflicted that she could not "get her anger out" and continued to idealize her husband, as well as other males, including the group leader. She also separated herself from them by alluding that she had nothing to be angry about although she could understand how they could become annoyed with men in their lives. She was perplexed that she seemed so different from these other individuals. To her, they seemed to be better by doing the very thing with which she felt no connection.

In retrospect, these confrontations were instrumental in helping Catherine face feelings that she had avoided throughout her life and which had been too overwhelming to surface in her previous treatment. Along with the willingness to confront their differences was a genuine concern for Catherine that was expressed openly by the members of the group. Once the group terminated, the clinical social worker accepted Catherine in individual therapy and worked with her in that mode for over two years. Initially, she was anxious and puzzled by what she perceived as the mystery of women in the group getting better by saying that they had faced and worked through angry parts of themselves that had been previously disowned. One of the instrumental vehicles helping her to become aware and to integrate her aggressiveness within herself was the relationship with the therapist. As she gradually took the risk of expressing her anger (initially in a passive/aggressive way) to important figures in her life, including the therapist, Catherine began to feel more and more comfortable about that disowned part of herself. This was a gradual and painful process and one that led to a deepening of her depressive functioning during the middle course of therapy. The first interview reported here took place as this process was beginning to unfold. During that interview, she talks about aspects of her history and her current feelings that had not been expressed before this time.

Two powerful dynamics emerged during the therapy. One dynamic had to do with her deep fear of going crazy if she became angry. This involved the central issue of control and stirred up many painful memories of her earlier hospitalization and electric shock treatment. Her family had similar fears. The second dynamic was a dread of being abandoned by people if she expressed her true feelings. To be pleasant even in unpleasant circumstances had become a syntonic part of her sense of self. The exploration of this hidden world of angry feelings and understandable resentments was facilitated by a therapeutic relationship characterized by acceptance, firmness about the therapeutic agenda and empathic exploration of this private level of her self.

As a result of changes, which occurred in the individual therapy, particularly in Catherine's confidence in being more assertive with people, the family equilibrium was seriously upset and there was pressure for her to withdraw from treatment. What was experienced by her and the therapist as progress, was experienced by family members, including her husband, as regression. They feared she might need to be hospitalized again, especially since she was no longer the compliant, pleasant and generous family caretaker who responded unquestioningly to the needs of others.

After two years in individual therapy, Catherine's husband, Joe, was invited to join her in conjoint marital treatment. Joe accepted her invitation to become involved in conjoint marital treatment. They were seen for about one year in this mode and then occasionally after that for some family crises. Two of these crises are notable: one was the death of Catherine's father who died desolate and isolated in a shelter. This was extremely painful for her since she was the only sibling who had maintained contact with the father and who attended his funeral. Other family members wished to have nothing to do with him even in death. She was pained as much by their reactions as she was by the death itself. The other crisis involved a serious life threatening illness of Catherine. At these times, both she and Joe returned to therapy for relatively brief periods. The conjoint phase of therapy seemed to consolidate gains that Catherine had worked to achieve in her individual and group treatment. The conjoint therapy also helped Joe to make some modifications in his relationship to her. In that respect, the marital work seemed to consolidate some of the shifts in the family system, particularly the marital subsystem, so that these two people could feel better about their life together as they negotiated middle age.

Excerpts with discussion from interview a few months into individual therapy

The first vignette occurs toward the beginning of the interview after there was some brief exchange about Catherine's short vacation for which her mother had paid. It illustrates exploratory/supportive work.

*****

C Well, it was good for me, but I feel like I didn't get anything from it, really. I didn't get what I was looking for. I thought I'd come back kind of refreshed and I didn't. I don't know what I'm looking for. I feel like I don't know what's wrong with me. I'm looking for something and I don't seem to get anywhere.

I You sound very disappointed.

C I do. I feel disappointed with myself. I felt anger with myself and sometimes I think I could hate everything and everybody. I don't know what's wrong with me. I'm looking for something, but I just don't seem to find it and I don't know what it is. It's . . . I thought when I came home from my vacation I would be refreshed and want to start and kind of get into the swing of things again, but I just don't feel like it. I just didn't get what I was looking for in my vacation, just to come back refreshed. I thought maybe if I didn't have to do dishes and sweep floors and all the rest for a few days, that I might be willing to come back and feel better about it. In fact, I feel this way every time I have a vacation and come back. I don't seem to feel refreshed and it's just all part of the whole thing, I guess. I guess I just can't seem to put my finger on what I want. I feel as though, "What am I looking for? What do I want? I don't know." I want satisfaction. I want to feel satisfied. In a certain sense, I do with what I'm doing, but it's more on my mind than it is in my feelings. I know what I'm doing is good. I'm being as good a mother and a wife as I can but I'm not getting this feeling of satisfaction out of it. Sometimes I wonder is everybody like me. I don't know. I feel a lot, I don't seem to feel a lot of satisfaction and I wonder what the heck's the matter with me. I don't know. I know sometimes I feel like . . .

I You've never really felt any satisfaction.

C Not really, no. When I was first married, somehow the newness of being a wife and a mother and a housekeeper. I enjoyed it. It seemed to satisfy me for many years, but as the time went on, it seems that when my children get older, something happens. For one thing, I don't know if I feel their love as much when they get older. I know when I have a new baby, I seem to come alive and I can feel my love for the baby, a tremendous amount. It almost like brings me alive and then . . .

I You can feel sympathy for children ... but not for adults.

C But not adults. I know when I was growing up I always thought love was just for babies. I know better now, but whether that changes my feelings, I don't know. I know that adults need love and nothing seems to break through to me except love for children. I feel like I'd like to feel for people, for adults, I don't even know if I have sympathy for adults. In my mind I feel sorry for people who are having hard times, but I don't deeply feel it, but I do for children. I really... this gets to me. I see children suffering and the love, like for a baby, just really breaks through. It's the only thing that does and I feel like I need satisfaction from feeling for people, adults, sometimes; but getting back to, this is what I guess I'm looking for. I feel like I'm looking for something, but I, and I'm not getting what I'm looking for... to get out of vacation at least a little bit refreshed when I come back and feel that I want to do these things.

*****

The flow of the interview shifted at this point to exploration of what Catherine was looking for. She began to express her underlying feelings of emptiness and low esteem for self. When the therapist picks up on the theme of her fear about her feelings, Catherine talks about the bleak emotional environment in her family

*****

I You sound very frightened about your feelings.

C I have always been.

I You're kind of giving yourself permission to feel now; as you talk, there's somehow some dread or some fright about your feelings.

C I've always felt afraid to feel and also afraid to show my feelings to other people.

I Afraid something might happen?

C If I show my feelings?

I Yes.

C I don't know. I think . . .

I What was it like when you were a child? Children generally are more free about showing their feelings than adults.

C Well, my parents didn't show very much emotional feeling toward each other, for one thing. That wasn't a very good start right there for me and I can't even remember my mother showing affection to her other babies, my brother, my youngest brother. It seems as though she took care of his physical needs. She cleaned him. I never remember seeing her loving him and holding him. Somehow I kind of took care of that when he was growing up. I was with him most of the time and I took him every place and took care of him, except my mother fed him and cleaned him, but I don't ever remember them showing attention or affection to us. They never did. My mother never kissed me. My father never did either ... There was absolutely no sign of affection when I was growing up and I'm sure this must have had a great deal to do with how I feel about affection.

I You could never give them affection either? You could never kiss them?

C No. No, I never did. I would feel uncomfortable. I would, I guess that was something silly or . . .

*****

Catherine talks further about the lack of affection from her parents and how she became a nurturing figure for a younger brother, the beginnings of an affectionate relationship that continues. As the theme of emotional poverty is explored, she confronts the emptiness in the memories of those experiences. One of her strengths was in not replicating those experiences with her children.

*****

C I know that affection is good and it's needed. In my own house, even my children, as big as they are, the oldest boys are 11, 9 and 10; they always put their arms around us and they kiss us and tell us they love us and love is very free in our family, with my children and my husband and I know this is, and I wanted it to be this way. I wanted to make sure they always felt free to love us and to tell us that they loved us and always made sure that I told them that I loved them, even when they were punished sometimes. We tell them we punish them because we love them and they know that.

I How do you feel about giving love to the kids, affection, hugging them?

C The older they get, the less ... I seem to want to pull away. My boys are getting bigger. The three boys are getting bigger and I seem inside, more or less, to pull back a little, yet I try not to show them that I do, and I don't know why. I don't know why I do this but I don't give them any indication that I do this. I just do it inside and

I What are you feeling?

C Now? When this happens, you mean?

I Or even as you talk about it now. What are you feeling?

C I don't know. I feel like, I don't know, just sort of a pulling back, as though I just don't want to get, don't want them to give.

I You don't want them to give?

C Well, I give myself and allow them to get. It's more that I don't want them to give, to show their affection to me more than I show affection to them. It's, and I find this with my husband very much, somehow I wanted to know that he loves me but I don't want him to show me he loves me. This is, it's the physical part of love that kind of makes me want to pull back. I feel like when I was a little girl, I think I would have enjoyed sitting in my father's lap, put my arms around him, and talking to him and I don't ever remember trying and being rejected. I just don't ever remember feeling free enough to do this and again, when I was very little, I don't know how it was, but I often thought I'd ask my mother what kind of a child I was, what kind of a little girl I was, if I was affectionate and spontaneous and I don't know if she would understand what I was trying to say. She might and if I was as a young child, I wonder where it all started or when it started that I just seem to hold back my affection or . . .

*****

The exploratory/supportive approach leading to further confrontation of feelings continues.

*****

C Nothing happened in my life, no terrible experience ever happened to me at this time in my life. I didn't lose love. I can't remember anything.

I Rather than losing it, maybe you're very frightened of it.

C Yes, I do feel afraid of it. I feel afraid of it ... Why am I so afraid of love? I don't know. I feel afraid to, almost like I'm afraid to let go and love somebody and let go and be loved by somebody, but I don't know why I feel this way ... there seems to be fear there and that keeps me from loving and being loved, but I don't know what it is ... I don't ever remember anything happening in my life that should make me feel this way except that love wasn't shown in my family when I was grown up. It always was, love always was shown to be something silly and ridiculous. I can remember my father always saying that this boy-girl stuff in school, teenage stuff, was silly and ridiculous and to me this was the start of love and learning to love in an adult way but of course then I didn't realize that. I just accepted what my father said that love was silly and ridiculous. I felt, because I wanted someone to love me, I was silly and there was something shameful about love or wanting to be loved and as far as love and marriage, my father would always say, "Any damn fool can get married." This is evidently what he must have felt about marriage and then when I got to school and learned that marriage, was raised to the dignity of a sacrament and I learned this is marriage. I know it's a very hard life because it isn't easy raising children and I know marriage has great dignity and I still know it can be beautiful, but it's hard too, and it just can't survive without love and I wondered how my marriage survived as it did. I want to change and I feel like I won't be satisfied until I can change and that's why I came here, but I still haven't broken through on this one area. I feel like maybe I never will, but there's just always that last ray of hope that maybe I will.

*****

As she talks about being stuck yet wanting to change by feeling love for adults and accepting love from them, Catherine expresses anger for the first time about herself and her situation. A big step for her is to confront the therapist with her feelings of disappointment.

*****

C I feel so angry at myself for not being able to change this and I feel a lot of anger and sometimes I think ... like during this week ... I felt anger at everybody and everything and I just don't know why I feel that anger at everybody because they haven't been making me feel angry. It's just like anger and I just don't know where to put it. Somehow I feel . . .

I Were you angrier this week than you have been the last few weeks?

C Yes.

I Has it something to do with your coming here?

C Yes, I think it has a lot to do with my hopes of feeling better and also sometimes when my husband's around ...he's off these two weeks ... sometimes when he's around, I feel angry, angry at him, yet he's not doing anything to make me angry. Somehow I feel as though I have more loving thoughts toward my husband when he's not near than when he is near. I don't think that's too good.

I But it also has something to do with your coming here and feeling disappointed.

C Yes, I feel disappointed ... because I didn't get what I was looking for. The same was like my vacation. I didn't get what I was looking for. I seem kind of angry with my mother and yet I'm not.

*****

As the end of the interview approaches, Catherine expresses the dilemma and threat that she faces by expressing feelings of anger to which she never felt entitled. Once the feeling is expressed, she immediately needs to take it back. Note how she avoids continuing to express anger at the therapist by shifting the focus to mother, who has also disappointed her.

*****

I What do you think you're angry about?

C I don't know, just angry because I'm not being satisfied. I'm not getting the satisfaction and ...

I You know people who don't get what they want feel angry.

*****

This is the first time that Catherine has expressed with words her anger at people who disappoint her. This interview was a turning point in her therapy. As she was able to express anger, not only at the therapist but more importantly, at her husband and other family members, she began to feel better about herself. As these disowned feelings were accepted in the therapy, she gradually was able to accept anger as an understandable and real part of herself. By the time that she and her husband started conjoint marital therapy, more than one year after this interview, she appeared more integrated while, at the same time, acknowledging that some things had not changed, notably her feelings about sexual relations. One of the important gains in her emerging self was to integrate new ways of expressing anger, setting reasonable limits and communicating her needs to important people in her life. She was able to accept that life was more satisfying for her and for others when she made an effort to express her feelings, even though she wished to disown them.

<u>Excerpts with discussion from interview one year later</u>

As noted earlier in this chapter, Catherine had made progress in aspects of her life and was weighing different options that included termination or marital therapy. In the following excerpts, she talks initially about the gains and disappointments of therapy.

*****

C Last week we were discussing about my leaving and I kind of summed it up and said that I felt that there was about two things I hadn't accomplished. There were many things I did accomplish, like learning to think for myself, as I've said so many times now, and this was a big thing to me because I hadn't done it, you know, when I was very little. I didn't have the chance to think for myself, and I learned to have a respect for my own opinion. In fact, I have an opinion of my own, which is another thing I really didn't feel like I had an opinion of my own. These are good things and I feel that these things I have accomplished and the things I haven't accomplished was of learning to concentrate well and I spoke to you last week about going to school maybe and taking a course in reading and this might help me. So in the fall I think I'll look into this and see what kind of a course I could take.

I Good.

C And the other problem was I didn't feel like, I don't know, I don't feel like I kind of broke this--it seems like a barrier I have concerning sexual feelings and, but I feel like I've tried very hard to overcome these feelings and somehow I feel this is just as far as I can go. I can't seem to go any further with this.

I How are you feeling about stopping and still having these feelings about sex and your sexual relationship with your husband?

C Well, I feel like, well I don't know, I feel partly it either has something to do with myself or maybe something to do with Joe's (spouse) personality. It's either that maybe I just can't love a man that way or I don't know because of the bad start I got with my father and also the very prudish way that I was brought up. All I can say is maybe it's just myself. I don't know, but maybe it's something, maybe I just don't love JOE that much or ... I feel it should be a very natural thing to enjoy sex life in marriage and I just don't ... I don't know . .

I You were talking last time, Catherine, about talking with Joe and you were saying, I think, that the two of you hadn't been talking as much lately about your sexual relationship as you were a few months ago.

C Yes, somehow, it seemed too, I don't know... we both became so involved in what we were doing, I guess. It doesn't seem, though, that there's too much more to talk to him about. I feel like he knows where I stand and how I feel about it ... I don't know if he really accepts the way I feel about it.

*****

The exploration of this theme continued and led to a discussion of how their relationship was more satisfying when they talked together about it. An attempt during the preceding year to refer Catherine to a behavioral therapist for treatment of their sexual concerns was not successful.

*****

C ... I feel like this is just the way it is, the way things stand now and I feel like, I don't know, I just feel like I'm going to have to live with the situation the way it is. I feel like it will be hard at times, I'm sure, but I feel like there's nothing I can do about it.

I We had talked about the two of you coming in together.

C Yes, but that didn't seem to work out too good. Joe isn't really interested in coming.

I He says he wouldn't come with you?

C Yes, well, I brought that up, I don't know if I brought it up last week. Yes, I did last week. I brought it up with him when I went home and he said at first he wanted to go because he thought it was going to help me, but he said he doesn't like to come and explain his feelings to anybody. He feels that, he says, "I'm the way I am and I'm satisfied with being this way" and he said that he doesn't like to talk about his own feelings to anyone else.

I That's very difficult for anyone to do.

C Yes, it is.

*****

The interview then focuses on how Catherine feels about ending her therapy and Joe's relief at that. As the issue of termination is explored, Catherine mentions that Joe seems unusually "anxious for me to get through." Since talking with him about the option for the two of them to come together, she thinks that he has been more distant from her and less talkative. I ask:

*****

I *Might it have something to do with your talking about the two of you coming in together?*

C *I don't know. I don't think so because I think that was kind of settled in his mind that he wasn't coming for some time anyway. So I don't think it had anything to do with that. I can't see any connection there.*

I *You don't think it has anything to do with that?*

C *I don't think so.*

I *That's the one thing, it seems to me, that's changed.*

C *Well, he had the idea he was coming to help me, but he didn't... it's like he didn't mind coming to help me but he didn't want to expose his own feelings and, well... maybe it might have had something to do, it could be that he doesn't want to get involved, you know.*

I *That could be a very frightening idea .*

C *Yes.*

I *And one way to end it is to try to have nothing to do or let anyone who's close to you have anything to do . . . with therapy.*

C *This could be too. I never put that together, but that could be true. But for myself, I feel like I do want to get through. I feel like I've gone as far as I can.*

*****

At this point Catherine expresses much disappointment at not being able to overcome her sexual difficulties and also mentions that she continues to be troubled by a chronic problem with concentration, which she thinks may be the consequences of electroshock treatments earlier in her life. She is following through with the suggestion to get an evaluation of the concentration problem and to enroll in a special reading program. Later in the interview, she returns to the issue of sexuality and the therapist comments:

*****

I *It seems to me like there was a period of several weeks in which you and he were making an effort to talk about the things that you're unhappy about, particularly your sexual relationship.*

C *Yes.*

I *And the more you were able to talk with one another about these things, the happier you seemed. And somehow over the last few weeks it seems like the amount of conversation between the two of you about the things in your marriage that you're somewhat unhappy about, has diminished. And along with that seems to come more of a feeling of unhappiness or pessimism.*

C *You think that because we don't talk about it, you mean it makes it more unhappy?*

I *Yes. How do you feel?*

C *Well, I know we haven't talked too much about it because it seems like it's a dead issue now. It seems like, it seems as though we have talked about it and somehow I get the feeling Joe doesn't want to talk about it too much. I think he feels like when we talk about it, we just don't get anywhere. It seems like the problem's there and I tell him how I feel and he accepts it, I guess, or tries to accept it and this is the situation and it doesn't really change enough for us to talk about it. It seems like this makes it sort of a dead issue and there isn't very much more that we can say to help the situation any more. It just kind of just sort of remains that way.*

*****

The focus now shifts to exploring how marital therapy in which the two of them would be involved might help in opening blocked communication between them and how a third party might be useful in assisting them with that task:

*****

I *I think it might be better or more hopeful if you had a third party to talk with.*

C *You think so? You mean like Joe to come?*

I *The two of you to come. We talked about the two of you coming a few weeks ago . . .*

C *I don't know. Just the fact that I'm getting through, I don't think I could get Joe to come. I think he has it in his mind now that this is it and I don't think he would come. I could try, I could suggest this, but I don't think I would get very far . . .*

I *Well, how do you feel about the idea at this point?*

C *Well, I feel like if there was anything that possibly we could do to help this situation, I would be willing to give it a try and I kind of would like it too if Joe came. At first, when we discussed this before and I wasn't quite sure, but I feel I would be glad to have Joe come and have us discuss it together, but somehow I feel like I don't know what we could say or do that would help the situation or . . . because to me it does seem like a dead issue between us. It's there and that's it and it seems like there isn't anything to be done about it, but again, I would be willing to give it a try if Joe would . I can suggest it but I don't think it's going to get too favorable a comment from him. I'll try.*

I *I wonder if he knows how you feel about this. Really, it's the one big thing in your marriage right now that you still feel you haven't resolved or somehow made some progress with it.*

C *Yes. I can tell him how I feel about it and that's all I can do. And I'll see what he says and, but I'm sure he's going...I feel like he's going to be angry, but I'll bring it up anyway. He was angry last week when he thought that I was going to go on further and he has an idea that this is it. He's kind of glad that it's ended and to bring up more, I don't know if he's going to like this too well, but I'll mention it to him and tell him how much it means to me. But if you think it would help, I'm willing to give it a try. How do you think it would help? What would it bring out? How could a third, you said a third party would help. How could it help?*

*****

The directness of Catherine's questions reflect the progress that she has made in therapy in being more assertive and in feeling entitled to express her thoughts with another person. This part of herself had emerged in therapy as her feelings of shame and guilt about these issues were attenuated. Rather then explore the matter further, it was appropriate to respond in an educative way. I said: "a person like myself perhaps could help the two of you to see things that you're not seeing now" and be "available regularly to work on those things in your sexual relationship that you're not very happy about ... to try to understand what it is that prevents you from having more satisfaction in your marriage and to bring out how each of you feel about your relationship."

Initally, Catherine responds by blaming herself and taking all responsibility for their sexual difficulties. She then goes on to describe what happened when she was able to express how she "really felt" about sex.

*****

C *In fact one time I did tell him how I really feel. He didn't think it was that important in our marriage, that it shouldn't separate us in any way but as I said I brought out just about everything to Joe how I did feel and just bringing it out didn't seem to resolve the problem, but I'll bring it up to Joe about us both coming and see.*

I *Well, what happens when you express yourself that way?*

C *Well, when, it was like, it's funny how things come to you at different times. I was just doing my dishes on Sunday morning and I was thinking about it and how I felt and I just came to the conclusion this is how I feel about it and so the children were out playing and Joe was resting and I went in to talk to him about it. I just kind of laid it on the line and told him how I felt and it felt good to me ....it was sort of a relief. I don't have to pretend that I want this or enjoy this and I feel like I could be myself and I could just express myself and say how I felt and it felt good to me to say just how I felt about it. It was like a relief to be able to just express myself that way and somehow I feel relief... it gave me a feeling as though maybe I could enjoy it almost. It's like well maybe someday that I would.*

I *When did this happen?*

C *Months ago: two or three, three or four months ago.*

I *Have you been talking since then about it?*

C *A little bit. This is one of the times when we were talking a great deal about it, but it was very frightening to me because I felt like maybe I would lose everything I had by just expressing myself because I didn't know how Joe was really going to feel. I told him if I'm like this and he doesn't want me this way, then it would be all right if he didn't have to accept me this way. As I said, it was frightening but it was sort of a relief to know that I could be myself anyway and . . .*

I *It didn't make things worse?*

C *No it didn't. I thought Joe would be quite angry with me and feel like there was no way out for him, but he didn't seem to feel that way and he gave me the feeling that it wasn't all that important to him, that the other part of our relationship was more important than sex ...*

*****

Catherine was courageous in struggling to give up a false and defensive facade that was not true to her inner self. As she says, it was frightening to change from a passive and compliant falseness (whom everyone loved) to an individual who was able to assert her genuine feelings. A different sense of self emerged. As she explored what she would do about termination or continuing in therapy as a couple, Catherine observed that Joe was able to respond with how he felt about the change in her.

*****

C *... when I discuss things with him, he gets very uneasy and he admits to himself, he says: "When you discuss things, I see my faults" and he says: "I don't like this and it's uncomfortable and I don't want to discuss it."*

I *I wonder still if your stopping doesn't have a lot to do with how he's feeling about your progress.*

C *It might have.*

I And the fact that for the first time in your marriage you've been able to sit down and tell him quite honestly and openly how you feel about a very important issue ... that might be very upsetting to him.

C To him, yes. It could have something to do . . .

I Regardless of what you do about therapy, it's something that you're both going to have to work on and talk about with one another.

C I suppose you can't keep pushing it away. I tried to . . .

I It's really up to the two of you, but I think you've tried very hard and you've done a lot of good work and the other thing is that when you both work at talking with one another and listening to one another, it somehow helps your marriage, helps you to feel better about yourself, about one another, and that's the only thing that really counts.

*****

In this ending part of the interview, there was more confrontation and psychoeducational links made between different dynamics. For example, Joe's resistance to Catherine's continuing in therapy was connected to the effects on him of the changes in her. Both were frightened of what might lie on the other side of their new ways of communicating with each other. They dealt with their anxieties by avoiding discussions of the very issue that kept them apart in the first place, a very common collusive defense. Another confrontation occurred as they developed the courage to express how each of them truly felt about highly charged issues in their relationship, such as sex. While the problem could not be talked away, they experienced new levels of satisfaction with their relationship. The psychological intimacy gained in such a relational shift was a result and the principal contributor to marital satisfaction. It illustrates what we discussed in chapter 3 about the significance of meaningful relationships to the emerging self during adulthood.

Discussion

This case raises several issues about therapy, the role of the psychotherapist, and the biopsychosocial dynamics at play in the life of this woman. The complexity of the diagnostic picture is also of much interest. Despite the severity of her symptoms and the harshness of her expectations about herself, this person functioned remarkably well in social roles that were important to her and to others. She was a good mother and was able to nurture her children with great empathy. She appeared to be a woman who used her own suffering as an empathic tool to help her children find their way from infancy through adolescence. Although Catherine was most comfortable in the mothering role when her children were young and most dependent on her, she was able to deal with her anxieties about later development and to allow the older children more psychological space as they struggled through early adolescence.

There were also powerful remnants of attachment issues that intruded into her everyday functioning and in her relationship with the therapist. The feelings emanating from these issues were contained by an extremely punishing superego which defined her role as a woman as one of service to others, always putting herself last and never asserting her rights to have her own needs met. As the therapeutic relationship unfolded and offered her an opportunity to explore inner levels of herself so unacceptable that they were sealed off from consciousness, she was gradually able to express what had been inexpressible. The experience of having these forbidden feelings accepted allowed Catherine to modify her behavior in relationships outside the safety of therapy.

The therapeutic relationship seemed to echo developmental issues. Basic values such as acceptance, attempts to understand and not to judge her, and maintaining the focus on the therapeutic contract facilitated the development of an alliance which subsequently provided the resource for the client to examine more triangular conflicts. The process of therapy moved from primarily supportive to educative modes of intervention; the shift from dyadic to conjoint therapy reflected, as well, a change in the client's functioning, particularly her capacity and confidence to engage in reflective and confrontive work.

Another issue was related to the question of change. There is no single explanation that helps to explain the nature of change and why this person was able to achieve some shifts in her sense of self and modifications in her relationships with important people. One dimension of understanding change was, no doubt, the experience of therapy; that is, as she was accepted and respected by the therapist she could experience herself in a different kind of way and begin to think of herself in more positive terms. Another explanation may be related to how reflective discussion and understanding of her history resulted in freeing her, at least partially, from impairments of a very depressing nature. A third aspect of change is the impact of group therapy, particularly her observation of change in other women, which was initially experienced as confusing and later as a catalyst for her to modify her own behavior. That empathic confrontation by peers may have been a catalyst for Catherine to identify with new models of being a woman in the world and to engage in the process of individual therapy in order to modify her sense of self.

Finally, what needs to be entertained is the impact of conjoint marital treatment on opening channels of communication and giving this couple permission to talk about issues between them which they had always felt were forbidden and were a threat to the survival of their marriage. Modifications took place in the quality of their discussions about parts of themselves that were not likely to change significantly. This resulted in higher levels of mutual empathy and acceptance. Interestingly, our subsequent research on lasting relationships found that spouses in marriage do not change significantly in their conflict management styles over the years and that these elements are very important in understanding why relationships last. Also, our research suggests that a new sense of psychological intimacy becomes a reality as couples are able to find ways to communicate openly about their differences and to give up the fantasy of changing the partner. (see chapter 6).

This case illustrates the courage and resiliency of an individual despite serious difficulties with depression. At times, sectors of her life seemed to be severely damaged while other aspects of herself engaged the world in a highly adaptive way. Her cognitive functioning and feelings about self were quite impaired although her capacity to transcend her suffering and to be an empathic mother tended to remain intact. More than any other factor, acceptance, empathy and the maintenance of a focus on mutual and realistic goals by the therapist facilitated the emergence of a modified sense of self in important roles and relationships.

Summary

The helping process takes place within a relationship that is the medium through which therapeutic skills of exploration, support, confrontation and psychoeducation are employed to assist the adult client in her/his journey toward a richer sense of self. The professional self of the therapist is a resource for restoring impaired functioning and for facilitating the integration of new learnings, which may enhance adaptive behaviors in social roles and relationships. To be professional is to have a genuine regard for the well-being of that other person, an empathic acceptance of his/her suffering and a respect for the integrity of that person as another human being equal in spirit yet different in knowledge and skills. The most effective clinical work is done, I believe, by individuals who value themselves as beings in the process of becoming and who also are open to new learnings about current realities while holding on to timeless humanistic values. These existential values along with the clinical skills outlined here are the core for the practice of psychotherapy. They leave enough room within the professional self for individual style unique to the personality of each therapist as well as different theoretical orientations to emerge.

References

Davanloo, H. (1980). Short-term dynamic psychotherapy. NY: Jason Aronson.

Hughes, D. (1997). Facilitating developmental attachment: The road to emotional recovery and behavioral change in foster and adopted children. NY: Jason Aronson.

Kernberg, 0. (1975) Borderline conditions and pathological narcissism. NY: Jason Aronson.

Kernberg, 0. (1980). Internal world and external reality: Object relahons theory applied. N Y: Jason Aronson,

Kohut, H. The restoration of self. NY: International Universities Press, 1977.

Nasar, S. (1998). A beautiful mind: The life of mathematical genius and nobel laureate John Nash. NY: Simon and Schuster.

Scott, J., Williams, J. and Beck, A. (1992). Cognitive therapy in clinical practice: An illustrative casebook. NY: Routledge.

Chapter 06 - Couples Therapy

Conflict in meaningful relationships, especially those that last for many years, is inevitable. As therapists, we often encounter couples that are in stress and unhappy about their relationships, a particularly critical challenge in view of the importance of intimate relationships to the emerging sense of self in adulthood. This chapter uses the data from our study of adaptation among couples in lasting relationships to explore how partners cope with relational conflict as a result of interpersonal differences. Based on these findings, treatment implications for marital therapy are discussed.

Relationships characterized by the development of psychologically intimate communication between partners are critical to the emerging self in adulthood. A major challenge for couples is how to deal with relational conflict. Conflict that festers is undermining of individual well being, satisfaction with relationships and the realization of a more integrated sense of self. Our research suggests that unresolved festering conflicts may compromise psychological intimacy between partners, which is instrumental to the developing self in adulthood.

Conflict between partners in meaningful human relationships, such as marriage, is inevitable (Canary, Cupach and Messman, 1995); further, constructive conflict is not an "oxymoron" (Markman, 1991). These two axioms, which emerged from the results of several studies that focused on conflict in human relationships, underscore the importance of understanding the meaning of conflict in relationships rather than to frame conflict only as an undesirable element to be eliminated. The axioms encourage us to focus on styles of conflict management between spouses. By studying relationships that last, we may learn how spouses adapt to interpersonal conflict over time, which may assist in the development of new models of psychotherapy for couples (Gottman, Coan, Carrere and Swanson, 1998).

This chapter is based on our studies of lasting relationships and focuses on the conflict management styles of 144 spouses in 72 marriages that had lasted an average of 35 years (Mackey, Diemer & O'Brien, 2000). Although we focus on the marriages of heterosexual couples in this chapter, the findings apply, as well, to same sex couples who have made a commitment to their relationships. For details about the research methodology, the reader may consult Appendix B.

Most previous studies of conflict and its management have focused on younger subjects in relationships that have not lasted as long as those in our study. In contrast to the White, middle class samples utilized in many studies of marriage, we focused on couples in long-term relationships who were diverse in their race, ethnicity and socioeconomic status. By design, all of the heterosexual couples were parents, so we had the opportunity to assess how child-rearing may have affected conflict management styles during later years. Our focus was to identify factors that were related significantly to reported styles of managing conflict in recent years, defined as the years after the youngest children in these families reached their eighteenth birthday; a period that has been referred to as the empty nest years.

Richard A. Mackey

In this chapter our definition of conflict and its management is presented, a review of recent studies of conflict management styles among couples, and their relevance to our work are discussed. Factors that contributed to the reported conflict management styles of interviewees in recent years and their observations of their spouses' styles are discussed. Based on the data, a model of psychotherapy with couples is discussed.

Research on how couples manage conflict

Differences between human beings in close relationships, such as marriage, may result in interpersonal conflict. When interpersonal differences and the accompanying negative feelings remain unresolved, they appear to have a corrosive effect on the quality of relationships. For example, Gottman and Krokoff (1989) as well as Vaillant and Vaillant (1993) found that unresolved conflict fed and reinforced negative interactions between spouses. The resulting defensive behaviors perpetuate dissatisfaction and estrangement between them.

Other researchers have suggested that interpersonal conflict may offer opportunities for development of intimate relationships if spouses learn mutually acceptable ways of negotiating and managing differences between them (Canary, Cupach and Messman, 1995). Rather than a threat to the integrity of relationships, conflict may be a catalyst for reaching higher levels of adaptation and an avenue for the development of the self.

We considered conflict as a state of reported disharmony in relationships that developed because of differences between spouses that may have been triggered by any one or a combination of issues such as negotiating roles, handling finances, child-rearing practices, personality clashes, difficulties in expressing one's needs and communicating one's expectations to the spouse. Our approach to developing an understanding of conflict in these marriages was to ask spouses to tell us about differences and problems in their relationships. They were asked to describe examples of conflict during the early, child rearing and recent years. We focused on understanding disagreements from the perspectives of individual spouses. Because all interviewees reported at least minimal conflict in their relationships, the challenge for us was to assess the severity of conflict. If conflicts were assessed to have minimal impact on marital relationships, they were assessed as minor. If interviewees described disagreements as highly distressing to them personally and as having significantly disruptive effects on their marital relationships, they were assessed as major; the latter were reported most frequently during the child rearing years.

Research on conflict management styles

According to Canary, Cupach and Messman (1995), research on conflict management styles has focused on three important behavioral dimensions. The first dimension is how individuals respond when conflict emerges; a spouse may adopt an engaging style characterized by direct verbal confrontation of the other spouse, or she/he may attempt to avoid face to face engagement by use of avoidant behaviors; these behavioral mechanisms have been referred to as the fight-flight and the demand-withdrawl responses. Second, conflict management may be characterized by the nature of affect that is triggered; commonly, affect has been classified as negative or positive. The third dimension refers to whether conflict management behaviors are understood as constructive or destructive: if behavioral responses repair any disruption in relationships, they are considered to be constructive or integrative; if responses undermine the relational connection between spouses, then they are considered destructive.

Based on a review of several studies, Markman (1991) hypothesized a sequential model of conflict management that may lead to adaptation, rather than deterioration in marital relationships. The model assumes that "all couples experience disagreements and conflict" (p. 91), which result in negative affects, such as anger and resentment. To manage negative affects, spouses need to develop skills for expressing their feeling and linking them to "specific behavioral events" and to be able to "hear and validate" the negative feelings of the spouse. Markman posited that the handling of negative affect is "one of the key predictors" of adaptation in subsequent years. He suggests that future adaptation is related to the skill of wives in expressing negative feelings "constructively" and to the ability of husbands to respond in a reciprocal manner to the initiatives of their wives. Markman suggests, further, that the expression of negative affect that is "associated with marital distress," while upsetting at particular points in time, may result in satisfaction with relationships in subsequent years.

Gottman, Coan, Carrere and Swanson (1998) focused on similar issues to Markman in understanding constructive responses to conflict and the importance of gender in managing responses to differences. They studied the conflict management styles of 130 couples in a laboratory setting. Based on observations of these couples over a six year period, the research team reported that divorce was predicted by the following sequence of relational behaviors:

a "negative start-up" by wives in which anger occupied center stage in an encounter with their husbands;

in response, husbands refused to "accept influence" from their wives;

these initial negative encounters were followed by reciprocal negativity by wives and the "absence" of de-escalating responses from the husbands.

Different processes characterize happy marriages that lasted: wives were able to initiate encounters with their husbands by constructive expressions of affect and, husbands responded by listening to their wives and accepting their "influence." Humor helped to de-escalate negative affect and had a soothing effect on spouses, especially on husbands. Expressions of positive affect, despite the presence of conflict, were associated with long term happiness and stability in these marriages.

Other studies have also contributed to our understanding of conflict management styles, which, along with the above research, may be useful in thinking about approaches to therapy with couples. A common way of organizing data on conflict management styles has been to conceptualize a continuum with avoidant behavior at one pole and confrontive behavior at the other pole (Cahn, 1990; Gottman, 1990). Confrontation is characterized by the expression of thoughts and feelings about differences and disagreements directly to the spouse. Cahn (1990) suggests that a confrontive style, which is valued more highly by spouses than avoidance, increases the likelihood that differences would be resolved and had the potential to enhance intimacy between spouses.

Avoidance involves evading face to face discussion of thoughts and feelings about differences. Denial, flight and fight are examples of avoidant mechanisms. As a pattern of conflict management, avoidance may result in chronic relational tensions between spouses and dissatisfaction with marriages (Baucom, Notarius, Burnett and Haefner, 1990). In general, avoidant behaviors, especially when they become chronic patterns, have been predictive of dissatisfaction with marriage (Gottman and Krokoff, 1989).

Conflict management styles and gender

Several studies have found an association between gender and conflict management styles. Wives are more likely than husbands to adopt confrontive modes of conflict management (Heavey, Layne and Christensen, 1993; Mackey and O'Brien, 1995; Mackey and O'Brien, 1998). The explanation for these gender based patterns of conflict management has focused on socialization experiences of males and females. Women are socialized to develop an identity within meaningful relationships (Gilligan, 1982; Surrey, 1984). Males are socialized to develop an identity that values autonomy (Levant, 1996). As a consequence, relationships may take on different meanings to males and females. Women in marriage may value modes of dealing with conflict that enhance expressive, direct and intimate attachments with their spouses. Because their socialization to relational roles is different, husbands may experience more anxiety then their wives in dealing with conflictual matters in a face to face manner (Levant, 1996).

Another explanation for differences in conflict management styles of husbands and wives was offered by Gottman and Levinson (1988) who found physiological differences between males and females as they responded to stressful stimuli. Males reacted physiologically to stress differently than women and the differences were hypothesized to shape their social responses to conflict; they tended to adopt flight-flight responses. Because women were less reactive to stress physiologically, it was hypothesized that they adopted social responses that were tolerant of negativity and of face to face modes of dealing with conflict. However, according to Feeney, Noller and Roberst (1998), the potential link between physiology and the social responses of males and females to stress has not been replicated in other studies. Regardless of the reasons for gender differences, the evidence supports the idea that husbands and wives are different in how they manage interpersonal conflict. As a group, wives tend to be confrontive while husbands tend to adopt avoidant conflict management styles.

Therapeutic models

There are various approaches to helping couples deal with conflict. Crane (1996) suggested that approaches be classified into "behavioral marital therapy, emotionally focused therapy, insight oriented therapy," (and) "minimal marital therapy" (p.28). The latter, which is based on the work of Gottman and his associates, focuses on helping spouses to develop skills at mutual soothing, listening, and validating communication (Crane, 1996).

Others propose similar ways of classifying approaches to helping couples cope with marital conflict. For example, Young and Long (1998) identified cognitive/behavioral, object relations, structural and strategic approaches for working with couples in contemporary practice.

Based on a review of trends in marital therapy and research during the 1990's, Johnson & Lebow (2000) observed that, few models have been "subject to research validation" (p. 25). The researchers noted that most of the studies were based on cognitive/behavioral and emotionally focused models of marital therapy. Despite variations in theoretical orientations, different approaches generally seemed to produce positive results (Snyder, Castellini & Whieman 2006). However, the positive effects of therapy tended to diminish over time, especially if behavioral interventions alone were used. That research also identified elements of effective therapy that cut across models, such the development of communication skills between spouses, strengthening mutual acceptance, and cultivating mutual empathy (Johnson & Lebow, 2000).

Research on couples therapy since 2000 has focused on the effectiveness of different treatment approaches. In their review of this research, Snyder, et al (2006) concluded that various approaches resulted in "statistically and clinically significant improvements for a substantial proportion of couples," but also noted that a "sizeable percentage of couples fail to achieve significant gains from couples therapy or show significant deterioration afterward" (p. 1).

Jacobsen and his colleagues (2000) studied the effectiveness of traditional behavioral couple therapy with integrative behavioral couple therapy. The latter approach added a relational dimension to the behavioral work in which emotional acceptance played a significant role. Therapists communicated to the partners by "empathic joining, unified detachment and tolerance building" (p. 353) techniques in addition to the change oriented techniques of traditional behavioral therapy. In a preliminary analysis of therapy with 21 couples, the integrative approach resulted in higher levels of marital satisfaction and greater improvement in relationships compared to the behavioral approach alone, data that resonated with that of Johnson and Lebow (2000). The data suggested that an integrative approach to marital therapy, which included change oriented along with empathic and accepting elements, facilitated and strengthened the potential for lasting behavioral modifications and positive adaptation in relationships compared to behavioral strategies alone. The integrative model resonates with the model of therapy discussed in this book

As a result of these findings there has been an emphasis on identifying factors common to different approaches and in encouraging the adoption of "plurastic models" of treatment, which include diverse techniques rather than those based on a single theoretical model. Two principals emerge from the research:

1. Approaches to working with couples that are distressed by relational conflict need to be grounded on factors that cut across different models of treatment, and
2. Clinicians who work with distressed couples need to be equipped with various techniques including those based on cognitive behavioral and psychodynamic theories.

Although these principals apply to both heterosexual and homosexual couples since they are similar in various aspects of their relationships, there are differences that have been reported in the literature both in terms of overall functioning and in therapeutic approaches. For example, satisfaction with and frequency of sexual relations vary both in terms of sexual orientation and the length of relationships (Mackey, O'Brien,& Mackey, 1997; Peplau & Fingerhut, 2007). There are also social stereotypes and prejudices about homosexuals with which heterosexual couples do not have to contend and which may stress relationships (Blais, Collin-Vezina,, Marcellin & Picard, 2004). To neutralize social forces that may undermine the efficacy of therapy, Kundso - Martin and Laughlin (2005) proposed a relational model (of therapy) "based on equality rather than gender."

My research colleagues and I wonder if the recent findings discussed above pick up on themes that are "natural" to couples as they struggle to cope with conflict. That is, individual partners may modify discrete behaviors, which may be maintained only within relationships characterized by mutual acceptance and support. In other words, does effective therapy, regardless of the sexual orientation of couples, need to focus on and strengthen the natural adaptive capacities of couples as they struggle to cope with challenges in their relationships. It's another way of suggesting that therapy, to the extent that it is effective, needs to resonate with the natural adaptive strengths of individual couples. If that assumption is correct, we need to understand from the inside out – i.e. from the perspectives of individual partners - how adaptation unfolds as individuals view their relationships over time. That observation is very important to understanding how intimate relationships serve as a valuable resource for the emerging self during adulthood.

We adopted a developmental, life span perspective (Dilworth-Anderson and Burton, 1996) to explore how spouses in lasting relationships managed conflict. Three periods defined the life span of these marital relationships: the early years prior to the birth of the first child, the child-rearing years that began with the birth of the first child, and the recent years which began when the youngest child reached 18 years. Our approach was organized to explore the potential links between conflict management styles and several dimensions of marital relationships during each of these periods; these dimensions included: decision making, sexual relations, role behaviors, psychological intimacy, parenting, communication and satisfaction with relationships. The focus of our inquiry was on predominant modes of conflict management rather than on specific and discrete incidences of conflict and its management. The goal was to develop an understanding of factors that shape conflict management styles, especially in the recent years of these relationships.

As we have already pointed out, research highlights differences between wives and husbands in how conflict is managed. With the exception of the work of Gottman and his associates who suggest a link between conflict management styles and physiological responses to stress, these differences have been framed within the context of socialization theories. Although we are in the midst of changes in cultural expectations about the roles of males and females in marriage, the effects of these changes on couples that remain together are unknown.

Listening to how couples manage conflict

In responding to the emerging consensus among researchers who study relationships, we have developed a "naturalistic" model of therapy based on what partners told us about their relationships. Toward that end, the conflict management styles of interviewees and their observations of the styles of their spouses are discussed in the following pages. Then, the results from a correlation analysis of the significant variables associated with conflict management style of interviewees in recent years as they reported them are presented; based on those data a theoretical model was constructed and tested with logistic regression. Next, a correlation analysis of the conflict management styles of spouses in recent years as reported by interviewees is presented. Based on those findings, a second theoretical model was constructed to identify factors that may predict the conflict management styles of their spouses in recent years. Last, we re-examine the interview data to find clues to understand adaptation in these marriages, especially in view of the relative stability in conflict management styles over the years.

CMS during recent years

Interviewees were asked to describe how they handled differences with their spouses and how they observed their spouses handling differences with them. The focus of these explorations was on the predominant modes of conflict management styles; in other words, how interviewees usually handled differences with their spouses and their observations of how their spouse usually handled differences with them. Initial examination of the data revealed several different styles both about interviewees' modes of handling differences with their spouses and their observations of their spouses' modes. These styles were conceptualized along a continuum with avoidance at one pole and confrontation at the other pole. Direct or face to face discussions were coded "confrontive." Compared to avoidance, a confrontive style was more straightforward. If interviewees reported that they did not or could not discuss their thoughts and feelings in face to face encounters with their spouses, such as denying their feelings or leaving the scene, the style was coded as "avoidant."

The evolution of conflict manage styles between spouses is illustrated in the following interviews with an African-American couple who had been married for 48 years. The wife commented on the change in the marriage:

He didn't always want to listen. Instead of discussing something, he'd get irritated because I didn't agree with him. But I think we do better now. As I said, at first, he wouldn't discuss anything, just leave. Rather than talk about it. So I'd have to persuade him that we needed to talk, we just had to talk. And I think as the years have gone by, I see that it's better. We can talk things out.. I think it's been a gradual process really...I think we finally found out how to talk ... I would have to remind him: "I'm on your side." And it finally got through ... you have to keep on trying ... It's an ongoing thing.

Her 71-year-old spouse, described the process of change from his perspective:

She always tells me I never hear anything she has to say. She says: "You don't listen to me"... I guess there are times when I don't. I don't do it with the intent of being insulting or whatever. I guess just sometimes things come through and they just keep right on going ... Early on, it probably did cause problems, but the longer we live together, the less I've done it. And I often hear a lot of things she doesn't think I hear.

The observations of these spouses reflect a predominant theme in the data: compared to wives, husbands had more difficulty with face to face or confrontive modes of managing conflict. Although no dramatic changes in conflict management styles occurred over the years, there were modifications in styles that were evident in the excerpts from interviews with this couple.

Factors that shape CMS

The following factors had significant relationships to conflict management styles of interviewees in recent years:

*gender,

*conflict management styles during the early and child-rearing years,

*the predominant role behavior of interviewees over the years,

*the quality of communication between spouses in recent years, and

*the reports of interviewees about the quality of their sexual relations during recent years.

The following factors had a significant relationship to the observations of interviewees about their spouses' conflict management styles in recent years:

*gender,

*conflict management styles of spouses during the early and child-rearing years,

*the quality of communication between spouses in recent years,

*the reports of interviewees about the quality of their sexual relations during recent years, and

*their observations about the level of psychological intimacy in their relationships during recent years.

Role behavior was coded either expressive or instrumental, depending on how individuals described themselves. If they viewed themselves predominantly as task centered and oriented primarily toward action in their marital role behavior, this variable was coded instrumental. If they saw themselves as primarily oriented toward verbalizing their thoughts and feelings in attending to relational issues, their role behavior was coded expressive.

Assessment of the quality of communication was based on responses to questions, such as: How would you describe the communication between you? Communication in recent years was coded "positive" when interviewees spoke affirmatively about their ability to converse with each other. Otherwise, communication was coded as "negative or mixed." An example of the quality of communication along with role behaviors is taken from interviews with a couple that had been married about 26 years. The husband, who was highly instrumental in his role behavior, talks about his guarded nature:

I have a tendency to play the cards very close to the vest ... it's probably the role model that was cast for you from early childhood that you were expected to be the bread winner, take on the burdens, and whatever pressures you were suppose to suffer them in silence. The Irish Catholic upbringing where you certainly didn't cry in your beer. It wasn't acceptable...I guess it was my lack of having a warm and charming personality and being very close mouthed and it bothered the hell out of her ... I never fessed up to anything.

As counterpoint to her husband, the wife related the following:

When it comes to that personal feeling level, neither one of us really ever, ever, learned too much about what it's like to let the other person know what you're feeling and what your needs are. He stifled and stuffed a lot.. I'm sure that there's a lot of things about me that I do that he would change but he's never said anything about it, so I have no way of knowing what makes him unhappy or what he'd like to do different ... I do think that we have grown... we both probably think too much but overall, it's probably pretty good communication now.

Psychological intimacy, which was discussed in chapter 3, involved being able to share inner thoughts and feelings not expressed customarily in other relationships, such as those at work. While this factor included effective communication, the distinction between communication and intimacy was a matter of degree. One could have effective communication with a partner without experiencing psychological intimacy, which was characterized by mutuality of understanding, acceptance, trust and respect based upon an openness and honesty of thoughts and feelings not customarily shared in other relationships. It is important to clarify that psychological intimacy was not a constant in these relationships (as it is not in any relationship) but a sense that one could usually count on having an accepting, open and honest exchange with the partner about personal matters if the need arose.

A couple in their 50's reflected on what intimacy meant to them. The wife described her husband as:

My best friend, best lover. The person I can come home to when something bad happens to me. Unfortunately, we have not had parents for many years. He is my parent as well as my friend. He is the person who most cares what is happening to me. The same as in the past ... I can be completely honest.

The meaning of intimacy to the husband was as follows:

I don't like to have my own space. You might as well be by yourself... the important thing is to like being with the other person ... If you don't have that feeling, I think there is a piece that is missing. I think we are our own people, but we do it together. You just have to respect the other person...trust their decisions and beliefs and want to be with them.

Other dimensions of intimate behavior that were explored included physical affection which referred to bodily touching, such as hugging, the quality of sexual relations and the importance of sexual relations over the years.

Based on the results of the correlation analysis of each factor with conflict management styles in recent years, a theoretical model was constructed of factors that shaped conflict management styles in recent years and tested using regression procedures. The results showed that the strongest factor in predicting the conflict management styles of interviewees in recent years was their style of managing conflict during the child-rearing years. The relationship between earlier conflict management styles and styles during recent years suggest that personal conflict management styles did not change appreciably from the child-rearing to recent years. Even before the child-rearing years, the majority of wives were confrontive in their conflict management styles and the majority of husbands were avoidant. In the early years, 63% of wives and 32% of husbands reported a confrontive style, which increased only slightly during the child-rearing years. In recent years, the percentages of interviewees who reported their styles as confrontive was 76% and 46% respectively.

Other factors that contributed to styles of managing conflict in recent years were the role behaviors of interviewees during the child-rearing and recent years as well as the sex of interviewees. Wives, who reported more expressive orientations than did their husbands, were far more likely to report face to face or confrontive styles of managing conflict.

Based on factors that were related to the reports of interviewees about the conflict management styles of their spouse, a second theoretical model was constructed and tested with regression procedures. The results show that the strongest predictor of conflict management styles of spouses as reported by interviewees was the style of managing conflict by spouses during the child-rearing years. During the child-rearing years, 31% of wives and 78% of husbands reported their spouses as confrontive; by recent years, 43% of wives and 81% of husbands reported their spouses as confrontive.

Adaptation in relationships

There was relative stability in styles of managing conflict over the thirty year span of these relationships. So, we re-examined the interview data to understand how these couples adapted over the years. Three themes emerged from that examination:

*communication about communication,

*selective understanding, and

* balances between spouses.

Communication about communication occurred when a spouse was able to let the other spouse know about their difficulties in expressing their feelings about differences. To put one's difficulties about expressing feelings about differences into words and to have the communication accepted by the spouse may have been sufficient to maintain or restore a sense of connection in a relationship. That process of communicating about communication may result in selective understanding of the reason(s) for specific interpersonal behavior, such as being raised in a family that did not encourage or tolerate open discussion of feelings about interpersonal conflict. As a result, gradual acceptance of behaviors that had been an irritant between spouses emerged in these relationships. When husbands felt less pressure from their wives to change, they may have experienced less defensiveness about their avoidant behavior. Concurrently, wives felt less conflicted about their husbands' avoidance.

Communication about communication along with selective understanding is apparent in interviews with the following couple who were married for 40 years. The husband said:

In the beginning communicating was tough .... I used to say to myself, well, she's not Italian. And she doesn't know my moods as an Italian. I grew up with 10 brothers and sister and a mother and father, in a very stable home with big meals and friends and relatives and open house and that type of thing. And then you look back at her house...it was cold. It was a mother and father who drank. It was a mother and a kid sister. It was not knowing what she's going to find when she comes home. So, I used to try to take that into consideration. I think it's caring for the person more than anything else ...We know each other's anger now. We've never been physical. But, I know by the tone of her voice when it's time to stop and she knows by the tone of my voice when enough is enough ... that's the point when we walk away ... because I respect her feelings about being angry and there's no sense in pursuing it because it's just gonna get worse so either I walk away or she walks away.

For the wife, respect and determination to let her husband know how she felt were central to the viability of their relationship:

I think respect is a very important thing ... when you get pushy and that sort of thing then that's not good and there's a lot of misunderstanding because you don't talk. You've got to talk. You've got to talk. You've got to tell the person, even though you're afraid it's gonna hurt their feelings, you've just got to let him know.

This couple illustrates how communication about communication may result in selective understanding and enhanced satisfaction. The process of communication about communication and selective understanding may modify what Gottmann and his associates identified as a "negative start-up" by wives. The words of these interviewees also illustrate how spouses found ways of dealing with conflict that helped their relationship.

An outcome of success at communicating about communication and selective understanding was the recognition of qualities in a spouse that may have been obscured by negativity. When individuals are not angry and defensive about differences, they may become freed-up to recognize strengths in their spouses that were previously obscured. Not infrequently, that recognition led to the acknowledgement of balances in relationships. The following two couples describe how recognition of complementary qualities offered balance in their relationships. A Mexican-American husband reported:

We are opposites. She's over here as the strong decision-making disciplinarian type person. I'm over here and I want to have fun. I'm still a teenager ... we complement each other. She keeps things in order, making sure everything goes right, and I get the fun part of it.

His spouse offered the following observations:
He's understanding of me and my problems and background. His supportiveness in everything that I wanted to do or not to do, his patience ... I'm very fortunate.

Couples with different personality traits talked about differences bringing a balance to their relationships. A husband described complementary aspects of his relationship with his spouse:

I consider myself as rather reserved, and she is outgoing...she makes friends automatically and immediately. I am not that way...it takes me a while to get close to people...and she has made our marriage much easier by her being the way she is.

In discussing the relationship, the wife talked of how developmental experiences shaped the fit between them. Her selective understanding brought meaning to their relationship, which allowed for acceptance of differences and recognition of strengths:

[husband] is really very fair...and very lovable but he can't show it. But that is not his fault...it was his upbringing. If you dig long enough you get everything out of him...at times he is like a little kid. He is a good husband but his needs are different...he missed some of it growing up and he is looking for it now. He is a very kind man...and I usually get what I need from him.

Building a relationship based on balances was a reciprocal process. In responding to the spouse, whether those needs were grounded in traits, developmental differences or both, individuals also experienced a fulfillment of their own needs. The stability of conflict management styles may be related to fundamental qualities within the self, which are not likely to change as relationships mature. Such stability seemed to be the case with this husband. Communicating about communication and selective understanding enabled this couple to find and maintain a relational balance that apparently met their needs.

Discussion

Psychotherapists who treat couples for relational conflict may benefit from studies that focus on understanding conflict management styles from the perspectives of spouses in stable and satisfying marriages. In our research, conflict management styles were explored by asking interviewees to talk about their ways of handling differences and managing conflict. Several variables were related significantly to their conflict management styles: the sex of interviewees, their conflict management styles in the early and child-rearing years, whether their predominant marital roles reflected instrumental or expressive behaviors from early to recent years and the quality of communication.

Interviewees were also asked for their observations about the conflict management styles of their spouses. The following variables were related significantly to the observations of interviewees about the conflict management styles of their spouses: the sex of the respondent, observations of the conflict management style of their spouses in the early and child-rearing years, psychological intimacy with their spouses in recent years, the quality of communication and the quality of sexual relations in recent years.

Based on these data, two theoretical models were constructed, one based on the conflict management styles of interviewees and the second based on their observations of their spouses' styles. What emerged from the regression of each model was the powerful role that conflict management styles in previous years had in shaping the styles of interviewees and their observations of their spouses' styles in recent years. Although other factors were identified as having a shaping effect on conflict management styles in recent years, they paled next to conflict management styles of interviewees and their observations of the styles of their spouses during the child-rearing years.

Changes over the years in conflict management styles of spouses tend to reflect modifications in styles and not dramatic shifts. Conflict management styles remain relatively stable from the early to recent years when less than one out of two husbands and slightly more than three out of four wives report a confrontive style. In adapting to various aspects of their relationships, including the relative stability of conflict management styles from early to recent years, the interview data revealed that couples use communication about communication and selective understanding to maintain a balance in their relationships.

A model of couples psychotherapy

The data about the impact of previous conflict management styles in shaping the observations of interviewees about their own styles as well as the styles of their spouses in recent years add to the dialogue about the goals and focus of couples therapy initiated by Gottman, Coan, Carrere and Swanson (1998). They propose a model of therapy that departs from a focus on resolving "disagreements" between spouses to a model that reflects "what real couples do" (p. 5), and suggested a new approach to marital therapy that places less emphasis on active listening between spouses and more emphasis on the development of mutual empathy, respect and acceptance. Enabling couples to respect genuine differences, to accept what they cannot change and to work toward mutual understanding are valued in this model, similar to the approach with individuals already discussed earlier in this book.

Our approach does not purport to engage spouses in a collaborative effort to change their behavior but, rather, to engage them in a process of mutually exploring their needs, expectations and roles with the goal of enhancing mutual acceptance, respect for differences and empathic understanding. In the approach that we are proposing, strengths emerge as one of the central features. The process of exploring the needs of spouses, their expectations of getting these needs met through their marital relationships and the roles that each spouse adopts in relationships underscores mutual respect for differences and builds upon their strengths. Rather than the target of interventions, modifications in marital behavior, such as conflict management styles, may emerge from a therapeutic process that values what "naturally occurs in well-functioning marriages" (Gottman, Coan, Carrere and Swanson,1998, p. 20), which, we suggest, may include communication about communication, selective understanding and recognition of balances. These processes help to nurture a relational ambiance in which spouses may feel accepted and all right about their marriages. Such an ambiance may allow aspects of the inner self to emerge so that spouses do not have to maintain a defensive outer shell that may not fit with how they really feel. Coincidently, the model that we have constructed based on what couples tell us about how they cope with conflict is very similar to the model of acceptance therapy (Jacobsen, N. et. al., 2000; Jacobsen, N. and Christensen, A., 1996).

In supporting spouses to identify their needs, the first step in the model, the role of the marital therapist is to develop a context within which spouses may begin to feel safe enough to express their inner feelings to their spouse that may have remained obscure. Important in the process are responses by therapists that underscore respect for the feelings of each spouse. The goal is not change or the learning of new social skills but the mutual exploration of individual needs within a context of acceptance, respect and support.

A second step in the approach is to focus on specific expectations that spouses have of each other. Gottman and his associates (1998) identify "soothing" as especially critical for husbands who may have a stronger need than wives to deny the validity of that psychological state. To identify and to confront an inner feeling that has remained obscure in the relationship and have it validated through genuine acceptance by the spouse may become a soothing experience. The process is similar to the one in integrative couple therapy (ICT) being developed by Christensen at UCLA (2000).

A third step is to examine the roles that spouses have adopted as a consequence of not having their needs validated and their disappointment at not having their expectations fulfilled. Rather than dwell on anger, resentment and guilt, the exploration is oriented toward the negotiation of different role behaviors based on clarity about the needs and expectations of each spouse. The learning and adoption of new relational skills may follow.

In summary, we have constructed a model of marital therapy based on empirical data that emphasizes an empathic and strengths oriented approach in which spouses are supported to identify their needs, their expectations of the spouse and to negotiate marital roles to meet needs and satisfy expectations. The goal is to enhance communication about communication, especially needs and expectations, to develop selective understanding, to learn new relational skills and to work toward marital roles that will be responsive to the individual needs and expectations of each spouse.

Conclusion

This chapter is based on data from our research, which focused on how spouses adapt in lasting relationships. Current research points to the importance of understanding the conflict management styles of couples and developing models of therapy based on that evidence. We explored how wives and husbands perceived their own conflict management styles as well as their perceptions of the styles of their spouses. The evidence suggests that spouses in these lasting marriages did not change their conflict management styles significantly over the years. These couples have much to teach therapists about the process of adaptation in relationships, especially the value of good relationships to the emerging sense of self in adulthood.

The data suggest an empathic model of couples therapy characterized by the development of mutual acceptance, respect, and understanding of individual needs, expectations and roles that spouses adapt in their relationships. Therefore, acknowledgement of behaviors that will not change along with a focus on strengths are important parts of the therapeutic process. This exploratory, supportive and educative approach to working with couples may enhance individual well being and the consolidation of a positive sense of self as people negotiate the adult years.

Reference

Baucom, D. H., Notarius, C.I., Burnett, C. K., and Haefner, P. (1990). Gender differences and sex role identity in marriage. In F. D. Fincham & T. N. Bradbury (Eds.), The psychology of marriage: Basic issues and applications (150-171). NY: Guilford.

Berscheid, E. and Reis, H.T. (1998). Attraction and close relationships. In D.T. Gilbert, S.T. Fiske & G. Lindzey (Eds.), The handbook of social psychology (4th ed., Vol 1, pp. 391-445). NY: McGraw-Hill.

Blais, K., Collin-Vezina, D., Marcellin, K. and Picard,A. (2004). Current reality of homosexual couples: Clinical implications in the context of partnership counseling. *Canadian Psychology* 45 (2). 174-186

Cahn, D. (1994). Conflict in personal relationships. Hillsdale NJ: Lawrence Erlbaum Associates, inc.

Christtensem, A. and Jacobson, N. (2000). Reconcilable differences. NY: Guilford.

Canary, D., Cupach, and Messman (1995). Relationship conflict. Thousand Oaks, CA: Sage Publishers.

Crane, D. R. (1996). Fundamentals of marital therapy. New York: Brunner/Mazel Publishers.

Dilworth-Anderson, P. and Burton, L. (1996). Rethinking family development: Critical conceptual issues in the study of diverse groups. Journal of Social and Personal Relationships, 13 (3), 325-354.

Feeney, J., Noller, P. and Roberts, N. (1998). Emotion, attachment and satisfaction in close relationships, ch.18: 473-505, In P Anderson and L Guerrerd (eds.) Handbook of communication and emotion: Research, theory, applications and contents. San Diego, CA.: Academic Press.

Gilligan, C. (1982). In a different voice: Psychological theory and women's development. Cambridge, MA: Harvard University Press.

Gottman, J.M. and Levenson, R.W. (1988). The social psychophysiology of marriage. in P. Noller and M.A. Fitzpatrick (Eds.), Oerspectives on marital interaction (pp. 182-200). Philadelphia: Multilingual matters.

Gottman, J.M., Coan, J., Carrere, S. and Swanson, C. (1998). Predicting marital happiness and stability from newlywed interactions. Journal of Marriage and the Family, 60, 5-22.

Gottman, J.M. (1990). How marriages change. In G.R. Petterson (Ed.) New directions in family research: Depression and aggression. Hillsdale NJ: Erlbaum.

Gottman, J.M. and Krokoff, L.J. (1989). Marital interaction and satisfaction: A longitudinal view. Journal of Consulting and Clinical Psychology, 57(1), 47-52.

Heavy,C.L., Layne, C. and Christensen, A. (1993). Gender and conflict structure in marital interaction: A replication and extension. Journal of Consulting and Clinical Psychology, 61, 16-27.

Jacobson, N. *et al.* (2000). Integrative behavioral couples therapy: an acceptance-based, promising new treatment for couple discord. Journal of Consulting and Clinical Psychology, 68 (2), 351-355.

Jacobsen, N. and Christensen, A. (1996). Acceptance and change in couple therapy: A therapist's guide to transforming relationships. NY: Norton.

Johnson, S. and Lebow, J. (2000). The coming of age of couple therapy: A decade review. Journal of Marital and Family Therapy, 26 (1), 23-38.

Knudson-Martin, C. and Laughlin, M. (2005). Gender and sexual orientation in family therapy: Toward a postgender approach. *Family Relations,* 54 (1), 101-115.

Karney, B.R. and Bradbury, T.N. (1995). The longitudinal course of marital quality and stability: A review of theory, method, and research. Psychological Bulletin, 118 (1), 3-34.

Levant, R. (1996). The new psychology of men. Professional Psychology: Research and Practice, 27, 259-269.

Mackey R. and O'Brien, B.A. (1999). Adaptation in lasting marriages. Families in Society: The Journal of Contemporary Human Services, 80 (6), 587-596.

Mackey R. and O'Brien, B.A. (1998). Marital conflict management: gender and ethnic differences. Social Work: Journal of the National Association of Social Workers, 43(2) March, 128-141.

Mackey, R.A., O'Brien, B.A. and Mackey, E. (1997). Gay and Lesbian Couples: Voices from Lasting Relationships .. Westport, CT: Praeger Publishers.

Mackey, R.A. and O'Brien, B.A. (1995). Lasting marriages: Men and women growing together. Westport, CT: Praeger.

Markman, H. (1991). Constructive marital conflict is not an oxymoron. Behavioral Assessment, 13, 83-96.

Peplau, L and Fingerhut, A. (2007). The close relationships of lesbians and gay men. *Annual Review of Psychology,* 58, January, 405-424.

Snyder, M., Castellini, A. and Whisman, M. (2006). Current status and future directions in couple therapy. *Annual Review of Psychology,* 57, January, 317-344.

Surrey, J.L. (1984). The "self-in-relation": A theory of women's development.Work in Progress, No. 13. Wellesley, MA: Stone Center Working Papers Series.

Vaillant, C.O. and Vaillant, G.E. (1993). Is the U-curve of marital satisfaction an illusion? A 40-year study of marriage. Journal of Marriage and the Family, 55, 230-239.

Young, M. and Long, L. (1998). Counseling and therapy for couples. Pacific Grove, CA: Brooks/Cole Publishing Co.

Chapter 07 - The Value of Personal Therapy to the Emerging Professional Self

Practice wisdom as well as anecdotal evidence supports the value of personal psychotherapy for clinical practitioners. Although a few surveys of clinical social workers, psychologists and psychiatrists have found that most therapists enter personal psychotherapy at some point in their careers, little research has focused on the potential meaning of personal therapy to the development of a professional self. This chapter is based on a study that used in-depth interviews to explore the significance of personal psychotherapy to the professional roles of experienced therapists and advanced graduate students.

From the beginnings of my career, I have always worked in settings and have been associated with colleagues, regardless of their individual professional disciplines, who view personal psychotherapy as an invaluable resource in the development of their professional selves. Such an idea is of particular relevance to this model of psychotherapy, which underscores the professional use of self in relationships with adult clients. Awareness of the self and the developmental roots of one's behavior, the centrality of empathy in the therapeutic process and the capacity to contain personal thoughts and feelings that might undermine one's effectiveness, may be enhanced by personal therapy.

Beginning in the formative years of psychoanalysis and extending into the present, personal treatment has been viewed as a valuable, if not indispensable qualification for clinical practice. In psychoanalytic training institutes, a personal analysis is required. Among many professionals engaged in the practice of psychotherapy, personal treatment is highly valued. However, personal psychotherapy is not generally required in the professional training of psychiatrists, psychologists, counselors and social workers.

Previous Research

Although theory, experience and anecdotal evidence support the value of personal therapy for therapists, relatively little research has been done on the subject. When I undertook the research on which this chapter is based, there were only a few studies reported in the social and behavioral literature, primarily in psychology and none in social work. Among the studies reviewed (Buckley, 1981; Grunebaum, 1983; Guy. 1986; Clark. 1986; MacDevitt. 1987; Norcross, Strausser & Faltus, 1988; G; Guy & Liaboe, 1988) was a national survey of mental health professionals which included social workers from the 1985 NASW Register of Clinical Social Workers (Norcross, Strausser-Kirtland & Missar, 1988). Seventy- nine percent of female and fifty-eight percent of male social workers reported having been in personal treatment at some point in their careers. The most common form of treatment, identified by over half of all respondents, was psychoanalytic-psychodynamic therapy oriented to self awareness and insight. Asked to identify how their experiences in personal treatment shaped their values about doing therapy, most respondents referred to the importance of non-specific factors such as empathy, warmth, patience and acceptance, as well as understanding transference and countertransference dynamics.

Richard A. Mackey

Findings of other studies (Buckley, 1981; MacDevitt, 1987; Guy, Stork & Poelstra, 1988) resonate with those of Nocross. Generally, professionals who have had therapy, regardless of its duration, value it as a critical, if not essential, component for practice. Most frequently, the value lies in developing insights into one's self which may enhance one's role and skill as a psychotherapist.

Other empirical studies suggest that the effect of personal treatment of psychologists and psychiatrists on their patients is inconclusive (Clark, 1986). No relationship was found between the personal treatment of therapists and outcomes for their patients in five out of seven studies. In one study, treatment may have been detrimental to clients. As with much research, these studies suffered from numerous defects in sampling, design or measurement and cannot be considered conclusive. At best they suggest no empirically verifiable connection between personal therapy of clinicians and therapeutic outcomes for their clients.

What emerges from these studies is the importance of understanding the topic within the context of several variables: the timing of therapy or when it occurs in one's life and career, the motivation of a person to pursue treatment, the mode(s) of intervention, the theoretical orientation(s) and competence of a therapist. These dynamics are difficult to control and become even more problematic when hidden contextual forces, life experiences, as well as imprecision in measuring instruments are considered.

Our research (Mackey, & Mackey, 1994; Mackey, & Mackey, 1993; Mackey, Mackey, & O'Brien, 1993) explored the meaning of personal psychotherapy to advanced students and experienced clinical social workers who were practicing psychotherapists. This was timely in view of the dearth of research on the subject, especially in social work, as well as its potential significance to practice. By including both students and practitioners, the value of personal treatment was explored for those who were at the beginning of their careers as well as those in professional practice. The focal question was: Do graduate students and practitioners see a connection between their personal psychotherapy and their practice and if so, how do they understand the nature of that connection?

Listening to psychotherapist talk about their own therapy

Personal interviews organized around the focal question were conducted with thirty respondents: 15 students in the advanced year of MSW graduate study in clinical social work and 15 MSW clinical social workers. A qualitative approach in which clinical interviewing skills were adapted for a research purpose was utilized for exploration of the topic, a methodology appropriate for studies which focus on relatively unexplored territory and which we were using in the lasting relationships research (see chapters 03, 06 & Appendix B)). We were interested primarily in discovering what meaning personal therapy may have to individuals in their professional roles even though no one entered therapy to learn how to do psychotherapy. Essentially, this was a phenomenological question explored most effectively through focal question interviews, an approach quite different from the few existing studies on the topic. Although previous studies offer some understanding of the empirical connection between one variable and another, they did not elicit the type of information which is possible to explore with this approach. That is, a qualitative mode of research provided room within structure to explore the significance of personal psychotherapy to practice and the development of a professional self.

Respondents were recruited through publicity, which included an advertisement in a professional newsletter. The goal of the study was stated briefly and individuals were invited to volunteer if they had been in personal psychotherapy. The criteria were simple: one had to be in the advanced clinical year of graduate training or be an MSW clinical practitioner. No attempts were made to control for other variables such as the mode(s) or type(s) of personal therapy. Of course, the way in which people were recruited for the study clearly implied a connection and very likely implied further that the connection was a positive one.

Interviews lasted forty-five minutes, more or less, and were tape recorded. By listening to each recording, detailed process notes were prepared. Established procedures for coding and categorizing data as well as conceptualizing themes were followed (Strauss & Corbin 1990). Transcriptions provided detailed examples of these themes as they were found in the interviews. Working as a team, we checked, clarified, retained or discarded observations and inferences. A team approach enabled us to deal with biases and other subjective phenomena, which may have contaminated the integrity of the findings.

Sample

The mean age of students was 32 years and that of practitioners 42. Practitioners had an average of 7 years of professional experience. Eighty percent of the sample was female and 20 percent were male.

Reasons for entering personal therapy were similar for both groups. Fifty percent of all respondents identified something within themselves as precipitants. Frequently, this included personal reactions to some critical life event such as a developmental or career transition, which triggered anxiety and/or a reactive depression. Twenty-three percent reported that interpersonal conflict within a significant relationship led them into treatment. Often, that involved the termination of an intimate relationship, such as marriage. This was different than the loss of a loved one by death and different from intrapersonal precipitants only in the way in which people talked about how they were troubled at the time of entering therapy. Ten percent entered therapy as a consequence of stress associated with their MSW program and an equal percentage because of substance abuse, usually alcohol.

Half of the sample was currently in treatment with clinical psychologists and 40 percent with social workers. The remaining 10 percent were seeing other professionals. Fifty-seven percent of therapists were women. The orientation of 87 percent of their therapists was described as psychodynamic in which the goal was the development of self-awareness and insight through an exploratory and reflective modus operandi.

All respondents were in individual treatment with 23 percent of them also in another mode such as group or conjoint marital counseling. Two thirds of the sample were in treatment for more than three years: 60 percent of students were in therapy less than three years and 93 percent of practitioners for more than three years.

In summary, students and practitioners were similar in the ratio of women to men in each group, their reasons for entering personal therapy, the profession of their therapists (although more students were treated by psychologists), the mode of treatment and the theoretical approach of their therapists. They differed in age and in the length of their personal therapy.

Narrative themes from interviews

After data for students and practitioners were coded and analyzed independently, the data for the sample as a whole were analyzed again to determine if the significance of personal psychotherapy to each group was substantially different. Coding had produced five themes within each group, which appeared to capture the significance of personal psychotherapy to their professional use of self as therapists. Although themes were similar for both groups, differences became apparent as we examined the codes and resulting categories under each theme. For example, each group referred to their therapists as models for practice; most talked about therapy as an experience that enhanced empathy; all respondents talked of how personal therapy had helped them to understand the therapeutic process. However, students focused more on how personal therapy was a complement to their supervision and how therapy had helped them to integrate theoretical concepts in a personally meaningful way. Most practitioners focused on specific awarenesses of self that had emerged through their personal therapy. For them, integrating these awarenesses of self into their practice was central to their professional identities.

Differences appeared to be shaped principally by contextual variables; that is, the professional life-space at the time of the study. Students were about to launch their professional careers. The significance of personal psychotherapy needs to be understood within the context of their role as learners and emerging practitioners of psychotherapy. The practitioner sample had moved beyond that beginning stage of orientation to their profession. The significance of personal therapy reflected an investment at integrating personal dimensions of themselves into their psychotherapeutic roles. Although that theme was also found in the responses of students, they were more invested in connecting theory with skill within the context of searching for their professional identities.

In thinking about context as it shapes the meaning of personal psychotherapy to practice, it is important to recall that there were no substantial differences between students or practitioners in their reasons for being in personal therapy. Because of the nature of the study and the definition of its parameters, we did not focus on the significance of psychotherapy to the personal lives of respondents. This was explored only if respondents mentioned it and, then, only if they indicated a specific connection between their personal lives and their clinical practice.

Three themes emerged from the data. The first theme, therapist as model, included any references to identification with the modus operandi of therapists as well as adopting their skill in working with clients. The second theme, understanding the therapeutic process, included a wide range of responses, which spoke to how personal therapy enabled respondents to comprehend and master elements of clinical practice. Frequent references were made to the dynamics of the therapeutic relationship, especially transference and counter transference. There were also references to understanding technique and to gaining an appreciation of what was therapeutic about therapy. The third theme, integration, included responses that addressed the inter-relationship of personal and professional dimensions in one's self.

Their therapists as models

All practitioners and 14 out of 15 students talked about their therapists as objects of identification to be emulated in their clinical work. Perceptions of therapists' qualities such as genuineness, acceptance and empathy served as the foundation for the development of safe and trusting therapeutic relationships within which their identifications developed. As a result, respondents found themselves internalizing many aspects of the modus operandi of their therapists that included non-verbal mannerisms as well as verbal techniques. To many students and, to a considerable extent, the inexperienced practitioner, therapists represented the therapeutic ideal, whole objects of identification to be emulated. A student speaks to that aspect of modeling:

It's been a learning tool to sit with someone else who is a therapist; sometimes I even find myself responding to clients in a way that my therapist would respond, asking questions or phrasing certain things as he does; that's been very valuable.

A practitioner recalls:

When I began to practice, I made interpretations using his phrases, I could hear his tone of voice, it amazed me constantly and delighted me to hear it coming out of me just the way he said it.

That level of modeling was tempered by two factors: the length of time in therapy with the same therapist and the sense of competence which one had internalized as a result of success in practice. When these two factors were joined, respondents became selective about their identifications and internalizations. Imitation and idealizing, more common among students, seemed to give way to differentiation of qualities, some of which fit and some of which did not fit with the individual style of a practitioner:

It's positive as well as negative, in terms of being a model. There are a lot of things that I think she handled really well that I have found myself sitting in a therapy relationship thinking: "How would she deal with this? Well, she has dealt with this with me and this is what she did." That was helpful to me so, I might do the same thing. Of course, going back and talking to her about that is interesting.

Changes in the nature of modeling were also connected to the observations among several individuals about their perceptions of therapists as treatment unfolded. Rather than ideal objects to be imitated, therapists became competent human beings with both good and not so good qualities (although none of them were experienced as bad). As that shift occurred in the relationship, respondents reflected about the fit of therapists' characteristics with their own individuality as practitioners. While this cannot be separated from a change in the transference, there is evidence that therapists respond differently to patients the longer the latter were in treatment. In other words, the shift was reciprocal in nature.

Despite variations in identifying with therapists as models for professional practice, there was constancy to how therapists were experienced regardless of how long one had been in treatment. The basis of identifying therapists as models was in the experience of being accepted by them as well as their empathic and patient modes of behaving within their therapeutic roles. Prominent themes of constancy, availability and belief in the patient, especially when esteem for self was shaky, were evident in responses. The mutual and collaborative nature of therapy was also important in understanding modeling. That is, the concept of the therapeutic alliance was central to change even though there were many variations in specific behaviors of therapists the longer one was in treatment.

Finally, a difference was found in the nature of identifications depending on the discipline and gender of therapists. Among some women who were seeing female psychotherapist, the gender and professional aspects of modeling were joined; specific references were made to identifying with qualities perceived in female therapists to which female practitioners aspired in their professional roles. This was similar for two males who were also seeing male therapists. Because the numbers were small, any potential patterns need to be treated with caution.

Understanding the Helping Process

All practitioners and 14 of 15 students reported that therapy had helped them to understand the therapeutic process. This theme included the enhancement of empathy, the learning of specific techniques, understanding dynamics such as transference and gaining confidence in being able to confront issues which had been intimidating to them.

Perhaps because of their closeness to formal learning about the helping process, students, more than practitioners, talked specifically of gaining an intellectual appreciation of therapy as having a beginning, middle and end. Those in therapy a long time reflected on the importance of time in the beginning phase as a period in which they could gradually feel trusting and comfortable enough to explore very troubling inner conflicts. They recalled the beginnings of their treatment, often extending over weeks or months, as a time when they did most of the talking with therapists primarily adopting a listening mode. Most felt that this complementary relationship was appropriate to their needs at the time. All experienced their therapists as supportive, attentive and caring. Not infrequently, respondents talked of being in crisis during this period so that much of the beginning stage was focused on helping them to express their thoughts and feelings about recent events, which had overwhelmed them. Once this initial period was negotiated, therapists were described as becoming more interactive, offering observations and actively engaging them in exploration, reflection and thinking about their conflicts. A student noted that shift when she observed:

The boundaries in my individual therapy have changed somewhat. It's not like he offers information but he's more likely to answer question directly now then when I first started. That's probably because he knows me a lot better and knows what's behind my questions.

No one reported that therapists had acted inappropriately, nor did any feel that they were not seeing a professional person whose role was to help them. While these observations may reflect changes in the nature of transference and counter transference dynamics, they appear to reflect, as well, a real shift in the subject's sense of relatedness to another human being.

Students referred frequently to the value of therapy in helping them become more empathic with clients, especially to the meaning of the client role. They talked of their own vulnerability as patients, especially in the beginning phase of therapy, and how those experiences had enriched and deepened their appreciation of what it meant to apply for and accept help. Several references were made to how they used feelings associated with their experiences in working with clients:

Without therapy I wouldn't have been as attuned to my own feelings, to be able to use them in sitting with a client. Its an intuitive kind of thing to know where the client is by how I feel; without my therapy I wouldn't be able to do that.

There were frequent references to identifying with the soothing and empathic functions of therapists, which enabled students to be available to their clients in a similar way. To have been accepted and respected by their therapists was a vehicle for their treating clients in a similar manner:

I didn't realize it until now that one of the big things I've learned from this person who I idolize is just being very calm, taking things in a calm, cool and collected manner.

Although similar themes were evident among practitioners, a different level of understanding was apparent in their responses. Often, therapy helped to consolidate values about doing therapy. One practitioner comments on this gain as she describes how therapy had helped to enhance her listening skills:

I think the most important characteristic of being a good therapist is being able to listen. I've been listened to and I can listen because of that. I've been encouraged to consider the depth of what I say and what I think about and to look beyond superficial meanings of things. That came through his listening to me. I think that that's what I do with my patients more than anything else.

An important aspect of understanding the therapeutic process was the new sense of discipline which respondents brought to their role as therapists. For students, this often involved new skills at being able to tolerate pain in clients without needing to do something about it. In that respect, a student talks of confidence in being able to tolerate silences which was linked to her reflection on the meaning of silence in her own therapy:

I was very uncomfortable with silences and would always jump in. It would raise so much anxiety for me that I would try to ask a question or fill the silence in some way or another. In my own therapy I find that when there's a silence, I'm able to utilize that and really get some stuff from the gut. Sitting in my own therapy and being able to do that, how useful it's been to me; now, when I'm working with clients, I remember that it is useful for them to sit with that silence and that it's OK.

Practitioners often talked about the significance of therapy in clarifying and reinforcing fundamental therapeutic principles. For one practitioner, this underscored professional discipline:

I wanted to be gratified as a patient and didn't get gratified. What growth came from that! It taught me that gratifying the client out of my needs is not a good thing to do; it might feel nice for both of us and we might leave today with smiles on our faces, but it isn't going to change anything. This person is here for change, whether they are fully aware of it or not. Otherwise, they wouldn't have come here; that's hard work and it's not always fun sticking to the business. That's something I learned in my own therapy.

Another practitioner expressed similar thoughts in the following way:

An important impact on my work is what it feels like to sit on the other side; to me that is so important. I know how it feels to have somebody really listen and really care and also how anxiety provoking the whole experience can be. You come to know real resistance and how important it is for a therapist to respect somebody, to understand that you can't push people too much but you have to push them somewhat. I know now that being a nice person is not enough to make a therapeutic relationship move. No matter how many books I read, sitting in that other seat is what made that alive to me.

One area which students talked about more than practitioners was how personal therapy served as a valuable complement to supervision in their field internships. Interestingly, little ambiguity was reported among students about the boundary between these two modes of practice. In their minds, therapy was differentiated from supervision in its attention to personal dynamics while supervision focused more on learning how to do clinical work. Therapy often served as a vehicle for exploring issues that had been identified in supervision as counter-transference problems. A student speaks to that differentiation:

In therapy, I'm able to talk about my past and what's making me think like this now or respond in this way. In supervision that's touched on but not nearly as much as in my therapy where I spend a lot of time talking about counter-transference issues that come up in my placement. That's very important in the work that I'm doing. I need a third hour, therapy, to be able to connect that to my own developmental and family issues.

Finally, respondents from both groups talked about personal therapy as an anecdote to burn out. This often involved understanding their histories as caregivers and how elements of that history were played out in their professional roles in clinical practice. Frequent references were made to establishing and maintaining appropriate boundaries with clients based on understanding themselves. Since students were not confronted with as long a professional history as practitioners in working with very needy clients who often made extraordinary demands on their sense of narcissistic integrity, they did not talk as much about this aspect of the therapeutic process as did practitioners. A practitioner speaks to that theme:

Therapy has been very helpful, especially when people relapse and not to take it personally. I call it the Messiah complex; you have to go out and save all these alcoholics; you're not that powerful. You're an aid that they can use to help them get sober or help them sort through their issues. You're not going to be the person saving them; they're going to save themselves. Therapy, I think, has been helpful in terms of preventing burnout, just knowing what you can and can't do as a therapist, as a human being.

Integration of a professional self

Although everyone spoke of the integrative value of personal therapy, practitioners focused more on the inseparability of one's identity as a human being with how one is in professional roles with clients. Many practitioners spoke of how therapy had helped them to find and to preserve a central part of themselves that remained constant despite different roles which were adopted in practice. Students talked somewhat differently about integration although they were also concerned about its importance to their professional identity. They focused more on finding a professional identity which included how to behave in professional relationships with clients whose needs differed, how to tolerate and sit with pain and how to respond in ways that would be truly helpful.

Professional and personal integration may become a nodal issue once one reaches a plateau of adult development, which may occur several years after receiving the professional degree and entering practice. Not uncommonly, the developmental shift of moving from one plateau to another was often fueled by new awareness of self achieved in personal therapy. Often, these breakthroughs acted as a catalyst to spur professional/personal development as in the following:

For a long period of time, I never realized anyone else was depressed. Nobody was ever depressed that I saw and then I realized through treatment that I had a real hard time recognizing my own depression. I was more comfortable being anxious and so half my clients were anxious; I was not realizing what I was doing; I had a real blind spot to see other people's depression. My therapist really helped me see that as we talked about my work.

Students referred to similar connections but the foci of insights and the specific value of self awareness in shaping professional responses were quite different. An important aspect of integration among students was in being able to understand concepts, which may have eluded them in the past. Feelings associated with ideas, which had been in conflict with cognitive understanding, no longer undermined the process of learning. Thus, therapy became a framework for integrating thoughts with feelings as well as theory with practice. Ideas that had been tinged with conflict were experienced differently in the context of empathic, psychotherapeutic relationships. As a result, students talked of being freer to think about theory, evaluate its significance to their emerging professional selves and to be less intimidated by the process of intellectual discovery. A student comments on being able to process learning in ways that were previously unavailable to her:

I couldn't tolerate ambiguity before. That's been a major change in my life and it's affected me emotionally and intellectually. My writing is much better because I used to feel like I had to know what the right way to do something or say something was. Now, I can think in more complex ways. Complex ideas are ambiguous.

An important aspect of integration for students was in being able to understand theory in the context of their therapeutic experiences, a theme reflected in the following:

Being in therapy has helped me to understand object relations theory and self psychology in a very personal way. I know what that feels like to have somebody containing your feelings and performing functions that you can't do for yourself, like when you're depressed, distorting things and not able to soothe yourself; the therapist does that for you. For a while, I couldn't do it for myself. I would wait every week to see the therapist to do it for me and now I do it for myself.

Among practitioners, integration was often a matter of bringing together personal development with their sense of a professional self. As a catalyst for personal development, therapy became a central resource in the journey toward professional competence. Metaphorically, a practitioner captured that theme when she said:

My analyst used to leave the window open all the time, and I would lay there, a brand new patient, my legs outstretched and the wind blowing on my legs, freezing. I wanted to be a good girl, put up with it but the bottom line was I wanted the window closed and I was afraid to ask. There's something about that memory: how a patient feels, their fear not so much that they'll be disappointed but how will they handle the rage and deal with the therapist? I feel that so profoundly. I know when a patient is going through that and I know not to help them, not to get up and close the window. It's not because I delight in watching them squirm, but I know that until they ask me, "Is it OK to close the window?," they will not have confronted that central issue.

Conclusions

This final chapter explored an important, yet little understood, dimension of psychotherapeutic practice: the meaning of personal treatment to the clinical work of graduate students and experienced practitioners. Building on previous studies mainly of clinical psychologists, the findings support the hypothesis that personal therapy may be a valuable resource in development of a professional self and in becoming a competent psychotherapist. Although the research focused on clinical social work students and practitioners, the results are relevant to other disciplines in the human service field that are also engaged in the practice of psychotherapy.

The mode of research, in which clinical interviewing skills were adapted to the goal of the study, enabled us to explore the unique meanings which personal therapy had to individuals. This included contextual aspects such as the life space of students who were about to launch their careers and of professional clinical social workers with several years of professional experience. Indeed, context seemed to account for most of the qualitative differences found between the two groups.

The findings offer some important indicators of how personal treatment may enhance practice by being a resource in the development of a professional self. For these respondents, therapy helped to nurture knowledge, values and skills by way of identification with psychotherapists who became models of professional practice. No doubt, the good-enough fit between patients and therapists explains the quality of these highly positive results although previous relationships with other therapists were not always experienced as positively. What their current therapists seemed to have in common was a talent for integrating paradoxical themes into their therapeutic roles: they were experienced by respondents as supportive yet confrontational, connected yet separate, and empathic yet sticking to the agenda of therapy. Identification with and internalization of these characteristics led to a progressive sense of competence within the professional selves of the individuals in this study.

The experience of personal treatment also was a vehicle for understanding, cognitively and emotionally, the helping process and the dynamics of psychotherapy. However, these so-called secondary gains did not compromise the primary motivation for and focus of therapy, the amelioration of personal conflict. Rather, the treatment experience appeared to be reframed as an opportunity for continued development in adulthood, a significant aspect of which included their clinical practice. Respondents talked of therapy as an indispensable resource for integration of their professional selves, something more meaningful than through other means such as reading, supervision and education. Their therapists were valuable allies and catalysts in that process.

Although the data help us to understand how personal treatment may be a resource in the development of a professional sense of self, they do not resolve a major question: Should all clinicians be required to be in personal treatment? Respondents were split on the subject. About half thought that such a requirement would undermine essential pre-conditions for successful treatment: motivation and readiness. The other half pointed to other pre-requisites for professional practice, including a graduate degree and a license, which they felt were no more important than personal treatment. Despite those differences all were in agreement about the value of personal psychotherapy to their roles as psychotherapists.

Personal psychotherapy is one of several resources that may support an individual in the development of a professional self. Among these resources are professional education through which one is grounded in the theories, techniques and ethics of clinical practice. Supervision, consultation and continuing education are other resources available to practitioners after their graduate education. While all of these resources may contribute to one's professional competence, personal therapy appears to have a special maning in responding to the challenges that confront us today.

I observed in the prologue to this book that "it is the self of the practitioner interacting with the selves of clients that constitute the essence of professional practice." The empirical evidence now available about the centrality of the therapeutic relationship to effective psychotherapy (Lambert & Barley, 2001) underscores the critical importance of our responsibility for managing the therapeutic encounter with troubled people. Cultivation of core skills along with a wide range of techniques, which are grounded on sound theory and research, are important especially as we make the effort to integrate them into our sense of a professional self. For many practitioners personal therapy may be a valuable resource in responding to that challenge.

As we learn more of how "the person of the psychotherapist is inextricably intertwined with the outcome of psychotherapy" (Norcross, 2001, p. 346), we will make progress in unraveling the mysteries of how one human being may actually make a difference in the life of another human being through the vehicle of a psychotherapeutic relationship. To that end this book may stimulate exploration and discussion of how and why psychotherapy may serve as an invaluable resource in the development of the emerging self during adulthood.

References

Buckley, P., Karasu, T. and Charles, E. (1981). Psychotherapist view their psychotherapy, Psychotherapy: Theory, research and practice,18, 299-305.

Clark, M. (1986). Personal therapy: A review of empirical research, Professional psychology: Research and Practice, 17, (6) 541-543.

Grunebaum, H. (1983). A study of therapists choice of a therapist, American Journal of Psychiatry, 140:10, 1336-1339.

Guy, J. and Liaboe, G. (1986). Personal therapy for the experienced psychotherapist: A discussion of its usefulness and utilization, The Clinical Psychologist, 39, (1) 20-23.

Guy, J., Stark, M. and Poelstra, P. (1988). Personal psychotherapy for psychotherapists before and after entering professional practice, Professional Psychology: Research and Practice, 19, (4) 474-476.

Hesse-Biber, S., Dupuis, P. and Kinder, T.S. (1992). HyperRESEARCH: A tool for the analysis of qualitative data. (Computer Program). Randolph (MA: Researchware

Kaslow, F. (Editor), (1984). Psychotherapy with psychotherapists, New York: Haworth Press.

Lambert, M. and Barley, D. (2001). Research summary on the therapeutic relationship and psychotherapy outcome. Psychotherapy: Theory / Research / Practice / Teaching, 38 (4), 357-361.

MacDevitt, J. (1987). Therapists' personal therapy and professional self-awareness, Psychotherapy, 24, (1) 693-703.

Mackey, R. and Mackey, E. (1994). Personal psychotherapy and the development of a professional self. Families in Society: The Journal of Contemporary Human Services 75(8), 490-498.

Mackey, R. and Mackey, E. (1993). : The value of personal psychotherapy to clinical practice (1993) with E. Mackey. The Clinical Social Work Journal. 21(1), 97-109.

Mackey, R., Mackey, E. and O'Brien, B. (1993). Personal psychotherapy and the social work student. Journal of Teaching in Social Work. 7(2), 129-146.

Norcross, J. (2001). Purposes and products of the task force on empirically supported therapy relationships. Psychotherapy: Theory / Research / Practice / Teaching, 38 (4), 345-356.

Nocross, J.,Strausser, D. and Faltus, F. (1988). The therapist's therapist, American Journal of Psychotherapy. XLII (1) 53-66.

Norcross, J., Strausser-Kirtland, D. and Missar, C. (1988). The process and outcomes of psychotherapists' personal treatment experiences, Psychotherapy. 25 (1) 36-43.

Strauss, A. and Corbin, J. (1990). Basics of qualitative research; Grounded theory procedures and technique, Newbury Park, CA.: Sage Publications.

Appendix A

Summaries of the lives of Maya Angelou, Eleanor Roosevelt and Frank McCourt

One way of appreciating the adaptive potential of the emerging self is to examine the lives of individuals whose adult years have been characterized by generativity rather than stagnation (Erikson, 1963). These are human beings who experience significant adversities in their lives yet are able to move beyond these adversities in adulthood to make remarkable contributions to others and to society. In the following appendix, the lives of three individuals, who are discussed in chapter 1, are summarized. Each of them transcended various adversities - racism, trauma and poverty - to make important contributions to the world.

Maya Angelou

Maya Angelou has had a celebrated career as a writer of several books and collections of poetry. She is the recipient of many awards and has been the Reynolds Professor of American Studies at Wake Forest University since 1981. In the first volume of her autobiography, I Know Why The Caged Bird Sings (1993), Angelou writes about her life up to the mid-adolescence.

At the age of three years she and her brother, Bailey, moved from California to Stamps, Arkansas to be reared by their grandmother because their parent's marriage had ended. Her book is a poignant account of poverty and racism in a small southern town. More importantly, it is the story of a Black family anchored by a stern devout grandmother who owned and operated a general store. The narrative of Angelou's childhood in 1930's America depicts a poor human environment that was full of enriching characters that cared genuinely about her well being. It also depicts the fear and oppression that White America inflicted on Blacks

At the age of eight years, Maya along with Bailey, one year older and her closest friend, moved to St. Louis to live with their mother. During the year that they remained in St. Louis, Maya was raped by the mother's boyfriend who threatened to kill Bailey if she told anyone. Because of injuries that were impossible to hide, the rape was discovered and the boyfriend was sentenced to a jail term. Before beginning the sentence, he was murdered. Characteristic of how children may experience trauma, Maya blamed herself for the death and vowed never to talk again.

Soon after these events, Maya and Bailey returned to Stamps where they remained until Maya graduated from the eighth grade at the age of twelve. Her autism, which she says describes as an unwillingness to talk, was tolerated for awhile by adults. After more than one year of not talking, Maya formed a relationship with Bertha Flowers a refined, beautiful and talented Black woman. One of Maya and Bailey's great loves was reading; Mrs. Flowers, whom Maya admired, invited Maya to use her personal library, which included novels and volumes of poetry. The only condition was that this gifted 10 year old child read them aloud. Maya soon regained her ability to speak. The caged bird began to sing.

Richard A. Mackey (Ed.)

As she was approaching adolescence, the grandmother took Maya and Bailey to live with their mother in San Francisco by way of Los Angeles where their father lived. They stayed in an apartment with their grandmother and saw their father regularly. After six months, the grandmother returned to Stamps; Maya and Bailey moved to San Francisco to live with their mother and the mother's new husband who Maya describes as the first father she ever knew. She enrolled in a school with Whites for the first time in her life and was inspired to cultivate her love of learning by an unusually gifted and caring teacher.

The following summer she returned to Los Angeles to stay with her father and his girlfriend who was quite young and immature. After accompanying her father on a wild trip to Mexico, Maya returned to spend the remainder of the summer with her father and his girlfriend. It was a disastrous arrangement, which resulted in physical violence after a heated skirmish between Maya and this woman. Maya left and remained homeless for several weeks. She was befriended by a group of White, Black and Mexican-American adolescents with whom she lived for a month in a junkyard. In contrast to her earlier experiences with people who were not Black, Maya's acceptance into this mixed group of societal outcasts had a profound effect in shaping her identification with what she refers to as "the brotherhood of man."

After returning to San Francisco, she continued to experience success in school but was caught in a serious family conflict. Her special friendship with Bailey continued, as did the relationship with her mother, whom she admired for her gaiety, beauty and competence. The growth in the mother-daughter relationship contrasted with mother's relationship with Bailey that deteriorated into constant tensions and arguments. As a consequence, he left home at 16 years of age.

During her adolescence, one of the remarkable accomplishments of Maya was to be hired as the first Black conductor on the San Francisco streetcars. She accomplished this feat by shear perseverance and creative deception when she was only 15 years old.

Maya is candid about her sexual maturation during adolescence, which triggered personal conflict as she struggled with physical changes, confusion about her sexuality and identity as a young woman. She was able to rely on the trusting relationship that had developed with her mother to ask questions about the changes that were happening to her body and her confused sense of self. To deal with what she refers to as an "uneasy suspicion" that she "might not be a normal female" accompanied by her "awakening sexual appetite" she resolved to seduce an attractive young man in the neighborhood. Her plan worked but she became pregnant. Within a few weeks of receiving her high school diploma, she gave birth to a baby boy. Mother, stepfather and Bailey were very supportive throughout this major transition in her life.

The story ends here but subsequent volumes narrate the story of Maya Angelou's adult life.

Eleanor Roosevelt

Although there are several biographies on Eleanor Roosevelt, the one by Blanche Wiesen Cook, Eleanor Roosevelt: Volume one, 1884-1933 (1992) offers an insightful glimpse into one of the most remarkable woman of the twentieth century. A second volume has recently been published. Roosevelt was remarkable, not only for her contribution in setting a new direction for the role of first lady, but for her creative work in behalf of women's rights and the rights of Blacks and other oppressed groups. Yet, her developmental experiences were not predictive of her generativity in adulthood.

In contrast to Maya Angelou, Eleanor Roosevelt was born into a prestigious American family from the privileged class of nineteenth century society. In numerous ways, Angelou and Roosevelt were vastly different. Their race and socioeconomic backgrounds are the most obvious differences. Yet, they shared a history of loss, betrayal and trauma by very important people in their early lives. Those experiences did not defeat them; rather, they appeared to be the basis for an adult lives full of service to others and remarkable literary achievements.

Eleanor Roosevelt was the first of three children born to an immature 20-year-old mother, Anna, who was not prepared to accept the responsibilities of parenthood. A beautiful young woman, Anna is described as being narcissistically preoccupied with herself to an excessive degree, even for her age, and concerned primarily with her social status in upper class society. At best, she appeared ambivalent about being the mother of a child, perhaps related to an unhappy family background and the burden of caring for five younger siblings after their father's untimely death. There is evidence of a pattern of rejection by her mother found not only in Eleanor's writings about herself but also in the observations of others who surrounded the family.

Eleanor's father, Elliott was the younger brother of Teddy Roosevelt, a future president of the United States. A highly competitive relationship existed between the two brothers. Increasingly, throughout later childhood and into adolescence, Elliott experienced persistent doubts and preoccupations about his adequacy. From descriptions of his behavior, Elliott may have suffered from chronic depression or, more likely, manic depression. The inner turmoil was obscured with an excessive use of alcohol in adolescence and adulthood along with unusual periods of travel that separated him from the family. Despite or in spite of these inner conflicts, those in the family and in his social circles regarded Elliott as a congenial, charming and generous individual.

When Eleanor's parents met, Elliott idealized Anna as the perfect partner with whom to spend his life although she had some ambivalence about making a commitment to him. Not long after their marriage, he resumed drinking alcoholically and traveling to distant places without Anna, a theme that characterized their unhappy relationship for almost a decade. Her inner turmoil led to unpredictable violent outburst that endangered his wife and, later, their 3 children. Despite the serious pathology, Elliott was affectionate and attentive toward Eleanor in his sober moments when they were together. In contrast to memories of her mother that are tinged with references to being "scolded and scorned," Eleanor referred to her father in an adoring way. Partly, her thoughts were based on the good times with him but also on her need to deny the suffering and pain that he had brought to the family. Even in her adult years long after her parents had died, Roosevelt never seemed to make peace with the memories of her mother, particularly Anna's struggles to protect Eleanor and her two brothers from an increasingly destructive and potentially dangerous father.

The turmoil of her family life ended in a series of traumatic deaths over an 18 month period when Eleanor was in mid latency. Her mother died first followed by a younger brother six months later. Her maternal grandmother and other relatives cared for Eleanor. During this period, Elliott was forbidden by a legal settlement to have contact with his two surviving children but did carry on a regular correspondence with Eleanor. As in previous letters to her, Elliott expressed affection for his only daughter and his hopes for her happiness. Eighteen months after Anna's death, Elliott Roosevelt died estranged from his family. As in the other tragic losses, Eleanor who was not allowed to attend his funeral service apparently had to live through the death of her idealized father in isolation and loneliness.

Life after the loss of her parents and one of two siblings in such a short period of time was "dominated" by relatives who apparently took great care to attend to her physical and educational needs. Eleanor experienced relative tranquility, compared to her first nine years of life. For the following five years, she studied in small private groups of upper-class peers where there was considerable support to develop her knowledge, skills in the arts, languages and other subjects "appropriate" for a female member of the aristocratic social class.

One of the most significant turning points in her young life began at the age of fifteen years when Eleanor went to England to enroll in a small private school, Allenswood, "dedicated to offering the daughters of Europe's liberal aristocracy and America's leadership class, a wide-ranging education that emphasized social responsibility and personal independence." In part, this unusual move was triggered by the emergence of more pathology in the maternal family, as her two uncles, who were alcoholics, became increasingly unpredictable.

For three years she studied and traveled under the direction of the school's progressive founder, Marie Souvestre, an experience that Roosevelt would later describe as the most critical transition in her life. Souvestre became a new figure for identification not unlike the idealization of her father that never changed. With Souvestre, however, her identifications were based on daily involvement with an individual who represented a new and challenging model for what Roosevelt would become as a woman. She responded to the new perspective on womanhood, which, even in our day almost a century later, would be considered progressive. In her day, it was revolutionary. Her cognitive and emotional development flourished during these years.

After returning to New York at the age of eighteen years, Eleanor was involved in the social scene that accompanied a young woman of her social position. In contrast to the openness of Allenwood, she was confronted with family and societal expectations to become a debutante. In some ways, there appeared to be an expectation that she would take up the torch of womanly respectability that her mother had carried with so much social approval. Despite these social constraints, Roosevelt was determined to engage in meaningful activities rather than simply fit into what was expected of a young woman of her social class. She volunteered to work in settlement houses as well as in other social service programs in New York City. She used public transportation and often walked to and from work through poor neighborhoods.

At the age of 18 years, she again met her fifth cousin, Franklin, whom she had last met when she was fourteen. They married on Saint Patrick's Day in 1905.

Frank McCourt

Angela's Ashes: A Memoir tells the story of Frank McCourt's life beginning with his birth in New York City, his experiences living in dreadful poverty in Limerick Ireland from five to nineteen years of age when he returned to New York. The book was published in 1996 after he had retired from teaching English at Stuyvesant High School in New York City.

McCourt observes that "while people everywhere brag and whimper about the woes of their early years ... nothing can compare with the Irish version: the poverty; the shiftless loquacious alcoholic father; the pious defeated mother; pompous priests; bullying schoolmasters; the English (p. 11)." In telling his story, McCourt integrates the themes of sadness with humor, economic impoverishment with human richness, hope with despair, pathos with strength. It is a remarkable story of the struggles of one family to survive the tragedy of having three of their six children die of diseases nourished in the filth of poverty, the persistence of a mother who lived for her children when she probably would rather have died, the denigration of a father who was unable to face life without poisoning himself with alcohol, and the hidden strengths of their children in contending with the overwhelming odds against them.

One of the most remarkable aspects of this memoir is the richness of life that an adult in middle age may see in reconstructing a forlorn childhood existence. McCourt describes vividly the emptiness, oppression and degradation of being trapped in poverty. One must look beyond the obvious facts to appreciate the creativity and resiliency of an individual in contending with the assault of severe poverty and family pathology on his emerging sense of self.

The McCourt family, all five of them, departed from New York with the hope of finding a better life in Ireland than they had during the midst of the economic depression of the 1930's. They had recently suffered the death of their youngest child and would experience the death of two additional children in the next few years. The wretched house, which they rented in Limerick, was surrounded by filth and squalor. The children had to beg and steal food and the mother regularly had to plead with the civil authorities for a dole and with religious charities for handouts. As miserly as that assistance was, all of them may have perished without it.

The chronic alcoholism of the father, Malachy, victimized his wife and children. When he obtained work, Angela rarely received any of the money to feed the children and herself, since Malachy had already spent it to feed his addiction. The father is a difficult character to understand since he appeared to enjoy his role as father when sober and was not verbally or physically abusive to Angela or the children at any time. When he was not drinking, he commonly related to the children through the telling of stories mostly about the glories of an Ireland alive only in legends, especially the folk hero, Cuchulain. Perhaps, he wished to be someone of importance and power, like Cuchulain, and was too filled with shame for his failures to relate to Frank and the other children in any other manner. As is true of many alcoholically addicted individuals, his life was controlled by a closed cycle of pain, escape, broken promises, shame and more pain.

Angela defined herself only in terms of child bearing and caring for the children, no matter what the circumstances. She appeared as a woman who never allowed herself to think of any other alternatives. The reality was that there were few, if any, alternatives. There were no places to go. No one else wanted her. While physically close and responsive to her needs in the numerous crises that occurred, Angela's family maintained a psychological distance from her and a detachment from her pain. Except for the concern of Frank as he grew older, there is no evidence of any genuine support for Angela. No doubt, Angela's determination to survive, her faithfulness to her marriage vows despite the pain and potential damage to her the children, were shaped substantially by her religious beliefs. There seemed to be an unquestioning acceptance of the teachings of the Catholic Church blended with Irish superstitions. She was impoverished in many ways.

Until recent times, the Catholic Church had a powerful hold over the Irish people. Even its role in dispensing charity in this poor neighborhood of Limerick was tinged by its power and control over the minds and lives of Catholics. The spirit of Christ is hard to discern in most of the relationships with religious figures with whom the family came in contact. Some of the most positive encounters are those that evoked humor, even though they may not have been humorous at the time. Indeed, the memoir is full of very humorous occurrences in the midst of religious oppression by a church that appeared to be preoccupied with its power and control over people rather than its love for them.

There were several instances when individuals recognized something within McCourt and reached out to help him. When Frank was 11 years of age, he worked for Mr. Hannon in his coal delivery business. It was an extremely dirty job but one that fueled Frank's dream of escaping the imprisonment of childhood by being a "workingman." Mr. Hannon, with whom Frank developed a fatherly-like attachment, tells the boy not to be like him but to "go to school … get out of Limerick and Ireland itself." Not long after that encounter, Hannon was mortally ill in the hospital and his wife told Frank that her husband felt like Frank was the son he never had, "a joy to him." Although it is impossible to discern the effect of this man on Frank's future life, he probably had a positive impact, especially since McCourt refers to their relationship with poignancy not characteristic of his encounters with other men.

A second individual who saw strengths in this pubescent boy who yearned to leave school to become a workingman was the stern schoolmaster, Hoppy O'Halloran. He calls Angela to the school, which, to Frank can only mean big trouble. To their surprise, O'Halloran observes that Frank is a "bright boy" who "ought to be going to secondary school" and to a university. He refers them to a well-regarded secondary school run by the Christian Brothers. Reluctantly, Frank accompanied his mother to the school, only to have the door slammed literally in their faces. Despite the outcome of the schoolmaster's efforts, it was probably the first time in this young boy's life that a respected figure identified and validated a positive quality within him.

The third individual was a Franciscan priest who Frank encountered at the age of fourteen. He had gone to a church where he sat begging God's forgiveness for having sexual intercourse with a sixteen year old young woman who died of "consumption" (i.e. tuberculosis), not long after they had committed the mortal sin of sex before marriage. A highly sensitive and scrupulous adolescent, Frank was consumed with guilt that the girl was condemned to hell for eternity because of the seriousness of the sin on her soul at the time of death, so serious that he was ashamed to confess it to a priest. The priest suggested that Frank tell St. Francis what was troubling him; he, the priest, would only listen like "a pair of ears for St. Francis." McCourt not only confesses the sin of sex before marriage that condemned his friend to hell but all of the other thoughts and actions for which he is deeply ashamed. The priest offers him absolution without a comment except to assure Frank that God has forgiven them both and that his friend is in heaven forever. This simple act of kindness by a priest who represented an institution that had great power over this scrupulous adolescent seemed to free McCourt to move on with his life.

Five years later he returned to the United States

Appendix B

Research Methodology

We have been studying marital and same sex relationships that last. The goal of our research focused on heterosexual and homosexual relationships that last is to understand how couples adapt over the years from the perspectives of individual partners. In-depth interviews with 216 partners in 108 relationships that have lasted for an average of 30 years have been conducted. The data have substantial implications for understanding how meaningful relationships contribute to individual well being and to the emerging sense of self in adulthood.

Based on our assessment of the existing research literature and our goal, we decided to use the following approach: A semi-structured interview format was developed and pre-tested by the researchers. The resulting interview guide consisted of focal questions that were designed to elicit how participants viewed several dimensions of their relationships. Collaborative researchers conducted additional pilot testing and provided feedback that led to further refinement of the interview guide.

The guide, which was used in all interviews, was divided into four sections:

*the relationship,

*social influences including economic and cultural factors,

*the relationships of their parents' marriages (all participants had been reared by heterosexual parents), and

*the experiences of participants as they reported their observations about their relationships from the early to recent years.

T he recent years were the last 5-10 years prior to the interviews. The early years were the years prior to the birth of the first child for couples who had children or the first 5 years for those without children or those who adopted children after being together for 5 years. The middle years were the years in between the early and recent years or the child rearing years.

The interview structure was designed to acquire in-depth information from the point of view of individual participants in order to develop an understanding of how each partner adapted over the life span of their relationships. An open-ended style of interviewing allowed for freedom of expression in order to elicit information from the perspectives of participants about interactions with their partners. The approach, which adapted clinical interviewing skills to the needs of the research, explored the experiences of individuals within relationships as they remembered and reported them. (Note: A similar approach was used in the study of psychotherapy reported in chapter 7).

Interviewers, who were advanced doctoral students with extensive clinical experience, were trained in the use of the interview guide. They were respectful and accepting of the uniqueness of each participant's perceptions. Their empathic interviewing skills were a valuable resource in collecting the data (Hill, Thomson and Williams, 1997).

The interviews were held in the homes of participants, which provided additional information about lifestyles and environments. Prior to each interview, participants were told about the purpose of the study, given an overview of the interview schedule and were assured their identities would remain anonymous. Informed consent for audiotaping and the research use of interviews was obtained. Each partner was interviewed separately; the length of each of the interviews was approximately two hours.

Sample

Couples were recruited through business, professional and trade union organizations as well as through churches, synagogues, and a variety of other community organizations. Most couples resided in the northeast part of the country

The sample was chosen purposively to fit with the goal of developing an understanding of a diverse and older group of heterosexual and same sex couples in lasting relationships. Couples were recruited who met the following criteria:1. married or in a committed same sex relationship at least 15 years; 2. diversity of race/ethnicity, education, religious background and sexual orientation.

Of the 216 partners who were interviewed, 76% were White and 24 % were people of color (African-Americans and Mexican-Americans). Religious background was as follows:

46 % were Protestant; 34 % were Catholic; and 20% were Jewish. Fifty-six percent were college graduates and 44% were non-college graduates. The mean age for the sample as a whole was 57 years (S.D.=10.24): 27% of participants were in their 40's, 33% in their 50's, 26% in their 60's, and 14% in their 70's. Sixty-seven percent of couples were heterosexual and 33% in same sex relationships. The mean number of years together was 30.22 (S.D.=10.28): 18% of couples had been together 40 years or longer; 29% between 30 and 39 years; 34% between 20 and 29 years; and 19% less than 20 but more than 15 years. Seventy-seven percent of couples had children; 23% did not have children. By total gross family income, 7% of couples earned less than $25,000; 25% between $25,000 and $49,999; 29% between $50,000 and $74,999; and 39 % had gross incomes of $75,000 or more.

Coding

Each interview was tape recorded and transcribed to facilitate coding and to prepare the data for both quantitative and qualitative analysis. Interview passages were coded for relational themes that were then developed into categories (Strauss and Corbin, 1990).

Initially, a research team (2 women, 2 men) coded eight transcriptions blindly and individually. Detailed notes were kept and categories were generated. A relationship coding sheet was developed and used in subsequent coding of eight additional interviews. As new categories arose previous interviews were re-coded in keeping with the constant comparative process. Having both genders involved in that process helped to control for gender bias and contributed to the development of a shared conceptual analysis. Using this method, a scoring system was developed to identify themes that evolved from each section of the interviews. There were over 90 categories in 24 topic areas for every participant.

Once the Relationship Coding Sheet was developed, each interview was coded and scored independently by two raters (one male and one female) who noted themes and categories as they emerged from the transcripts. One member of the research team coded all 216 interviews to insure continuity in the operational definitions of variables and consistency of judgments from case to case. The agreement between raters, determined by dividing the number of identical judgments by the total number of codes, was 87%. Cohen's kappa, used as a measure of inter-rater reliability, ranged from .79 to .93. When discrepancies occurred, the raters met to discuss their differences and to re-examine the original transcripts until a consensus was reached as to how a particular item was to be scored.

HyperResearch software (Hesse-Biber, Dupuis and Kinder, 1992) enabled the researchers to do a thorough content analysis of the interview transcripts, which totaled over 8,000 double-spaced pages, and to identify, catalogue and organize specific interview passages on which categorical codes were based.

In the second phase of the study, we re-examined the codes so as to prepare the data for quantitative analysis. Many variables were re-coded into dichotomous categories. For example, psychological intimacy was coded originally into three categories (positive, mixed and negative). The positive category was retained and compared with a re-coded mixed/negative category.

<u>Data analysis</u>

The coded data from the scoring sheets yielded frequencies, which were analyzed using SPSS software. Chi square analysis was used to examine the relationship between the independent variables - which included personal, demographic and participants' reports of various dimensions of relationships - and the dependent variables. The Alpha criterion was set at .01 for the chi-square analysis.

The chi-square statistic was appropriate since certain conditions were met. First, it hss been very difficult to ensure randomness of samples in social and behavioral research, especially in studies that focus on new territory. This non-probability sample was selected deliberately to include a diverse group of older couples who have been understudied in previous research; namely, heterosexual and homosexual relationships that had lasted an average of 30 years; rather than to test hypotheses, the goal was to identify and to develop an understanding of factors that contributed to adaptation from the perspectives of individual partners. Second, compared to other tests of statistical significance, chi-square has fewer requirements about population characteristics. Third, the expected frequency of 5 observations in most cells was met.

Variables that were related significantly to important dependent variables, such as psychological intimacy and conflict management styles, in the chi-square analysis and which had been identified in previous studies as having importance to understanding adaptation were selected for building theoretical models, which were tested with logistic regression procedures, a useful tool in this exploratory research where the goal was to develop theory rather to test theory (Menard, 1995). The use of both qualitative and quantitative methods enhanced the goal of the research.

Bibliography

Adler, G. (1985). Borderline psychopathology and its treatment. New York: Jason Aronson.

Ainsworth, M. (1969). Object relations, dependency and attachment: A theoretical review of the infant-mother relationship. Child development. 969-1025.

Anderson, R. and Cissna,K. (1997). The Martin Buber-Carl Rogers Dialogue. Albany, NY: State University of New York Press.

Angelou, M. (1993). I know why the caged bird sings. NY: Bantam Books.

Attachment and related disorders (2005). Conference: Harvard Medical School, Department of Continuing Education, May 6-7 Boston, MA.

Baldwin, M. and Satir, V., Editors (1987). The use of self in therapy. NY: Haworth.

Bandura, A. (1977). Social learning theory. Englewood Cliffs, NJ: Prentice Hall.

Basham, K. and Miehls, D. (2004). Transforming the legacy: couple therapy with survivors of childhood trauma. NY: Columbia university Press.

Baucom, D. H., Notarius, C.I., Burnett, C. K., and Haefner, P. (1990). Gender differences and sex role identity in marriage. In F. D. Fincham & T. N. Bradbury (Eds.), The psychology of marriage: Basic issues and applications (150-171). NY: Guilford.

Berl, F. (1988). Social change and social work practice: Writings of Fred Berl. Hagerstown, MD.: Hagerstown Bookbinding and Printing Company.

Berscheid, E. and Reis, H.T. (1998). Attraction and close relationships. In D.T. Gilbert, S.T. Fiske & G. Lindzey (Eds.), The handbook of social psychology (4th ed., Vol 1, pp. 391-445). New York: McGraw-Hill.

Berzoff, J., Flanagan, L. and Hertz, P. (1996). Inside out and outside in: Psychodynamic clinical theory and practice incontemporary multicultural contexts. Northvale, NJ: Jason Aronson, inc.

Bettelheim, B. (l983). Freud and man's soul. NY: A. Knoff.

Blanck, G. and Blanck (1979). Ego psychology II: Psychoanalyhic developmental psychology. NY: Columbia University Press.

Blanck, G. and Blanck, R. (1974). Ego psychology: Theory and practice. NY: Columbia
University Press.

Blasband, D., and Peplau, L.A. (1985). Sexual exclusivity versus sexual openness in gay male male couples. Archives of Sexual Behavior, 14 (5), 395-412.

Blos, P. (1967). The second individuation process of adolescence. The Psychoanalytic Study of the Child, XXII, New York: International Universities Press, 162-186.

Bowen, M. (1978). Family therapy in clinical practice. NY: Jason Aronson.

Bowlby, J. (1980). Attachment and loss (Vol.3). NY: Basic Books.

Bowbly, J. (1973). Seperation: Anxiety and anger (vol.2). NY: Basic Books.

Bowbly, J. (1969). Attachment (vol.1). NY: Basic Books.

Brazelton, G. 'The infant as focus for family reciprocity." In Harvard Seminar Series, The American Family (cassettes). Cambridge, 1980.

Brown, J. (1998). The self. NY: McGraw-Hill.

Breger, L. (1974). From instinct to identity: The development of personality. Englewood Cliffs: Prentice-Hall, Inc.

Buckley, P., Karasu, T. and Charles, E. (1981). Psychotherapist view their psychotherapy, Psychotherapy: Theory, research and practice,18, 299-305.

Burch, B. (1982). Psychological merger in lesbian couples: A joint ego psychological and systems approach. Family Therapy, 9, 201-208

Cahn, D. (1994). Conflict in personal relationships. Hillsdale NJ: Lawrence Erlbaum Associates, inc.

Canary, D., Cupach, and Messman (1995). Relationship conflict. Thousand Oaks, CA: Sage Publishers.

Carey, E. (1984). Themes of adult development in women: Life history interviews with never married women over sixty, Boston College: Doctoral Dissertation.

Clark, M. (1986). Personal therapy: A review of empirical research, Professional psychology: Research and practice, 17, (6) 541-543.

Crane, D. R. (1996). Fundamentals of marital therapy. New York: Brunner/Mazel Publishers.

Chescheir, M. (1985). Some implications of Winnicott's concept. Clinical Social Work Journal, 13(2), 218-233

Colin, V. (1996). Human attachment. Philadelphia, PA: Temple University Press.

Cook, B.W. (1992). Eleanor Roosevelt: Volume one 1884-1933. NY: Viking.

Coombs, R.H. (1991). Marital status and personal well-being: A literature review. Family Relations. 40, 97-102.

Davanloo, H. (1980). Short-term dynamic psychotherapy. NY: Jason Aronson.

Dean, R. (1993). Constructivism: An approach to clinical practice. Smith College Studies in Social Work, 63, 2 (January), 127-146.

DeCecco, J.P., and Shively, M.G. (1978). A study of perceptions of rights and needs in interpersonal conflicts in homosexual relationships. Journal of Homosexuality, 3 (3), 205-216.

Dilworth-Anderson, P. & Burton, L. (1996). Rethinking family development: Critical conceptual issues in the study of diverse groups. Journal of Social and Personal Relationships, 13 (3), 325-354.

Feeney, J. (1999). Adult romantic attachment and couple relationships. In J. Cassidy and P. Shaver (eds.), Handbook of attachment: Theory, research and clinical applications. NY: Guilford Press.

Feeney, J., Noller, P. and Roberts, N. (1998). Emotion, attachment and satisfaction in close relationships, in P Anderson and L Guerrerd (eds.), Handbook of communication and emotion: Research, theory, applications. San Diego, CA.: Academic Press.

Feeney, J. and Noller, P. (1996). Adult attachment. Thousand Oaks: Sage Publications.

Duck, S.W. and Wright, P.H. (1993). Re-examining gender differences in same-gender friendships: A close look at two kinds of data. Sex Roles, 28: 1-19.

Elise, D. (1986). Lesbian couples: The implications of sex differences in separation-individuation. Psychotherapy, 23 (2), 305-310.

Elson, M. (1986). Self psychology in clinical social work. NY: W.W. Norton & Company.

Erikson, E. (1950). Childhood and society. NY: W. W. Norton and Co., Inc.

Feeney, J., Noller, P. and Roberts, N. (1998). Emotion, attachment and satisfaction in close relationships, ch.18: 473-505, In P Anderson and L Guerrerd (eds.) Handbook of communication and emotion: Research, theory, applications and contents. San Diego, CA.: Academic Press.

Felton, J.(1986). The Psychotherapist as the interminable patient, The Psychotherapy Patient, 3, (1) 101-110.

Fraiberg, S. (1977). Every child's birthright: In defense of mothering. NY: Basic Books.

Fraiberg, S. (1975). Ghosts in the nursery: A psychoanalytic approach to the problems of impaired infant-mother relationships. American Academy of Child Psychoanalysis, 14, 387-421.

Frank, A. (1952).The diary of a young girl. NY: Pocket Boohs.

Freud, A. (1946). The ego and the mechanisms of defense. NY:
International Universities Press.

Freud, S. (1966). The complete introductory lectures on psychoanalysis.
NY: W. W. Norton & Co., Inc., 1966.

Freud S. (1962). The ego and the id (Translated by Joan Riviere). NY: W. W. Norton
& Co., Inc.

Gardner, H. (1985). Frames of mind: The theory of multiple intelligences. NY: Basic Books.

George, K.D., and Behrendt, A.E. (1987). Therapy for male couples experiencing relationship problems and sexual problems. Journal of Homosexuality, 14 (1-2), 77-88.

Gilligan, C (1982). In a different voice: Psychological theory and women's development. Cambridge, MA: Harvard University Press.

Goleman,D. (1995). Emotional intelligence. NY: Bantam Books.

Goldstein, H. (1981). Social learning and change: A cognitive approach to human services. Columbia SC: University of South Carolina Press.

Gottman, J., Coan, J., Carriere, S., and Swanson, C. (1998). Predicting marital unhappiness and stability from newlywed interactions. Journal of Marriage and the Family, 60, 5-22.

Gottman, J.M. (1990). How marriages change. In G.R. Petterson (Ed.) New directions in family research: Depression and aggression. Hillsdale NJ: Erlbaum.

Gottman, J.M., & Krokoff, L.J. (1989). Marital interaction and satisfaction: A longitudinal view. Journal of Consulting and Clinical Psychology, 57(1), 47-52.

Greenberg, J. & Mitchell, S. (1983). Object relations in psychoanalytic theory. Cambridge, MA: Harvard University Press.

Grunebaum, H> (1983). A study of therapists choice of a therapist, American Journal of Psychiatry, 140:10, 1336-1339.

Guy, J. and Liaboe, G. (1986). Personal therapy for the experienced psychotherapist: A discussion of its usefulness and utilization, The Clinical Psychologist, 39, (1) 20-23.

Guy, J. (1987). The personal life of the psychotherapist, New York: John Wiley & Sons.

Guy, J., Stark, M. and Poelstra, P. (1988). Personal psychotherapy for psychotherapists before and after entering professional practice, Professional Psychology: Research and Practice, 19, (4) 474-476.

Hartmann,H. (1964). Essays on ego psychology. NY: International Universities Press,

Hartmannl H. (1958). Ego psychology and the problem of adaptation. NY:
International Universities Press.

Hazan, C and Shaver, R. (1994). Attachment as an organizational framework for research on close relationships. Psychological Inquiry, 5 (1), 1-22.

Headly, B. and Wearing, A. (1992). Understanding happiness: A theory of subjective well-being. Melbourne Australia: Longman cheshire.

Hegelson, V.S., Shaver, P.R. and Dyer, M. (1987). Prototypes of intimacy and distance in same-sex and opposite-sex relationhips. Journal of Social and Personal Relationships, 4, 195-233.

Hendrix, L. (1997). Quality and equality in marriage: A cross-cultural view. Cross-Cultural Research: The Journal of Comparative Social Science, 31, 201-225.

Heavy,C.L., Layne, C., & Christensen, A. (1993). Gender and conflict structure in marital interaction: A replication and extension. Journal of consulting and clinical psychology, 61, 16-27.

Hesse-Biber, S., Dupuis, P., Kinder, T. S. (1992). HyperRESEARCH: A tool for the analysis of qualitative data. (Computer Program). Randolph (MA: Researchware.

Hill, C.E., Thompson, B.J. and Williams, E.N. (1997). A guide to conducting consensual qualitative research. The Counseling Psychologist, 25(4), 517-572.

Hoffman, M. (1977). "Empathy, its development and prosocial Implications"
In C.B. Keasey (ed.), Nebraska Symposium on Motivation,. University of Nebraska Press, 1977.

Horner, A. (1984). Object relations and the developing ego in therapy. NY: Jason Aronson.

Hornstein and Murray (1994). The bell curve. NY: the Free Press.

Horwitz, A. V., White, H.R. and Howell-White, S. (1996). Becoming married and mental health: A longitudinal study of a cohort of young adults. Journal of Marriage and the Family, 58, 895-907.

Howard, J.A., Blumstein, P., and Schwartz, P. (1986). Sex, power, and influence tactics in intimate relationships. Journal of Personality and Social Psychology, 51 (1), 102-109.

Hughes, D. (1998). Building the bonds of attachment: awakening love in deeply troubled children. Northvale NJ: Jason Aronson.

Hughes, D. (1997). Facilitating developmental attachment: The road to recovery and behavioral change in foster and adopted children. Northvale NJ: Jason Aronson.

Jack, D. (1991). Silencing the self: Women and depression. Cambridge, MA: Harvard.

Jackson, H. (Ed.) (1991). Using self psychology in psychotherapy. New Jersey: Jason Aronson.

Jacobsen, E. (1964). The self and the objecy world. NY: International Universities Press.

Jacobson, E. (1954). "The self and the object world." The Psychoanalitic Study of The Child, Vol. IX. NY: International Universities Press, 75-127.

Jocobson, N. Christensen, A., Prince, S., Cordova, J., and Eldridge, K. (2000). Integrative behavioral couple therapy: An acceptance-based, promising new treatment for couple discord. Journal of Consulting and Clinical Psychology, 68 (2), 351-355.

Johnson, S. and Lebow, J. (2000). The coming of age of couple therapy: A decade review. Journal of Marital and Family Therapy, 26 (1), 23-38.

Jordan, J. et al (1991). Women's growth in connection: Writings from the Stone Center. NY: The Guilforg Press

Jourard, S.M. (1971). Self-disclosure: An experimental analysis of the transparent self. New York: Wiley.

Julien, D., Arellano, C. and Turgeon, L. (1997). Gender issues in heterosexual, gay male and lesbian couples. In Halford, W. K. amd Markman, H.J. (Eds.), Clinical handbook of marriage and couples interventions, (pp. 107-127). Chichester, England: John Wiley & Sons, Inc.

Kaplan, L.(1995). No voice is ever wholly lost. NY: Simon and Schuster.

Karney, B.R. & Bradbury, T.N. (1995). The longitudinal course of marital quality and stability: A review of theory, method, and research. Psychological Bulletin, 118 (1), 3-34.

Karr-Morse, R. & Wiley, M. (1997). Ghosts from the nursery: Tracing the roots of violence. NY: The Atlantic Press.

Kaslow, F. (Editor), (1984). Psychotherapy with psychotherapists, New York: Haworth Press.

Kernberg, 0. (1975) Borderline conditions and pathological narcissism. NY: Jason Aronson.

Kiecolt-Glaser, J.K., Fisher, L.D., Ogrocki, P., Stout, J.C., Speicher, C.E. and Glasser, R. (1988). Marital discord and immunity in males. Psychomatic Medicine, 50, 213-229.

Kohlberg, L (1964). "Development of Moral Character and Moral Ideology," in Review of Child Development Research, Edited by N. Hoffman and L. Hoffman. NY: Rossell Sage Foundation, 383-431.

Kohut, H. (1977). The restoration of the self. NY: International Universities Press.

Kohut, H. (1971). The analysis of self. NY: International Universities Press.

Kurdek, L. (1998). Relationship outcomes and their predictors: Longitudinal evidence from heterosexual married, gay male cohabiting, and lesbian cohabiting couples. Journal of Marriage and the Family, 60, 553-568.

Kurdek, L. A. (1988). Relationship quality of gay male and lesbian cohabiting couples. Journal of Homosexuality, 15(3/4), 93-118.

Kurdek, L. A. (1991). Correlates of relationship satisfaction in cohabiting gay male and lesbian couples: Integration of contextual, investment, and problem-solving models. Journal of Personality and Social Psychology, 61(6), 910-922.

Kurdek, L.A., and Schmitt, J.P. (1986). Relationship quality of partners in heterosexual married, heterosexual cohabiting, and gay male and lesbian relationships. Journal of Personality and Social Psychology, 51 (4), 711-720.

Lambert, M. and Barley, D. (2001). Research summary on the therapeutic relationship and psychotherapy outcome. Psychotherapy: Theory / Research / Practice / Teaching, 38 (4), 357-361.

Lane, R. E. (1998). Searching for lost companions in the groves of the market. In D. Kahneman, E. Diener and N. Schwartz (Eds.), Understanding well-being: Scientific perspectives on enjoyment and suffering. NY: Russell Sage foundation.

Lauer, R.H., Lauer, J.C. and Kerr, S.T. (1990). The long-term marriage: Perceptions of stability and satisfaction. International Journal of Aging and Human Development, *31,* 189-195.

Lazare, A. (1973). Hidden conceptual models in clinical psychiatry, New England Journal of Medicine, Fall, 345-351.

Levant, R. (1996). The new psychology of men. Professional Psychology: Research and Practice. 27, 259-269.

Levine, M. (1979). Gay male men: The sociology of male homosexuality. New York: Harper & Row.

Levinson, D. et. al. (1996). The seasons of a woman's life. NY: Alfred A. Knopf.

Levinson, D. (1978). The seasons of a man's life. NY: Alfred A. Knopf.

Lewin, T. (2002). A child study is a peek, its not the whole picture. The New York Times, 07/21/2002.

Lifton, R.J. (1993). The protean self: Human resilience in an age of fragmentation. NY: Basic Books.

Longres, J. F. (1996). Human behavior in the social environment. (2nd ed.).
Itasca, Il: F.E. Peacock Publishers, Inc.

Mackey, R., Diemer, M. and O'Brien, B. (2000). Psychological intimacy in the lasting relationships of heterosexual and same sex relationships. Sex Roles. 43(3/4), 2000, 201-227

Mackey, R., Diemer, M. and O'Brien, B. (2000). Conflict management styles of spouses in lasting relationships. Psychotherapy:Theory/Research/Practice. 37(2) Summer, 134-148.

Mackey R. and O'Brien, B.A. (1999). Adaptation in lasting marriages: A multi-dimensional prospective. Families in Society: The Journal of Contemporary Human Services, 80 (6), 587-596.

Mackey R. and O'Brien, B.A. (1998). Marital conflict management: gender and ethnic differences. Social Work: Journal of the National Association of Social Workers. 43(2) March, 128-141.

Mackey, R., O"Brien, B. and Mackey, E. (1997). Gay and lesbian couples: Voices from lasting relationships . Westport, CT: Praeger Publishers.

Mackey, R. and O'Brien, B. (1995). Lasting marriages: Men and women growing together . Westport, CT: Praeger Publishers.

Mackey, R. & Mackey, E. (1994). Personal psychotherapy and the development of a professional self. Families in Society: The Journal of Contemporary Human Services 75(8), 490-498.

Mackey, R., Mackey, E. and O'Brien, B. (1993). Personal psychotherapy and the social work student. Journal of Teaching in Social Work. 7(2), 129-146.

Mackey, R. and Mackey, E. (1993). The Value of Personal Psychotherapy to Clinical Practice The Clinical Social Work Journal. 21(1) Spring, 97-109.

Mackey R. (1989). Containment of self in the narcissistically vulnerable yet cognitively agile patient, The Psychotherapy Patient. also published in the Journal of the same title 4, 3/4 (1988), 119-138.

Mackey, R. (1985). Ego psychology and clinical practice. NY: Gardner Press, Inc.
also published by Boston College Press, 1992.

Mackey, R. (1976). "Generic aspects of clinical social work, Social Casework, December,
619-624.

Macoby, E.E. (1990). Gender and relationships. American Psychologist, 45, 513-520.

Mahler, M. et al. (1975). The psychological birth of the human infant: Symbiosis and individuation. NY: Basic Books, Inc.

Maier, H. (1965).Three theories of child development. NY: Harper and Row, 1965.

Markman, H. (1991). Constructive marital conflict is not an oxymoron. Behavioral Assessment, 13, 83-96.

Markman, H.J. and Kraft, S.A. (1989). Men and women in marriage: Dealing with gender differences in marital therapy. Behavior Therapist, 12, 51-56.

Maslow, A. (1962). Toward a psychology of being. Princeton, NJ:D. Van Nostrand.

Masterson, J. (l985). The real self: A developmental self and object relations approach. NY: Brunner/Mazel.

McBride, J. (1996). The color of water: A Black man's tribute to her/his White mother. NY: the Burkley Publishing Group.

MacDevitt, J. (1987). Therapists' personal therapy and professional self-awareness, Psychotherapy, 24, (1) 693-703.Kernberg, 0. (1980) Internal world and external reality: Object relations theory applied. NY: Jason Aronson,

McCourt, F. (1996). Angela's ashes: A memoir. NY: Scriber.

McGoldrick, M., Pearce, J., & Giordano, J. (Eds.). (1982). Ethnicity and family therapy. New York: Guilford Press.

Menard, S. (1995). Applied logistic regression analysis. Thousands Oaks, CA: Sage.

Monsour, M. (1992). Meanings of intimacy in cross- and same-sex friendships. Journal of Social and Personal Relationships, 9: 277-295.

Mroczek, D. K. and Kolarz, C.M. (1998). The effect of age on positive and negative affect: A developmental perspective on happiness. Journal of Personality and Social Psychology, 75, 1333-1349.

Nakkula, M. & Ravitch, S. (1998). Matters of interpretation: Reciprocal transformation in developmental relationships with youth. San Francisco: Jossey-Bass Publishers.

Nasar, S. (1998). A beautiful mind: The life of mathematical genius and nobel laureate John Nasn. NY: Simon and Schuster.

Noller, P. (1993). Gender and emotional communication in marriage. Journal of Language and Social Psychology, 12, 132-154.

Norcross, J. (2002). Psychotherapy relationships that work: Therapists contributions and responsiveness to patient needs. NY: Oxford University Press.

Norcross, J. (2001). Purposes and products of the task force on empirically supported therapy relationships. Psychotherapy: Theory / Research / Practice / Teaching, 38 (4), 345-356.

Nocross, J.,Strausser, D. and Faltus, F. (1988). The therapist's therapist, American Journal of Psychotherapy. XLII (1) 53-66.

Norcross, J., Strausser-Kirtland, D. and Missar, C. (1988). The process and outcomes of psychotherapists' personal treatment experiences, Psychotherapy. 25 (1) 36-43.

Osborne, R. (1996). Self: An eclectic approach. Needham Heights, MA: Allyn & Bacon.

Parks, M.R. and Floyd, K. (1996). Meanings for closeness and intimacy in friendship. Journal of Social and Personal Relationships, 13(1), 85-107.

Peplau, L.A. (1991). Lesbian and Gay male Relationships. In J.C. Gonsiorek & J.D. Weinrich (eds.). Homosexuality: Research implications for public policy, (pp. 177-196). Newbury Park, CA: Sage.

Piaget, J. (1952). The origins of intelligence in children. NY: International Universities Press.

Piaget, J (1948). The moral judgment of the child. Glencoe, Illinois: Free Press.

Piaget, J (1973). The child and reality. NY: Grossman Publishers.

Pinderhughes, E. (1989). Understanding race, ethnicity, and power: The key to efficacy in clinical practice. NY: The Free Press.

Prager, K.J. (1995). The psychology of intimacy. New York: Guilford Press.

Reilly, M. E., and Lynch, J. M. (1990). Power-sharing in lesbian partnerships. Journal of Homosexuality, 19(3), 1-30.

Rosenbluth, S.C. and Steil, J.M. (1995). Predictors of intimacy for women in heterosexual and homosexual couples. Journal of Social and Personal Relationships, 2(2), 163-175.

Rubin, L.B. (1983). Intimate strangers. New York: Harper & Row

Queralt, M. (1996). The social environment and human behavior. Boston, MA: Allyn and Bacon.

St. Clair, M. (2000). Object relations and self psychology: An introduction (third edition). Belmont, CA: Brooks/Cole.

Saari, C. (l986). Clinical social work treatment. NY: Gardner Press

Sass, L. (l988). The self and its vicissitudes: An archaeological study of the psychoanalytic avant-garde. Social Research, 55, 4 (Winter), 551-607.

Schaefer, M. and Olson, D. (1981). Assessing intimacy: The PAIR Inventory, Journal of Marital and Family Therapy, 47-59.

Scheibe, K. (1995). Self studies: The psychology of self and identity. Westport, CT: Praeger.

Schneider, M. S. (1986). The relationships of cohabiting lesbian and heterosexual couples: A comparison. Psychology of Women Quarterly, 10, 234-239.

Schore, A. (1994). Affect regulation and the origin of the self: The neurobiology of emotional development. Hillsdale, NJ: Lawrence Erlbaum Associates.

Scott, J., Williams, J. and Beck, A. (1992). Cognitive therapy in clinical practice: An illustrative casebook. NY: Routledge.

Shapiro, J. and Applegate, J. (2000). Cognitive neuroscience, nerobiology and affect regulation: Implications for clinical social work. Clinical Social Work Journal, 28, 1 (Spring), 9-21.

Slater, S., and Mencher, J. (1991). The lesbian family life cycle: A contextual approach. American Journal of Orthopsychiatry, 61, 372-382.

Smith, R. (1975). Martin Buber. Atlanta, GA: John Knox Press.

Spitz, R. (1965). The first year of life. NY: International Universities Press.

Stern, D. (1985). The interpersonal world of the infant. NY: Basic Books.

Strauss, A. & Corbin, J. (1990). Basics of qualitative research: Grounded theory procedures and techniques. Newbury Park, CA: Sage. Press.

Surrey, J. L. (1987). Relationship and empowerment. Work in Progress, No. 30. Wellesley (MA): Stone Center Working Paper Series.

Surrey, J (1985). Self-in-relation: A theory of women's development. Wellsley, MA: Stone Center for developmental Services and Studies.

Swain, S. (1989). Covert intimacy: Closeness in men's friendships. In B. Risman & P. Schwartz (Eds.), Gender in intimate relationships: A microstructural approach. Belmont, CA: Wadsworth.

Towle, C. (1955).Common human needs. NY: American Association of Social Workers.

Urdang, E. (2002). Human behavior in the social environment: Interweaving the inner and outer worlds. NY: Haworth Press.

Vaillant, G. (1993). The wisdom of the ego. Cambridge MA: Harvard University Press.

Vaillant, C.O. & Vaillant, G.E. (1993). Is the U-curve of marital satisfaction an illusion? A 40-year study of marriage. Journal of Marriage and the Family, 55, 230-239.

Werner, E. (1989). Children of the garden island. Scientific American, 106-111.

White, K., Speisman, J., Jackson, D., Bartis, S., Costos, D. (1986). Intimacy, maturity and its correlation in young married couples. Journal of Personality and Social Psychology, *50,* 152-162.

Winnicott, D.W. (1965). The maturational process and the facilitating environment. New York: International Universities Press

Winnicott, D.W. (1953). Transitional objects and transitional phenomena: A study of the first not-me possession. International Journal of Psychoanalysis, 34, 1-25.

Yahraes, H. (1978). Childhood environment and mental health: A conversation with Dr. Jerome Kagan. Rockville, MD: NIMH.

Yalom, I. (1989). Love's executioner and other tales of psychotherapy. NY: Basic books.

Young, M. and Long,L. (1998). Counseling and therapy for couples. Pacific Grove, CA: Brooks/Cole Publishing Co.

Index

Richard A. Mackey

www.ingramcontent.com/pod-product-compliance
Lightning Source LLC
LaVergne TN
LVHW070952210926
848482LV00002B/194